The Gardener's Eye

BY ALLEN LACY

Gardening with Groundcovers and Vines

The Gardener's Eye and Other Essays

The Garden in Autumn

The Glory of Roses

Farther Afield: A Gardener's Excursions

Home Ground: A Gardener's Miscellany

Miguel de Unamuno: The Rhetoric of Existence

EDITED BY ALLEN LACY

The American Gardener: A Sampler

Elizabeth Lawrence, *Gardening for Love:
The Market Bulletins*

Elizabeth Lawrence, *A Rock Garden in the South*
(co-edited with Nancy Goodwin)

TRANSLATED BY ALLEN LACY
(WITH MARTIN NOZICK AND ANTHONY KERRIGAN)

Miguel de Unamuno, *The Private World*

Miguel de Unamuno, *Peace in War*

THE GARDENER'S EYE

and Other Essays

ALLEN LACY

An Owl Book
Henry Holt and Company   New York

Henry Holt and Company, Inc.
Publishers since 1866
115 West 18th Street
New York, New York 10011

Henry Holt® is a registered trademark
of Henry Holt and Company, Inc.

Portions of this book appeared, in somewhat different form, in
*The New York Times, HG, Horticulture, Organic Gardening,
New Jersey Monthly,* and *Garden Ornaments,* a Brooklyn Botanic
Garden Handbook

Library of Congress Cataloging-in-Publication Data
Lacy, Allen.
The gardener's eye and other essays / by Allen Lacy.
p.   cm.
"An Owl book."
Originally published: New York : Atlantic Monthly Press, 1992.
Includes bibliographical references (p.   ) and index.
1. Gardening.   2. Gardens.   3. Plants, Ornamental.   I. Title.
[SB455.L35   1995]   95-1574
635—dc20   CIP

ISBN 0-8050-3952-X

Henry Holt books are available for special promotions
and premiums. For details contact: Director, Special Markets.

First published in hardcover in 1992 by
The Atlantic Monthly Press.

First Owl Book Edition—1995

Designed by Laura Hough

Printed in the United States of America
All first editions are printed on acid-free paper.∞

1   3   5   7   9   10   8   6   4   2

FOR HELLA

Contents

CONTENTS

[x]

CONTENTS

Preface

THIS BOOK HAS its forerunners in two previous collections of essays, *Home Ground: A Gardener's Miscellany* and *Farther Afield: A Gardener's Excursions,* but it differs in certain respects. *Home Ground* was half previously published articles from my columns in *The Wall Street Journal,* half new pieces, but in much the same vein. *Farther Afield* was entirely made up of columns from the *Journal* and several magazines, revised only slightly.

This new collection contains some previously published pieces from the column I have been writing since 1985 for *The New York Times* and from *Horticulture* and other magazines, but there have been extensive revisions in almost every piece. A goodly number of the essays are completely new, including the title essay and all but one of the others in the section it introduces. This collection differs from its predecessors in another respect. In addition to writing about gardening during the past decade or more, I have continued to teach philosophy and the humanities at Stockton State College and to work as an editor. Those activities are reflected in this book, in pieces dealing with my one venture to date in teaching a course in horticulture and with the pleasures and problems of editing Elizabeth Lawrence's posthumous book, *Gardening for Love: The Market Bulletins*, which was published in 1987 by Duke University Press. I have also included a slightly revised version of a lecture on Celia Thaxter and Louise Beebe Wilder that I delivered in Boston as part of a series on romanticism and gardening, under the auspices of the Museum of Fine Arts and the Arnold Arboretum of Harvard University. I believe that gardening has intellectual underpinnings, that it always goes beyond technical and practical questions of when to and how to, and I have allowed these philosophical foundations of the horticultural enterprise to show more clearly in these pages than they did in the earlier collections.

To write is to be indebted. My debts are headed by those I owe to my wife, Hella, for too many blessings to enumerate here, although they include failing on most occasions to mention that whenever I am working on a book my study looks like a landfill in its last days of operation. I am also grateful to my agent, Helen Pratt, for the unfailing personal and professional support she has always given, and for her friendship. As for my editor, John Barstow, I consider myself richly lucky that he has been my editor on two books, after earlier being my editor at *Horticulture* magazine. As all of the writers who have worked with him know, he is smart and good-humored, and a fine midwife in helping books find their way into the world. (Helen Pratt and John have also "just said no" to call waiting, setting a fine example for other agents and editors.)

I would like to thank my sons, Paul and Michael, for two things in particular. First, while adopting none of my bad habits, they have taken up the avid pursuit of gardening, enabling me to think well of either heredity or environment or both. Second, they gave me for Christmas last year a modem and a trial membership in an on-line computer service that maintains a gardening bulletin board, among its other features. This gift has proved to be a marvelous way of wasting time, in such pursuits as checking airfares and flight schedules between Atlantic City and Kuala Lumpur or getting the latest price quotations on stocks I do not own. The gardening bulletin board, however, has enabled me to make friends with kindred spirits across the country who have shared their experiences with me in ways that have influenced some of these essays. Among them I must particularly thank Marion Abajian, Margaret Biener, James Delahanty, William Hillman, Alan Kornheiser, Lynn Hoyt, Gail Martin, Joan Schimmelman, and Garry Williams.

I am grateful to the Committee on Research and Professional Development at Stockton State College for the help it gave in the form of a sabbatical from teaching during the spring of 1991, and to the college's dean of the Faculty of Arts and Humanities, Robert A. Regan, for reducing my teaching load by one course during the previous fall. Such support has made it possible to finish this book without feeling pressed by the demands of the classroom, in addition to those of editorial deadlines.

The list of other people who have given help and assistance is long, but I must mention here Martha Blake-Adams, Douglas Brenner, Allen Bush, Thomas Cooper, Stephen Drucker, Edith Eddleman, Joanne Ferguson, Nancy Goodwin, Peter Knapp, J. C. Raulston, Douglas Ruhren, Hannah Withers, and Linda Yang. I also owe special debts to Carol Rinzler and Elisabeth Woodburn, whose deaths late last year darkened the lives of many people, of whom I am just one.

ALLEN LACY
June 1991

THE
GARDENER'S
EYE

The Gardener's Eye

I DO NOT BELIEVE that it is a green thumb that sets true gardeners apart from other people, that distinguishes us as a tribe. I do not, in fact, believe in green thumbs. I do believe that there is such a thing as a gardener's eye and that it is a gift of what Christians call grace—a gift that comes from outside, that is apart from one's own intentions, and that can never be entirely fathomed. Gardening is, in other words, something religious. And its religion involves a point in time, a moment of conversion that separates things into before and after.

Whether the gift of a gardener's eye comes early or late in life, it comes all at once, or at least within a very brief span of time. One was not a gardener, because the gardener's eye had not yet been given. Then the gift comes, and one knows that one had been living in darkness, but that now there is suddenly a new world to see, a world whose beauties and wonders many lifetimes would not be sufficient to encompass.

In saying that the gardener's eye comes all at once or quickly, I do not mean to imply that once this gift is given we take up our hoes and pruning shears immediately, learn hundreds of Latin names overnight, and become active gardeners forthwith. I believe instead that receiving this eye is a moment of revelation, which may not be acted upon for a long time. A road has been revealed, a road into the world of gardening, but it may go untraveled until the time is right. My friend Allen Bush traces his own love of gardening to the day in the third grade when he planted some bean seeds—"*Bush* beans, of course," he adds—as a school project. Nothing else happened until one spring day during his college years at the University of Kentucky, where he was majoring in sociology. He walked to the top of a hill overlooking the Kentucky River and found himself in the middle of a grove of buckeye trees in full bloom. From that moment on, the love of plants filled his life. But there is no solid rule about the length of time between what I have called the moment of revelation and its fruition. Another friend, Edith Eddleman, lived during her childhood with a grandmother who was so ardent a gardener that once when Edith was a very young girl and was given some seeds to plant, the only spot she could find in the garden was under a pecan tree. The seeds never came up, and Edith thought, Well, so much for gardening. Then, when she was twenty, a friend took her to a greenhouse so bright with bloom that she was wonderstruck and plunged headlong into the world of gardening, trying to learn as much as she could as quickly as she could.

I began to be a gardener during a childhood now sufficiently distant that the circumstances of my conversion remain somewhat dim and unclear, although what I first saw when I began to see with a gardener's eye is vivid. It was April of 1943, shortly after my eighth birthday. My parents, my two younger brothers, one still a baby, and I were living on an eleven-acre farm west of Irving, Texas, between Dallas and Fort Worth. City suburb now, it was deep country then. We lived on Kit Lone Star Continuation Road, a mile after the macadam ceased and the dusty gravel began. We had a few acres of truck farm, which was poor in comparison with the Loopers' farm next door, where every square inch was well tended and abundant with produce.

I had some vague awareness of plants. My father gave me chores, including hoeing the weeds out of a long row of black-eyed peas, so I must have known what a black-eyed pea looked like and that anything that wasn't that was a weed. I knew that peach trees had long, thin leaves like green fingers, and that the leaves of plum trees were shorter, fatter, and more oval. I knew what spearmint and cress were, what ditches they grew in, and how one had a sweet spice, the other a sharper astringence. I knew what all children seem to know by instinct, that there's a trick with honeysuckle that yields for the tongue one tiny drop of a nectar never to be forgotten once tasted. I knew what bushes were likely to harbor wasps' nests and which others were abuzz with honeybees and bumblebees from earliest spring until latest autumn. I knew that the fuzz on our window screens came from the cottonwood trees in the river bottom down the road a bit from our place on Kit Lone Star. But I was not yet a gardener.

It may have come on two days right in a row, or there may have been a short time in between, but I know it was in April, the ninth April of my life. First it was Mrs. Harkey's iris fields, not far from our own farm near Irving. And then it was Mrs. Penn's azaleas, near my grandparents' house in Dallas.

Mrs. Harkey was an elementary school teacher, fourth grade, Irving Public School. She was a widow, and I think she had a son in the army, stationed in England a year before the invasion of Normandy. She was also a serious gardener who hybridized and raised irises and daylilies on her own small farm. Her farm was much tidier than ours, and it was in the service of beauty, not utility like the Loopers' farm next door. My mother wanted to buy some irises for her garden, and she brought me along one afternoon in our 1937 white Chevy with a running board and tires worn nearly bare from the gravel road to our house. She wanted to pick out her irises when they were in full bloom, to get the colors she wanted.

There was no sight so lovely, I thought, as a two-acre field of bearded irises in the slanting golden light of a Texas afternoon in high April. Deep purples; blues of every shade and hue; whites and creams; light-colored flowers edged with stipples and dots of a darker tone; yellows and coppers and bronzes; burgundies and orchids and lavenders—so wide is the palette of colors of irises that it seems inevitable that they should collectively take their name from the Greek goddess of the rainbow. The blossoms, moreover, are wonderfully constructed, with their erect standards and downward-flowing falls. Together they capture the eye, which then draws closer to examine them individually, to look at each blossom and each petal, and to admire the fringe of orange beard adorning each of their falls. Many of them have, furthermore, a sweet and subtle perfume reminiscent of wisteria and of vineyards when the grapes begin to ripen.

As my mother selected her irises, discussing her choices with Mrs. Harkey, I learned something else. Irises, like human beings and domestic pets, had names—'Queen of May', 'Cordelia', 'Mrs. Horace Darwin', 'Perfection', and many others. Mrs. Harkey grew five hundred named varieties, and she claimed to know each of them on sight. I thought this was a task that would take a long lifetime to achieve. I then asked the name of a yellow one that seemed to have some special quality and asked how much it cost. It was named 'Happy Days', and it cost twenty-five cents, a week's allowance. 'Happy Days', the first plant that was all my own, came home with me that afternoon in the pasteboard box with the six irises my mother had selected. An iris so named was a perfect choice for a child who would grow up to find that most of his days in a garden were full of pleasure.

It could have been the very next day, one of those Saturdays when I went to Dallas to spend the night with my grandparents, Pauline and Big Dave Lacy. But whenever it was, I remember Grandmother asking Big Dave to drive us over to see Mrs. Penn's azaleas. Mrs. Penn had a large estate on Preston Road in Highland Park. The property was walled on three sides but open on the fourth, where the land sloped down to Turtle Creek, a sluggish tributary of the Trinity River that had been dammed in that part of town to form a series of small lakes. There was a road running along the other side of the creek from Mrs. Penn's place. On the banks of the creek, which was shaded by two rows of evergreen oaks, Mrs. Penn had her azaleas— hundreds of them, maybe thousands, in April so covered with bloom that no foliage showed. No color known to azaleas was excluded from this planting: pale pink, watermelon red, coral, white, lilac, frank orange, deep reds, all tumbled together in a splash of heady color down the bank to the water's edge. There was nothing subtle about this riot of color, but the colors were more muted in their mirroring in the creek, where more azaleas seemed to be blooming beneath the dark waters. I imagined a world where in sunny places the iris fields went on to the horizon, and where by shady waters azaleas were in bloom forever. I didn't have a garden yet, but I had a gardener's eye.

It was about the same time that music entered my life, in such a way that it has always seemed to be connected with gardening. My parents' taste in music ran heavily to Dinah Shore, the Andrews Sisters, and Bing Crosby, but one of my uncles had several season tickets to the Sunday-afternoon concerts of the Dallas Symphony Orchestra. One day he invited me to go with him. The program began with a performance of Bach's *Magnificat*. I felt chills from the very opening bars the orchestra played before the chorus came in with the words "Magnificat anima mea." The strong rhythm, the bright sounds of trumpets, the surging quality of the music opened my ears to a new world as bright and beautiful in its own way and as filled with color as a sunny field of irises. The concert ended with Gustav Mahler's Fourth Symphony. I was transfixed by the tranquillity of the adagio movement, music that seemed to be born from beauty mirrored in dark calm waters.

*   *   *

I PLACE MYSELF somewhere between Allen Bush and Edith Eddle-man as regards the gardener's eye and the actual passionate pursuit of the gardening life. During the rest of grade school and then in junior and senior high, after we moved to Dallas from the country, I worked in my mother's garden. During college, at Duke University, I spent as much time as possible in the Sarah P. Duke Gardens. While in graduate school, after Hella and I were married and living in a tiny apartment, we borrowed land from friends living outside of Durham for a vegetable garden. When I began teaching, we lived in a succession of rented houses, at each of which we gardened in a modest way. Thus my experience of gardening has been continuous since childhood, but there came a great change in 1972: we bought an old house, with no garden, in southern New Jersey near the shore. I was free then to begin a serious, almost frightening and obsessive accumulation of plants to observe, love in some instances and despise in others, and to live with as dramatis personae, if bit players until our sons Paul and Michael grew up.

One may become a lover of gardening or of music in a single moment, but there is something more involved. First, the experience of conversion or initiation, perhaps of seduction, depends on many other people having been there first. Each of these arts is a special world with its long history of human creation, using the materials of the natural order. To enter either world is to accept an inheritance, a legacy left by Pliny, Linnaeus, Mendel, John Loudon, Gertrude Jekyll, Louise Beebe Wilder, or by Palestrina, J. S. Bach, Mozart, and Gustav Mahler, and also a legacy to which many others whose names are unknown have contributed. Second, the eye that looks on plants with absolute approval and acceptance comes first, and the knowl-edge of their habits comes later, accumulated over a lifetime. To outsiders, I imagine that music and gardening both seem sequential and rational. In music, someone starts by finding middle C on the piano and on a sheet of music, proceeds to finger exercises and then to Bach's *Two Part Inventions,* and finally, if the talent and the discipline are there, to Mozart sonatas and Brahms ballades. In gardening, one begins by learning the differences between herbaceous and woody plants, and between annuals and perennials and biennials, proceeding thence to an understanding of pH factors, urea-form fertilizers, and the merits of *Milium effusum.*

I don't think it works like that. The wonder of gardening is that one becomes a gardener by becoming a gardener. Horticulture is sometimes described as a science, sometimes as an art, but the truth is that it is neither, although it partakes of both. It is more like falling in love, something that escapes all logic.

"Though a very old man," Thomas Jefferson wrote near the end of his life, "I am but a very young gardener." I think I know exactly what he meant. The young child who puts a seed in a pot of dirt, waters it, and then watches with fascination as it becomes a living plant has as much claim to being a gardener as someone who writes a book of relentlessly practical advice telling us what we should be doing when, month by month throughout the year. Furthermore, no matter how long we have dug in the earth, there is always something to learn.

Finally, although I do not want to press the claim to the point of exaggeration, I suspect that more loving and caring people can be found among gardeners than among any other group united by a common interest. I think that the possession of a gardener's eye, which is primarily aesthetic in character, also has a moral effect. I have long been struck by two passages from British writers of the Victorian era who both combined a passion for the beauty of nature and art with the conviction that there is a quality of vision, a way of seeing the world, that has a broader ethical consequence. The first is Charles Kingsley, who in *Madam How and Lady Why* (1869), a book consisting of extended imaginary dialogues with his young son, Grenville Archer Kingsley, raises a question: why is the soil of a moor black and peaty, while the soil in fields and gardens is brown? His son counters with other questions: What good is there in wondering about the color of soil? Why does his father press him to answer? The conversation continues with this exchange, starting with the father's reply:

> I want you to look and think. I want every one to look and think. Half the misery in the world comes from not looking, and then from not thinking. And I do not wish you to be miserable.
>
> But shall I be miserable if I do not find out such little things as this?
>
> You will be miserable if you do not learn to understand little things: because then you will not be able to understand great things when you meet them. Children who are not trained to use their eyes and their common sense grow up the more miserable the cleverer they are.
>
> Why?
>
> Because they grow up what men call dreamers, and big- ots, and fanatics, causing misery to themselves and to all who deal with them. So I say again, think.

Convergent testimony comes from John Ruskin's *Modern Painters*. "The greatest thing a human soul ever does in this world," Ruskin wrote, "is to *see* something, and tell what it *saw* in a plain way. Hundreds of people can talk for one who can think, but thousands can think for one who can see. To see clearly is poetry, prophecy, and religion—all in one."

No one can garden well without seeing well—and habits of vision transfer to other areas of life. To see a garden is to see an intricate network of connections. It is, I believe, a healing kind of vision in a lunatic modern—or postmodern—world diseased by com- partmentalized habits of mind in a great many important areas of human endeavor: business, education, medicine, economics, and the foreign and domestic policies of governments. The ultimate wisdom is that of Candide in Voltaire's novel. After traveling the world, visiting the utopia of El Dorado, observing suffering and oppression on every hand—meanwhile guided by a mistaken philosophy that holds that all is for the best, no matter how horrible it may be— Candide learns his lesson from an Islamic farmer and adopts it as his own hard-won wisdom.

"We must cultivate our garden."

Indeed we must.

From a Window

AS SOMEONE who both writes and teaches, I spend many hours most weeks in my tiny and cluttered upstairs study. In front of me there's a computer screen and a blank wall beyond that. But from the window to my left I have an aerial view of one portion of my garden. The window overlooks part of the asphalt driveway that leads to the place where we park the cars near the walk to the kitchen door. (One car is red, the other gunmetal. We have no garage, so we have learned to think of the cars as pieces of outdoor sculpture that we can drive to the grocery store.) The driveway entrance is flanked on one side by a *Cornus kousa* of respectable height and spread and a twenty-foot-tall Russian olive tree that leans precariously toward the horizontal as a result of a brush with hurricane Gloria some years ago. On the other side of the driveway there is an eighteen-year-old *Viburnum plicatum* 'Mariesii'. The trees meet over the driveway to form an arch that from spring until early autumn is a cool-looking tunnel of gray and green.

From my window I can also see three half barrels that used to hold whiskey. Now they are planters, strategically placed to keep visitors from parking beyond the driveway. In my view there is a strip of lawn and one curving end of a deep perennial border that sweeps along three sides of the back garden. The front of the bed lies in full sun, but in high summer it recedes into the deep shade of a paulownia tree, two dogwoods, a dawn redwood, and a line of white pines marking the edge of our property. In winter, when the deciduous trees are bare, this border, heavily mulched with pine straw and decaying salt hay, is sunny most of the day.

Even in January, in the dead of winter, there is always something to see from my study. I can examine the structure of the woody plants outside: the branches of the paulownia stretched out widely, as if in supplication; the conical growth of the dawn redwood; and the arching habit of a *Hydrangea paniculata* this side of a white pine. I can see the color and texture of the bark. The paulownia is gray, with a slight greenish stain from some algae, and the bark is slightly channeled, with bumpy nobs where lower limbs have been removed. The dawn redwood is russet, and the bark hangs in long strips.

There is no true death here in winter. We have an abundance of birds that do not migrate southward, and it is always a joy to catch the sudden flash of color as a cardinal or a blue jay swoops in and out of view. The innumerable squirrels of the neighborhood use the paulownia as their jungle gym, chasing one another up and down its trunk and branches, and as their trapeze from which to leap through thin air to a nearby pine. In January the seed plumes of ornamental grasses, tall sedums, and astilbes are left standing for winter interest. These plants are all dormant, and wet snows eventually beat them into bedragglement, but other plants stay green and fresh in winter, forming colorful rosettes of foliage in the brown mulch. Primulas, foxgloves, and dwarf Chinese astilbes all are reminders that life endures and that there is always another growing season, with plants ready to explode into exuberance with the returning sun and the warming air and soil.

In early January, the most prominent herbaceous plants are adjacent colonies of several species of hellebores and of *Arum italicum* 'Pictum' at the base of the dawn redwood. One hellebore, the Christmas rose *(Helleborus niger)*, is both a literary childhood memory and a recent addition to our garden. One of the first things I read about gardening, in the 1940s, was the catalog of Wayside Gardens, when Wayside was still in Mentor, Ohio. Under the headline "The Christmas Rose—It blooms through the snow!" a black-and-white photograph showed the large single flowers of Christmas roses sticking up out of snow and ice. The Wayside catalog fudged the truth quite a bit. For one thing, *H. niger* isn't a rose, or even a near relative, but a member of the ranunculus family. For another, it doesn't really bloom through the snow. The truth is that snow may fall on it after it has started its long season of bloom of six weeks or more. And it's more likely to produce its white flowers, which are occasionally suffused with pink, in January or later, not in time for Christmas. (This hellebore got its common name, I suspect, from Germany, where the species is called *Christrosen*—"Christ's roses"—because of a bit of old plant lore. An angel, legend has it, took pity on a little shepherd girl who had nothing to give the Infant Jesus in his manger. The angel handed her a weed, but first transformed it into this beautiful flower of winter.)

Helleborus niger has the reputation of being the most difficult of all hellebores to grow. Mine, so far, is doing well because I took Nancy Goodwin's advice and watered it in midsummer of the year I planted it with Epsom salts, a tablespoon to the gallon. Two other hellebores in the colony are easier to grow. One is the bearsfoot hellebore *(H. foetidus)*, which generally blooms for me in January, putting up a great spike of pale apple-green buds and flowers whose color contrasts dramatically with its more somber dark green leaves. The other is the Lenten rose *(H. orientalis)*. Its black-green leaves are handsome all year, and when it blooms it is one of the wonders of the winter garden. The downward-facing blossoms range from creamy white to deep maroon, with intermediate colors of gray-green, blush, wine, and many other hues that have no name. The flowers are often stippled or brushed with other tints.

I got my Lenten roses from the garden of my friend Hannah Withers, in Charlotte, North Carolina, who in turn got them from the garden of her friend Elizabeth Lawrence. (Miss Lawrence was devoted to hellebores of any sort, writing in *A Southern Garden* in 1942 that "an established plant becomes an heirloom, for in all likelihood it will outlive the gardener who plants it.") Hannah also gave me my *Arum italicum* 'Pictum'—a variant form with more pronounced marbling of its pewter, silver, and deep green leaves. This arum is especially valuable for the way it goes against the tide of the seasons. Its arrow-shaped leaves, some six inches long, arise directly from the tuber when they unfurl in November. They keep their color right through the winter, and they are especially lovely when dusted with snow or covered with gleaming frost on a cold, sunny morning. The plant is of more than winter interest, however, considering its creamy green spring blossoms, much like those of its close kin, Jack-in-the-pulpit, and the tall spikes of bright red berries that follow in late summer, after the leaves have disappeared.

There is some added pleasure in the thought that when contemplating my hellebores and arums from my window I am looking at beauty with a sinister side. *Helleborus* means "a food that kills." The plants are poisonous in every part, containing a chemical called helleborin. In the Middle Ages its roots were used to produce a heart medicine that was often more quickly lethal than cardiac disease. As for the arum, it is loaded with toxic alkaloids. (The aroids, the family to which it belongs, are the mad chemists of the plant kingdom, producing delicious and valuable foods like taro in some genera, deadly toxins and powerful hallucinogens in others.)

In late January the light on sunny days becomes almost miraculous. The pallor of the winter sun is now departing. The length of the days has been increasing since the winter solstice, and now the few extra minutes each day add up to something substantial, a real turning point. The sun, moreover, moves closer and closer to the meridian. From the window, I see the strong sunlight, and the equally strong shadows it casts of the venerable swamp maple in the middle of the back garden. I cannot see more of the maple than a few twigs, but the long shadows of the tree's massive trunk and main branches paint their shapes on the lawn with great power and drama. At the winter solstice, when the sun lay low and southerly in the sky, these shadows pointed due north at midday. Since then, they have moved westward by daily degrees.

As the sun moves higher on its climb toward the summer solstice, it streams in through the windows at ever-changing angles to light up places it does not reach during most of the year. On the desk in my study, one corner never receives direct sunlight except for two days right before the spring equinox and two days after the autumnal equinox, always in late afternoon. A vase placed there with just one tulip in it will glow like a moment of epiphany, as will a chrysanthemum on the equivalent days in fall.

I am writing in late January, at the time of strong shadows of the maple on the lawn. Gardeners, like everyone else, live second by second and minute by minute. What we see at one particular moment is what is then and there before us. But there is a second way of seeing. Seeing with the eye of memory, not the eye of our anatomy, calls up days and seasons past and years gone by. The memory, Saint Augustine said, makes us who we are. It is a deep and mysterious well, and I think a well with living waters. Granting us knowledge of what has been in the orderly progress of past days and seasons, it gives us a fairly reliable prophecy of what will be. There is no tulip of epiphany on my desk yet, but it will come. The garden outside the window is moving toward resurrection.

By the first week of March—in some years before that—there will be early daffodils, the diminutive *Narcissus obvallaris* being the first to blow its golden trumpets. A few weeks later, most of the little bulbs—the scillas, the chionodoxas, the muscari, the puschkinias, and all the rest—will be at their peak. Many perennials, dormant since late November, will have awakened, sitting with little mounds of foliage in the mulch, like cats dozing in the sun. (Sometimes there are real cats, too, Geoffrey and Jeremy, both feral, who have adopted us to the point of allowing themselves to be fed though not touched, love to lie in the sun in this part of the garden.) The maple I cannot quite see will have covered itself with the crimson flowers that will change in early May to little tan helicopters, which will take to the air and land everywhere to sprout and be weeded out. Forsythia, the only one I have, a small shrub huddled between the driveway and the tall viburnum, will be in bloom, with its faintly disturbing shade of chrome yellow. But there still may be snowfall, like the one we had one year, starting on March 24. It snowed for two days, tiny icy flakes that glistened like infinitesimal diamonds the first day, huge fluffy and feathery ones the next. There was no wind and no drifting, and when the snow stopped and the sun came out, the snow lay four inches deep on the lawns and the beds. *Scilla siberica* and chionodoxa were blooming beneath the blanket, and for the first time I understood why chionodoxa in Greek translates to its English common name, glory of the snow. It and the little squill both looked like blue flames burning below the accumulated snow. The pale blue of their fire was unmistakable from the upstairs window of the room where I work. The forsythia was also transformed. Covered with snow, its bells were stilled from chrome brashness into a pale cream that glowed from within.

In April, tulips and large daffodils will dominate the scene. Under the paulownia several clumps of the fine double primula 'Mark Viette' will lift their heavy crop of flowers near the end of the month. Bearing both blue and pink petals, they have the look of African violets. Farther back, the pure white flowers of *Vinca minor* 'Miss Jekyll's White' will begin to open, more and more of them each day, until they star the pine mulch with a galaxy of blooms. By now, the garden I see from the window will be gathering force in a crescendo of growth. Large hostas like *Hosta sieboldiana* 'Elegans', 'Blue Umbrellas', and 'Sum and Substance' will put on muscle, taking less than two weeks to reach the size of washtubs by May 7 (most years). The latest daffodils will be in full cry, accompanied by *Phlox stolonifera* and other spring perennials. The mat of low *Veronica rupestris* that has insinuated itself into an equally low mat of golden moneywort will bloom to happy if accidental effect: a winsome contrast between the dark green leaves and violet-purple flowers of the one, the bright chartreuse foliage of the other.

There will probably be a mid-May lull, for there usually is—a time when only green seems much in evidence, except for the multitude of sparkling white bracts that cover the outstretched or tabulated branches of the viburnum next to the driveway, and except for some pink foxgloves. But the lull is short, and it is followed by astilbes, Siberian irises, peonies, Madonna lilies, and everything else that blooms then everywhere in the garden, including what I can see of it from my window—and what I would see, if I were sentenced never again to walk into the garden, but just to watch it from this second-story vantage.

Then spring will end, and summer will begin. I date this metamorphosis around the fifteenth of June, when our *Cornus kousa,* a dogwood of Asian origin, holds center stage next to the driveway and the sidewalk on Belhaven Avenue. This splendid small tree of earliest summer starts slowly in its move toward magnificence. The buds open in late May to display four small bracts of olive green. They steadily enlarge and pale toward white, until the tree exceeds in beauty our native eastern dogwood, as well as the white viburnum across the driveway. By this time of year, I am almost never in my study; in fact, each new stage of spring lures me farther and farther out of doors into the garden, to work, to take the fragrant air of fresh dirt and sweet flowers, or just to think how fortunate I am to be a gardener. As it happens, we have one of the few plants of *Cornus kousa* in the vicinity. Pedestrians ask about it. So do people in cars, who roll down their windows and ask what it is and where can they get it.

Summer will happen, as it always does. So will autumn, which all my friends know is my favorite time of year, and the best season in my own garden. In the summer and in the fall, I will be torn between the impulse to stay at home in the garden that Hella and I have made and the desire we share to see gardens others have made, in other places. My study, visited only because of the necessities people who write on gardening become heir to, will seem lifeless and sere. It is some small kin to Faust's study, too long inhabited by a man who after many years wearied of theory and burned with the passion to see life's living tree.

From mid-June to early October in my own study, I can see neither Faust's symbolic tree or any trees at all. I catch only the merest patch of sky and an electricity line—things a prisoner might see from the confines of a jail cell. My study is the only room in the house that is air-conditioned, not for my comfort but for that of my computer, which one August day, after a week when the temperature soared into the upper nineties and stayed there, suffered a serious and costly meltdown.

In the summer, I am much more likely to be in the garden than to be looking at it through a window, but I still enjoy the experience of seeing one part of the garden framed by a window. Only one window, in the living room, is entirely blocked, by a calycanthus bush festooned with sweet autumn clematis. The allspice odor of the calycanthus fills the room when the window is flung open on a fine June day. In late August, the flowers of the clematis give off a delicate perfume. Weeks later, the leaves of the calycanthus turn a deep yellow, which fills the room in late afternoon with a warm and golden light. The effect is delightful, but it was never planned. Our son Michael just decided one day to plant a calycanthus there, and the clematis volunteered. All gardeners need to know when to accept something wonderful and unexpected, taking no credit except for letting it be.

But in midautumn, there comes a day to return to the study window and the partial vision of a garden and of gardening that it affords. The air conditioner goes to the attic. Finally, pineapple sage *(Salvia rutilans)* is in bloom. I cannot smell the sweet and fruity perfume of its leaves, but I can see in late afternoon the uncanny incandescence of its slender scarlet torches of flowers, aglow with the sun behind them. I can also enjoy another salvia nearby, *S. involucrata* 'Bethellii'. Its deep rose flowers are pleasant enough, but its leaves own my heart, for they are a pale green, velvety even from this distance, with some trick, like stained glass, that makes them so glow from within that one could imagine they would look the same on a dead planet no longer lit by its cold star.

In October I will observe the steady progress of the season. The viburnum next to the driveway will turn to a sullen maroon, brightened by a scattering of white flowers out of season. Many of the needles of the white pines will yellow before falling to the ground and deepening the mulch with their copper hues. The dawn redwood, a deciduous conifer thought to be long extinct until it turned up after World War II in a remote part of China as a "living fossil," will drop its pale orange leaves, some of which will almost cover the clumps of white sweet alyssum that reliably self-seed at the front of this patch of garden. Our dogwoods, which are always holdouts, staying green when all the others in the neighborhood have turned, will finally change from green to port wine. One night will bring the killing frost that blackens the large leaves of the paulownia, which fall from the tree immediately, offering no ceremony of departure. The leaves of the old swamp maple will fall, more and more every day, until the last one has been raked from the yet green lawn and hauled to the compost bin.

Then will come the end of fall, the beginning of winter, although no winter of the spirit. An old French hybrid of *Rosa rugosa*, 'Blanc Double de Coubert', develops leaves in November that for four weeks are a golden fountain from the window. Suddenly the leaves turn brown and fall off. But by then, next to the hellebores, the arum leaves have unfolded their arrows of pewter and silver and green, to delight my eye in the winter weeks that lie ahead.

Small Wonders

IT IS SAINT VALENTINE'S DAY. On the table is a loose and informal bouquet Hella made from the flowers I got from the florist yesterday. The weather has alternated between dismal gray, with low clouds scudding across the sky, and brilliant light, when the clouds let the sun appear. Even when the sun shines, it is unpleasant outside, for the wind is chill and damp. I went into the garden this morning only briefly, bringing inside a few flowers that are in bloom on our own patch of earth on a late winter day when the thought of the coming of spring is almost feasible.

I have brought inside a few sprigs of winter heath, some with white flowers, some in several shades of pink. I have brought twigs of the Chinese witch hazel 'Arnold Promise', now at its height of bloom, its branches covered with clusters of wispy and twisted intensely yellow flowers that have a sweet yet spicy perfume. And I have plucked a snowdrop, just one, that was blooming next to the driveway.

The common snowdrop *(Galanthus nivalis)* is at first sight one of the humblest flowers of the garden. One wants to call it modest and unassuming, even if those words properly apply only to people. If snowdrops flowered in July no one would pay them the least attention. Their appeal lies in their January or February season of bloom, when there is not much competition and when, as befits their name, they may in fact push through an inch or two of snow to open their buds. Their appeal lies, further, in their apparent simplicity. Only two or three inches tall, they put up several stems per bulb, each bearing a pendant and nodding little flower of only three petals or segments, all milky white, drooping down from a little button of an ovary of pale lime green. Every year when I see the snowdrops in our garden, I note this fact and then forget it, lusting for the time when daffodils and then tulips will appear, putting on their grander show.

But the apparent modesty of snowdrops is a deception, based entirely on the way we look at them. Even a small human being is tall compared with a snowdrop, at three inches or under. And since these bulbs hold their blossoms facing downward toward the soil from which they just sprang, we look down at the back of those three petals, not into their heart, as an insect might. I was well into middle age before I thought to bring one snowdrop blossom inside and spend some time looking at it. Viewed properly—eye to eye, if you will—a snowdrop is as complex and subtle in its beauty as an orchid. There turn out to be six flower segments, not just the three we see from on high. The outer petals enfold and partly conceal the inner ones. These are shorter by half. They overlap to form a tube, which flares outward near its end. The inner petals are pristine white near the base, then banded with a contrasting shade of fresh lime green, then edged again with a thin band of white. On closer look, the band of green is not a solid band at all: it is composed of very narrow vertical green stripes, separated by even more narrow stripes of white. But green and white do not say everything about a snowdrop blossom. All six petals, inner and outer, surround a disk of overlapping honey-colored stamens, which in turn surrounds a white pistil. Snowdrops, it turns out, lay claim to a complicated and rich sort of beauty. If gods make flowers, as ancient peoples believed, then the tulip was made by a tyro, the snowdrop by a god who had mastered the craft, a god with no need to resort to look-at-me colors like crimson and scarlet. "God," someone said, "is in the details." Having looked deeply into a snowdrop blossom, I know better what that means.

AM I ACCURATELY reporting what I see in such a blossom? The answer is no . . . and yes.

For my first forty-five years, I had better than twenty-twenty vision. Near vision was okay, and long-range vision was so keen that I could see the twisted hooks on barbed wire from 150 feet away. But eventually, in order to read, I had to hold books at greater and greater distances, until, the length of my arms exhausted, I got reading glasses, and, when I turned fifty-five, bifocals. Even with glasses, if I looked into the heart of a snowdrop, I would see only that it wasn't quite as simple as it looked from outside and above. There was some green there somewhere inside, and maybe yellow in the very middle. Nothing to bring on thoughts about God or the gods being in the details.

The trick of seeing a snowdrop flower as something to admire and wonder over lies in an optical instrument called an Eschenbach *Leutchlupe.* Manufactured in Nuremberg, Germany, this device is in essence a flashlight illuminating the field of a lens that magnifies objects tenfold, revealing tiny details that the eye unaided cannot perceive. A powerful hand lens with a focused beam of light opens up an entire world below the threshold of the ordinary experience of seeing.

The flowers of winter heaths prove just as complicated in their beauty and strangeness as those of snowdrops. To the naked eye, these blossoms look like little ant eggs, white or various shades of pink, with something dark protruding from their ends. But at magnification on the order of ten, each flower has an unsuspectedly rich

architecture. At the base of the blossom four short, somewhat triangular petals encircle four larger petals, which, like those of the inner
flower segments of snowdrops, overlap. They form a tapering tube
with a minute opening at the end. But while the sexual parts of
snowdrop blossoms are inward, concealed and protected by the inter-
nal petals, they protrude beyond the petals in winter heaths. The
eight stamens vary in color from maroon to tan, depending on the
cultivar; the pistil is white in some, magenta in others.

The hand lens also reveals the probable cause of one of the
strange and useful features of winter heath in the garden—the ex-
traordinary longevity of its blossoms and its prolonged season of
bloom, from Thanksgiving to early April or even later. Under magnification, the blooms prove to have a glistening sheen, a waxen substance that I would guess protects them from desiccation in the
strong winds of winter and keeps them fresh for months.

Seen up close, my witch hazel also offers its surprises. From
several yards away this small tree is aglow with the deep yellow of
the fluffy petals borne close to its twigs and branches, contrasting
with the chocolate brown of the leaves that persist almost to winter's
end. Taking a twig in hand, I see that its flowers are borne in clusters
ranging in number from two to twenty. It is chiefly the petals that
are visible, and they intermingle and overlap to the extent that the
clusters seem to be flowers themselves, somewhat rounded in form,
like the flowers of a mimosa tree. The hand lens tells another story.
Each individual blossom bears four silken-textured golden petals,
faintly striped with translucent lines. The pistil and the stamens are
contained within a tiny chalice of reddish brown, which is covered
on the outside by a thick coat of down.

Her friends tell how Elizabeth Lawrence could often be found
outside in late winter on her hands and knees to take a closer look
at some tiny flower, all the more valuable because it was blooming
in a sparse season, with no spectacular competition from more obviously voluptuous flowers like tulips or cattleya orchids. I don't know,
but I rather hope that at some time in her life she happened onto

an Eschenbach 10x *Leutchlupe,* for this hand lens, it seems to me, evens out a couple of things quite nicely. It enables me to exchange human vision and its limits for something approaching the eye of a butterfly or a bee. It also demonstrates that viewed correctly, the flowers of snowdrops, winter heaths, and witch hazels are as ravishing as roses, as bewitching as the huge open blossoms of the southern magnolia. On this mid-February day, there is still more to bring inside and dive into with my fortified eye. A little white crocus— 'Snow Bunting', I think—is blooming everywhere in the garden, where I planted it years ago by the hundreds. Here and there are other crocuses, seedlings of uncertain ancestry, larger than 'Snow Bunting', pale lavender and growing in unexpected places.

I bring some crocus flowers inside for a closer and more intimate look. I turn the white one over, discovering that the green stem is stippled with pale lavender near the base of the flower. On the backs of the petals, the lavender changes to unmistakable and frank purple in a feathery pattern that spreads itself like the frost flowers on a window on an arctic-cold winter morning. Viewed from above, the cup of the crocus, which seems a pure and bridal white from just a few feet away, turns out to be just as rich and complicated as a snowdrop. At the center of the blossom, the petals are deep yellow with a slight olive overlay or cast. The three stamens are bright gold, with a dark blotch of black at the base of the pollen-dusted anthers. The pistil, with a three-forked stigma that has a feathered edge, is bright saffron, a reminder that an autumn-blooming species in the genus *Crocus,* the saffron crocus *(C. sativus),* gave us a name for a color as well as a dye and a spice. And as I study this tiny white flower, the hand lens brings another pleasure of the senses; in its slight warmth, the blossom gives off a delicate sweet fragrance. As for the pale lavender crocus, the purple markings on the back of its petal are even more pronounced. Again, the very heart of the flower is golden, and the pistil and stigma are mandarin red.

I have also brought inside a stem of *Jasminum nudiflorum,* the winter jasmine, whose only flaw is that it lacks the perfume most other species have. This lack is entirely forgivable at this time of year, for its green stems and deep yellow flowers bring cheer to a gloomy day, radiance to a sunny one. The flower seems to have entire simplicity, but appearances are, once again, deceptive, for the backs of the petals are washed with the red of fresh blood, color that spreads and changes to tones of rust on older blossoms about to fade. Under the light of the lens, the swelling buds, which can only be described as phalliform, are tipped with glossy bright crimson.

I have learned to think of the time that lies on the cusp of latest winter and earliest spring as the season of small or even tiny flowers, and also the season of the hand lens. Many a flowering weed turns out when viewed by a magnified eye to be exceptionally beautiful. Chickweed blossoms are a pure white garland of petals surrounding the dark pistil and stamens. The pale green buds, smooth to a more distant eye, are as hairy as Esau. As for an unidentified annual species of veronica that grows abundantly in my garden, hugging the earth but still managing to cover huge amounts of territory in no time flat, its tiny, almost insignificant flowers, mere specks of deep sky blue, prove through the hand lens to be more pink than blue, and to be as elegantly cupped as tulips.

In early March, I will have dandelions, just a few flowers at first, on stems so short that they rest on their rosette of leaves, not yet rising on tall stems to flower and then quickly disperse their seeds to float on the breeze. Dandelions on their first appearance are cheering to the spirit, but as they increase in number the mind quickly turns to thoughts of weeding them out with a hand digger to keep them under control. But a dandelion flower seen through an Eschenbach lens has wondrous complexity and beauty. The outer ray flowers of this composite only partially conceal the golden anthers beneath what we commonly, if mistakenly, call petals. Surrounding the very center of the blossom, around the disk flowers in the middle (the flowers that will produce the heavy crop of gossamer seeds), other anthers are borne on stamens arranged in a circle, like some sort of horticultural ring dance.

A week or two after dandelion season commences, there will be blossoms in my garden on daphne 'Carol Mackie', which has handsome evergreen foliage with a narrow band of silver on the edges of the leaves. The clusters of small pink flowers are delicious to behold, and even more delicious to smell, for their sweet spice. But seen ten times their size they become almost miraculous. The pink-tinged white blossoms have enormous substance. Seeming to be made at once of wax and of crystal, their petals are frosted like satin glass and covered with a scattering of diamond dust. They are reminiscent of a rosy dawn, of cotton candy, of sugared rose petals. There is more to see here than I or anyone else can ever say, except that I might mention that a tiny green speck on one petal is revealed by the lens as a tiny spider of remarkably ferocious aspect.

BUT THERE IS MORE to explore this way than flowers. Certain seeds are equally fascinating through a hand lens. Someone once gave me a peculiar gift—a lidded tray of clear plastic, filled with a hundred plastic boxes, all cubes measuring three-quarters of an inch along each side. Each was labeled with the name of a plant, and inside each there were several of its seeds. Some of these seeds are large enough that their individual characteristics can be noted and compared. The golden-tan seeds of moonflower vines, rather irregular ovoids, are smooth to the touch and the eye alike. Nasturtium seeds are corky. The black and light gray stripes of Russian sunflower are instantly recognizable by anyone who has ever filled a bird feeder. But the seeds of bird-of-paradise *(Strelitzia reginae)*, which were new to me, are immensely curious. Black, and about the same size as a nasturtium seed, they are topped with what looks like a tousled bright orange wig made from the same fibers used in a Tuffy pad. *Hortus Third* describes this physiological feature as "a filamentous aril," thus sending me immediately to its glossary. An aril turns out to be "a usually fleshy appendage of the funiculus." Digging a little deeper in the glossary I learn that a funiculus is "the stalk by which an ovule is attached to the placenta in the ovary."

I think I will stick with an orange wig made of the plastic in a Tuffy pad. For all its precision, the language that botanists speak is at its base highly metaphorical, but its poetic character is hidden to most of us in that its metaphors come from Latin and Greek. To name the elements of the world of seeds seen through an Eschenbach *Leutchlupe,* franker metaphors are called for. Thus, hollyhock seeds look like coal-black fossils of ammonites, the extinct mollusks whose name is itself a metaphor taken from the ram's horns associated with the Roman cult of Jupiter Ammon. Cleome seeds, far tinier than those of hollyhocks, echo this shape. The seeds of calendulas look like little caterpillars rolled into balls—and here again the depth of poetic language is astonishing, considering that the literal meaning of "caterpillar" refers to a hairy cat. Oleander seeds resemble sea cucumbers, the seeds of scabiosa bring to mind the shuttlecocks used in badminton, and the comparison between bachelor's-button seeds and old-fashioned shaving brushes with handles of polished bone is almost irresistible. The seeds of parsley could be tiny crookneck gourds, striped gray and tan. *Cynoglossum amabile,* the Chinese forget-me-not, has seeds like hedgehogs, and passion vines like avocados ripened almost to black. Catnip seeds are the heads of little black monkeys, with two white eyes open wide with curiosity. And the seeds of dandelions, still attached to the downy parachutes on which they travel so successfully, could be some delicate creatures of the ocean, floating gracefully in its currents.

Not all seeds bring other things to mind, but some that call forth no metaphors still offer interesting discoveries when seen through a hand lens in a sharp beam of light. Strawberry seeds, for example, vary considerably in color, from pale tan to mahogany to almost black. And the brown seeds of flax have a glossy varnish that should be no surprise, considering that flax is the source not only of linen fiber but also of linseed oil.

Even though my hand lens enlarges my vision to embrace many a small wonder—allowing me to examine otherwise imperceptible shapes and colors in tiny flowers and little seeds—it has its limits.

The almost infinitesimal seeds of lobelia, which look like mere specks of dust to the naked eye, still look like dust at 10x magnification. A much more powerful microscope might show their uncanny resemblance to almost anything—from the tusk of an elephant to a sandal to the moon pocked with craters. Or maybe just dust, after all.

But higher powers of magnification, I learned soon after I got my Eschenbach, are not desirable. In a camera shop one day I discovered another hand lens, which offered 30x. I bought it, tried it, and threw it away. At that degree of magnification, objects begin to lose identity; flowers and seeds, instead of revealing unsuspected beauties of color and form, become alien, no longer of the world that we inhabit with our fellow creatures. To describe what I see with an eye thirty times, instead of ten times more powerful than my ordinary vision, I would need a language I do not possess and do not want to possess.

Thistle
Sculpture

JUST BEFORE the advent of daylily season, several plants in a back
border draw considerable attention and comment from people walking by the driveway on our side street. Occasionally they will ask if
it's okay to walk into the garden for a closer look. They want to see
my thistles.

These are no ordinary thistles, such as the Canadian thistles
that plague farmers and home gardeners alike as their tiny seeds float
through the air on gossamer down to take hold as troublesome weeds
wherever they alight. Nor are they echinops or globe thistles, a fairly
common perennial whose round steely blue flower heads I much
admire, although I was long in learning that to grow them well a deep
mulch of salt hay makes a lot of difference. No, these plants that lure
strangers into my garden in early June are Scotch thistles *(Onopor-
dum acanthium),* and they are unmistakably the most commanding
plants I grow—and so well armed that the Pentagon ought to find
some use for them. Biennials, they germinate in July and spend the

next ten months as flat rosettes of prickly leaves a foot across. In the middle of the following May, they burst into growth so explosive that in a month they stand eight feet tall or higher, with flower buds popping into bloom all up and down the plant.

At its peak of bloom, before it begins to ripen its heavy seeds and then die, a Scotch thistle is impossible to ignore. From a distance, it is a dramatic accent, a tall pyramid of leaves up to two feet long. In blossom, it has two distinct tiers of leaves: the lower ones, up to the midpoint of the stem, droop slightly; the upper ones lift themselves on high, as if in jubilation. When a breeze rustles through the leaves, they shimmer and change their apparent color, now seeming silvery gray, now green, now a misty shade of blue. Up close, there's even more to see and also to touch. The sharp prickles along the serrated margins of the leaves are truly murderous, exceeded in their capacity to inflict pain only by the spines of the southwestern cholla or jumping cactus. But most of the leaf is covered with a thick white down that feels like velvet. And at dead of noon, when most plants look a bit boring in the flat overhead glare, a Scotch thistle remains interesting for the way each leaf casts a strong shadow of its prickly outline on the leaf below.

I don't talk to my plants, but I do like to visit some of them to see how they are doing, and I make a daily pilgrimage in early summer to check on my little colony of Scotch thistles. I have given them a spot at the front of a bed where I can walk around them, studying them like pieces of sculpture. Each leaf is attached directly to the single stem, and where the leaf and stem meet a thorny flower stalk emerges, bursting into rapid growth in early June. Near the top of the plant the flower stalks branch out like a huge candelabrum, bearing thorny blue-green buds whose yellow stamens show before the powderpuff of lovely and soft purple-lavender petals appears and bumblebees begin their work of pollination.

I never cut my thistles back right after they bloom. Instead, I let them bear seed. They die quickly, but they remain for a while a presence in the garden, brown skeletons of themselves, much visited by songbirds in search of their glossy brown seeds. I rescue a few of the seeds in July, planting them in the same spot to assure another spectacle the following year. In late summer, wearing heavy gloves and exercising gingerly caution, I cut back the thistles and put them in the garbage—not the compost pile, since thistle prickles can take years to decompose and lose their sharpness.

My love affair with Scotch thistles has been going on for years. So have the visits from strangers who stop in the driveway and ask for a closer look at these giants of the summer garden.

Edible Flowers, a Weed to Eat, and Handsome Vegetables

GARDENERS, except for those mere greenskeepers who live only for their lawns, come in three basic varieties. There are those who raise only flowers and other ornamental plants. These people buy the things they eat in grocery stores. There are those who raise primarily vegetables in tidy rows in their backyard patches. When these people say "I'll be out in the garden for a while," they mean that they'll be thinning out the carrots or checking to see how the corn is coming along. The third group consists of those of us who are mixtures of the first two, purer types. We are eclectic souls who value home-grown endive and lettuce none the less for loving our delphiniums and dahlias. No statistics back me up, but I would guess that the greatest number of American gardeners fall into this mixed group, provided that we count in it those whose flowers amount mostly to marigolds interplanted among their vegetables on the theory that marigolds repel insects, and those who give 99 percent of their attention to ornamental annuals and perennials, raising a few lettuce and tomato plants in odd corners for a simple salad.

But this tidy classification breaks down for the good and simple reason that the distinctions between flowers and vegetables are far from absolute and unambiguous. The mind's tendency to tidiness sometimes creates sharper distinctions, and thus it is with the things we eat. A pig in its pen is a pig, but when it comes to the table it is pork. Within the plant kingdom, we want to say that vegetables are vegetables, flowers are flowers, and fruits are fruits—even if some vegetables, tomatoes for example, turn out to be fruits.

As for flowers, we cultivate them for ornament and delight, a feast for the eye, not the palate. But the distinction between flowers and vegetables is, again, pretty shaky. *Vegetable,* a word that has existed in culinary English for a comparatively short time (in the late eighteenth century vegetable gardens were called kitchen gardens), means any part of a herbaceous plant that is edible and palatable. Beets, carrots, turnips, and their like are all roots. Rhubarb is a stem; in fact, the leaves it bears are painfully toxic, potentially lethal because of their high concentration of oxalic acid. Okra is a seedpod. Peas and dried beans are seeds; snow peas and string beans are immature seeds encased in edible pods. Considering that almost any part of a plant may turn out to be safe and tasty to eat, depending on the plant, it's not at all surprising that some of the vegetables we commonly eat are really flowers or their buds. Broccoli past its prime shows golden yellow petals as unmistakable testimony to its floral character.

Broccoli does not stand alone. The facts of history show that our ancestors, particularly if they were Europeans, had more flowers on their daily menus than seems imaginable, and for good reason. Before the discovery of the New World, many of the staple foods of today were unknown on the other side of the Atlantic. The list includes corn, squash, pumpkins, tomatoes, and potatoes, all of which were domesticated and brought into cultivation by the native peoples of the Americas. Europeans, who only since World War II have learned that sweet corn, or maize, is not only edible but also delectable, had in former times to stock their larders with vegetables that today seem suited only for the flower garden, not the kitchen garden.

They ate violets, for example—a practice that faintly survives in the candied violets sold in gourmet shops for sprinkling on top of ice cream or decorating cakes. They also made violet syrup and violet jelly, and traditional herbal lore held that violets had important medicinal properties. A garland of violets, the Roman naturalist Pliny advised, was a sure cure for hangovers. The Romans also ate violet leaves, which in fact turn out to be rich in vitamin C.

English books on herbs from the sixteenth and seventeenth centuries record many other floral foods in common consumption. One book published in 1600 states flatly that "no broths are well made without dried Marigolds," but a warning is in order here, lest someone be tempted to gather some marigold blossoms and toss them into a stockpot. The flowers we call marigolds are in the genus *Tagetes*, highly unpalatable because of their harsh odor and flavor. The old English marigold was *Calendula officinalis*, often used, wrote the great herbalist John Parkinson in 1629, in "broths and drinkes as a comforter of the heart and spirits." Roses also had a long run as flowers for both the table and the medicinal pantry. John Gerard, in the second edition of his *Herball* (1633), wrote of musk roses that "the leaves of the floures eaten in the morning, in the manner of a sallad, with oile, vinegar, and pepper, or any other way according to the appetite and pleasure of them that shall eate it, purge very notably the belly of waterish and cholericke humors, and that mightily, yet without any perill or paine at all."

Other flowers were eaten as well, or made into syrups and conserves, including the blossoms of clove pinks. Things that sound peculiar to us now had a way of turning up in "sallets" or "sallads," notably mint blossoms, peach flowers, hollyhock buds, and cowslips or primroses. Primrose salad was a special favorite well into Victorian times; the British prime minister Benjamin Disraeli is reported to have been passionate for it. I have seen eighteenth-century cookbooks with recipes for puddings made from primrose blossoms, lady-fingers, eggs, cream, and rose water.

In non-European cultures, other flowers are eaten. Chinese cooking sometimes makes use of *gum-tsoy,* the dried buds of day-lilies. Middle Eastern and Indian cooking is fond of jasmine blossoms and rose conserves, and a traditional Mexican soup is thickened with squash blossoms, which also make tasty fritters when battered and fried.

Flower eating has made no great inroads into American life, with one historic exception—the nasturtium. Very early in the nine-teenth century, Bernard McMahon wrote in *The American Gar-dener's Calendar,* the first truly American book on gardening, that the nasturtium "is very deserving of cultivation, as well as on account of the beauty of its large and numerous orange-colored flowers, and their use in garnishing dishes. The green berries or seeds of this plant . . . make one of the nicest pickles that can possibly be conceived; in the estimation of many, they are superior to capers." Thomas Jefferson agreed fully with McMahon. He planted many square yards of them every year at Monticello, and once, when his seed crop failed, he pleaded with a friend for whatever seeds he could spare, so that the summer salads served at his home in Virginia could be garnished with orange nasturtium blossoms and flavored by the pi-quant young leaves.

The idea of eating nasturtiums seems today a bit outlandish, since they are spectacularly beautiful annuals. Claude Monet de-lighted in growing the tall trailing or climbing sorts at Giverny, where in midsummer they climbed up turquoise arches and sprawled into gravel walks to delight the eye with their bright shades of yellow, orange, and scarlet. In the United States, the best display of nastur-tiums by any reckoning occurs in March in the enclosed atrium garden of the Isabella Stewart Gardner Museum in Boston. Growing in pots in open windows with pointed Venetian arches above the first story, they hang down twenty feet or more, their succulent large round leaves jeweled with crimson-orange blossoms that gleam as if afire.

The name by which these plants are commonly called sounds like botanical Latin, but it isn't. *Nasturtium,* which means "nose-twister," properly applies to *Nasturtium officinale,* the European watercress. The nasturtiums of the garden are really *Tropaeolum minor* and *T. majus,* both native to Central and South America. Gardeners merely borrowed the name of another genus altogether and used it as a common name, creating some confusion along the way. Real nasturtiums have in common with tropaeolums only one thing—a pungent-smelling and peppery-tasting foliage.

Tropaeolum, the name Carolus Linnaeus gave the genus, has its own meaning, with military overtones involving trophies captured in battle. Linnaeus thought that the round leaves, each with a slightly off-center pale dot near its middle where the veins radiate outward, looked something like shields. He also thought that the slightly cupped blossoms resembled burnished helmets. (In some of the many books on the language of flowers published in England and the United States during their vogue in the middle of the nineteenth century, a gift of nasturtiums meant "we share patriotic pride.")

It might be noted that in their enthusiasm for nasturtiums as an element of cuisine, Bernard McMahon and Thomas Jefferson were following in British footsteps. The English herbalists were un-commonly fond of this plant, which the Spanish physician Nicolás Monardes introduced to Europe in 1569. John Parkinson's *Paradisi in Sole* (1629) called the plant "larkes heeles." Parkinson claimed no medicinal properties for it but thought it of "so great beauty and sweetnes withal, that my Garden of delight cannot be unfurnished of it." In *Acetaria* (1699), the first book ever devoted entirely to salads, John Evelyn recommended adding shredded nasturtium pet-als to greens as a way of adding a sharp and tangy note. He also advised pickling nasturtium buds for similar uses.

If any flower regains popularity as something to eat, it is likely to be the nasturtium, thanks in part to upscale gourmet vegetable catalogs like that of Shepherd's Garden Seeds, which waxes lyrical in its praise. Several varieties are offered, the most beautiful being an old strain, 'Empress of India'. Its crop of flowers, abundant if the plants are grown in the lean, nitrogen-poor soil they prefer, are within hailing distance of true crimson, and they are set off perfectly by leaves of a decidedly bluish shade of green.

I grow, quite unwillingly, another plant that turns out to have a distinguished history as a vegetable for eating. It is purslane *(Portulaca oleracea)*. It is one of the most bothersome of summer weeds, because it seems to enjoy the rough treatment that would send less rugged plants right into weed heaven. When I pull it up, enough remains behind in the ground so that it will sprout anew, almost overnight. Furthermore, the succulent leaves and stems do not wilt when left in the hot sun, as crabgrass will. They can lie out in the open, separated from the soil and completely rootless, but still looking a bit too fat and smug, perhaps because they know a secret. After a few days, the stems make new roots, and the purslane resumes its growth as if nothing at all had happened to it. Meanwhile, being something of a demon at reproducing itself, it forms seeds, some of which germinate immediately, others of which remain dormant until the following summer. On purslane, I have long stood with Charles Dudley Warner, who in *My Summer in a Garden* (1870) said it was his most hated weed, "a fat, ground-clinging, spreading, greasy thing, and the most propagatious (it is not my fault that the word is not in the dictionary) plant I know."

My mother used to tell me to eat the okra on my plate, that it was good for me. Of late, I am getting the same advice about purslane. A recent catalog from another tony vegetable seed company, The Cook's Garden, proposes planting purslane for food. When I got the catalog, I called Shepherd Ogden, the company's owner, and he stood by his recommendation. He offers two varieties. One, called 'Green', is a selected version of the common weed, but more erect in habit and less inclined to sprawl. 'Goldgelber' is even more upright, with golden leaves so thick that they resemble those of the jade plant. Both, Mr. Ogden said, made very fine eating, succulent and slightly tart in a salad.

I did a little checking in the books in my gardening library, and Ogden proved to be on the mark. Purslane has been standard culinary fare in India and Persia for some twenty centuries. According to Mary Durant's *Who Named the Daisy? Who Named the Rose?* (1976) it was praised by an early eighteenth century New England divine, the Reverend Manasseh Cutler, as "little inferior to asparagus." Delena Tull's *A Practical Guide to Edible and Useful Plants* (1987) says that Europeans love purslane. She advises readers that after they've weeded their flower beds they should "save the purslane for the table rather than the garbage can." She calls it good raw or cooked or pickled and recommends it as a soup thickener. She offers a slight warning that its tartness comes from its oxalic acid content (about the same as spinach), so that it shouldn't be eaten to excess, especially by people who don't get enough calcium. It is quite rich in vitamin A.

I haven't gotten around yet to eating purslane, but I have it in fine supply. One of these days I'll try some. Maybe.

IF SOME FLOWERS turn out to have a surprising culinary history, the other side of the equation is that some vegetables are so damnably handsome that they deserve a place of honor among ornamental plants in a garden. I'll start with two that I in fact much prefer looking at to having on my plate. Eggplant is one. Cooked, it strikes me as slimy. I would argue that my long-standing negative feelings toward it are justified by its being kin to nightshade and some other deadly plants, except that so are peppers, potatoes, and tomatoes. But I am willing to admit eggplant to a garden for purely aesthetic reasons. Ordinary eggplant, with its smooth and glossy purple skin and its hint of pregnancy near full term, is beautiful to behold. I have seen it grown with great elegance and panache in twin terra-cotta planters flanking a doorway to a piazza of one of the houses in the historic district of Charleston, South Carolina—proof that the gardener who lived there understood how sublime something simple could be. As for okra, it's even slimier. The only way I will even consider eating a single bite is if it has been cut into slices, dipped into cornmeal, and then fried in bacon grease, southern style. But viewed objectively, it's an admirable plant. It bears a heavy crop of attractive yellow mallow flowers with wine-purple throats. The seedpods, once they ripen reassuringly past the point of being considered edible, are fetching things, green and fuzzy, with deep ridges running from base to tapering tip. Usually they are green, but there are maroon forms, and when the pods dry and open, they lend authority to dried winter arrangements. An okra cousin, the annual *Abelmoschos* 'Manihot' reaches over three feet tall and spreads as wide. The large, buttery yellow single flowers are lovely, showing up at a considerable distance. In the fall, the clusters of egg-shaped green seedpods bend toward the earth under their own weight. Covered with a soft gray down, they are extremely beautiful on a clear morning in early October when they glisten in a heavy dew.

Swiss chard, the varieties with red stems instead of green, holds its own as an accent in a flower bed. I have seen it used very simply and effectively in a long and narrow bed entirely filled with silvery dusty miller, except for individual plants of chard at intervals of three feet. The deep green of its leaves, the luminous ruby of its upright stems, and the gray of the dusty miller all combined with quiet but telling harmony. The place was Kew Gardens—hardly some backyard vegetable patch.

Ordinary rhubarb *(Rheum rhabarbarum)*, an extremely hardy perennial vegetable, commands a lot of attention when grown as a single specimen. The stems are ruby red, the bold foliage a luscious deep green, topped in late May by a foamy panicle of creamy blossoms. I first saw this splendid sight at the front entrance of Millstream, the home of the late Lincoln and Laura Louise Foster in Falls Village, Connecticut. The Fosters, beloved figures in the world of rock gardening, had such impeccable taste in plants that if they put rhubarb by their door the rest of us could know that to do so was fitting and seemly. But I am even more taken with another species of rhubarb, *Rheum palmatum* 'Atropurpureum'. Even the massive roots are gorgeous—substantial, somewhat woody, and cranberry red. When the first crinkled growth of leaves emerges at the crown, it is a glowing mixture of gold, lime, and scarlet. Well grown, this rhubarb can attain heights in excess of six feet, and the foliage turns a wonderfully petulant purple hue. A very suitable companion for it is another perennial vegetable, ordinary asparagus, which is tall and ferny, bearing red fruits in late summer.

My most recent discovery among vegetables is the cardoon *(Cynara cardunculus)*, which is not reliably winter hardy in regions much colder than Zone 9, so I buy it as small plants from a nursery down South. I grow it primarily for its bold, long, and arching leaves, a soft gray-green on top, downy white on the underside. In late summer this six-foot plant produces great stalks of thistle-like buds that open into flowers of a soft and gentle mauve. It grows with great distinction in the Conservatory Garden in Central Park, but it first caught my eye in Dan Hinckley's garden in Kingston, Washington, where it grows near a clump of miscanthus grass with peacock feathers stuck into the leaves. The cardoons suggest power, the miscanthus brings grace, and the feathers lend iridescent color, plus an agreeable touch of whimsy. If like Dan Hinckley I had a few peacocks strolling my grounds, I would borrow the combination, but I'm making do by growing cardoons with bronze fennel *(Foeniculum vulgare purpureum)*, another six-footer with ferny and delicate foliage. I agree with Nancy Goodwin, who says that its foliage captures the morning dew in a lovely way and that the sight of sunlight playing through the plant is unforgettable.

Plant Names:
The Poetic,
the Precise, and
the Giddy

IN THE SECOND CHAPTER of the Book of Genesis, God puts Adam in a garden and gives him a job to do—giving names to every living thing, including plants. Adam's instructions from on high weren't entirely specific, but I presume he was meant to give everything one name and one name only and not to assign the same name to two or more things. For the sake of precision and clarity, these criteria make a great deal of sense. We'd wallow in confusion if whales were also called pigeons or if we decided that a dog and a cat in the same household would share the name Spot between them. Giving names to things is a way of knowing them and of seeing them as well. Knowledge deals importantly in names, and naming requires the sort of vision that discerns that these two objects are of the same kind and those other two are not.

Adam apparently never got around to naming all that he was intended to in the plant and the animal kingdoms, for the history of plants is in part the history of their accumulation of names, in many different languages. These were extremely confused until the great eighteenth-century botanist Carolus Linnaeus came along to help us get them straight for once and for all. A tidy thinker, Linnaeus disliked the notion of multiple names for the same plant, clearly an uneconomical waste of names. Nor did he think much of several plants having to get by on just one name, a pure piece of stinginess. Latin names as they had been previously used by European herbalists such as John Parkinson, who called one little dianthus *Caryophyllus plumarius albus orbe rubro sive Stellatus,* struck him as needlessly wordy. To sort everything out, Linnaeus devised a system of binomial nomenclature, according to which every plant would be identified, in Latin, by the genus it belonged to and by its species within that genus.

Linnaeus and his system have triumphed, as is clear from the horticultural reference book I use most often, *Hortus Third: A Concise Dictionary of Plants Cultivated in the United States and Canada,* compiled by the staff of the Liberty Hyde Bailey Hortorium at Cornell University. Starting with *Abelia chinensis* and ending with *Zygosepalum labiosum,* it lists thousands upon thousands of plants by their scientific names.

At the very end of *Hortus Third* there's a long list of common or vernacular names, each keyed to the correct botanical name, and the list serves as ample testimony to the difficulties with common names. Let's take, for example, the plant that is unambiguously known in Latin as *Erythronium dens-canis.* Its common names of dog's-tooth violet and trout lily are misleading, for it's no true lily and it's certainly not a violet (nor are African violets). Elizabeth Lawrence once wrote that almost anything can be called a lily, and often is, and she was close to the mark. Like the trout lily, neither the toadlily nor the snake lily is really a lily—a member, that is, of the genus *Lilium,* like the Madonna lily or the regal lily. Neither is the spider lily, and in fact three unrelated plants in different genera show up under that name.

Then there's the houseplant known botanically as *Rhoeo spa-*

thacea, which would seem to have established a certain record in the common names it has gathered, including, that I know of, Christ-in-a-hamper, Moses-in-the-bulrushes, Moses-in-a-boat, Moses-on-raft, two-men-in-a-boat, and three-men-in-a-boat.

When I need to be precise about a plant, I use its Latin name, even if my nongardening friends sometimes look at me a little funny for using big words in a dead language—or in the kind of horticultural Esperanto that botanical names make up. Bleeding-heart isn't really bleeding-heart, but *Dicentra spectabilis.* Busy Lizzie (whose common name in German, *fleissige Liesschen,* echoes the meaning of its name in English, something that happens rarely: the common name for one species of hardy cyclamen is sowbread, but the German name translates to Alpine violet) is really a hybrid form of impatiens. But with all proper respect for Linnaeus and for the compilers of *Hortus Third,* it must be said that precision isn't everything. Poetry also has its place, and those anonymous souls who dreamed up many of our common names for plants were among the finest poets in the English language. Bleeding-heart may be technically incorrect, but it's an apt name for these graceful perennials of midspring, with their graceful arching stems bearing pendant pink flowers shaped like the stylized hearts of St. Valentine's Day. And busy Lizzie is also a fine name, conveying the constant and incessant flowers the impatiens produces for months on end, until the first good frost finally blackens it and turns its leaves to mush.

I find no poetry in the correct botanical names of plants. My imagination responds not a whit to *Dierama pendulum,* but its common name, angels'-fishing-rods, makes me want it for my garden. I've seen pictures of it; the name is apt, for the rosy bracts of this summer-blooming bulb do look a bit like fishermen's flies and they hang on long stems that sit at an angle reminiscent of a fishing pole dangling over the water. And while I'm dreaming of plants called angels'-fishing-rods, I might also think about getting the three different plants that are all called angel's-tears—*Brugmansia sanguinea, Narcissus triandrus,* and *Soleirolia soleirolii*—for a garden with a truly heavenly theme. Or I could have an entire garden of plants whose names have biblical overtones—Adam and Eve plant, Solomon's seal, Jacob's ladder, Our Lord's candles, and heart-of-Jesus, which happens to be a caladium. And to give the Old Nick his due, I could also plant devil's nip (a less frequently used name than Jack-in-the-pulpit, which *Arisaema triphyllum* is also called).

The meanings of some common names are fairly easy to figure out. *Ornithogalum umbellatum* is star of Bethlehem; the blossoms in its flower clusters are in fact star shaped. It's also called Jack-go-to-bed-at-noon and eleven o'clock lady, both names referring to the way the flowers fold up by late morning. I feel adequately forewarned to avoid the trillium that goes by the common name of stinking Benjamin. I would feel similarly warned to expect little or nothing from a plant known as May-blob, except that it happens to be *Caltha palustris,* also known as marsh marigold and meadow bright, a Eurasian perennial that has made itself so common in America that most people take it to be a wildflower and one of the best that blooms in moist places in the spring.

Common or folk names are often highly imaginative and poetic. They may describe plants with a vivid or intriguing image, like Venus fly trap, bouncing Bet, or butter-and-eggs. Even crabgrass is aptly descriptive of this hated weed, for it does scuttle quickly through a lawn. Some common names, however, point to their namesakes' uses; scouring rush was often used to clean cooking pots, in the days before SOS pads came along. Other names identify the medicinal properties, real or imagined, of certain plants, like woundwort, pleurisy root, boneset, and so on.

Other names simply puzzle me. Creeping Charlie for *Sedum acre* is easy to understand, since this low ground cover takes over wherever it is planted, but why it should also be called he-comes-home-drunk-but-she-loves-him-still is likely to remain a mystery forever. As for mind-your-own-business *(Soleirolia soleirolii),* I have no idea, but I note that this plant has gathered a great many names, some of which seem to contradict one another. They include Pollyanna vine, Irish moss, Japanese moss, Corsican curse, peace-in-the-home, and, as we've seen already, angel's tears.

TO OVERCOME the imprecision of common names, it has long been realized that an alternate system is needed, which must do several things at once. It must give one name, and one name only, to every plant (although not all plants actually have been given names; many plants growing in the highly endangered habitats of the earth's tropical rainforests are vanishing into extinction without even being discovered, much less named). This alternate system must give the same name to only one plant. It should indicate relationships among plants when they are different sorts of the same kind of plant (like those lilies that really are lilies). It should enable people who speak entirely different languages to call plants by the same names, so that a Spaniard and a German and an Englishman may all have a significant part of their horticultural vocabularies in common, even if the Spaniard eats *pan*, the German *Brot*, and the Englishman bread. For all these reasons, there is a great need for an orderly system of botanical nomenclature.

This system is sometimes called the Linnaean system, for Carolus Linnaeus, who dreamed it up and hustled it among his fellow scientists. It is also called binomial nomenclature, for it gives to plants (and all other living things) two names and two names only. The principle of binomial nomenclature is not at all strange, since many of us have two names ourselves, one (the surname) that identifies us as belonging to a group of people with some ancestors and other things in common, the other (the given name) that identifies us as an individual person, with all the quirkiness that that may involve. As Allen *Lacy*, I am located within a group of kinfolk; as *Allen* Lacy, I am distinguished from John, Robert, Paul, Michael, and some other Lacy relatives. And as *Allen Lacy*, I can go to a meeting with Allen Bush, Allen Summers, Allen Paterson, Alan Bloom, and Stephen Lacey (all real people, who share my horticultural interests) without confusing anyone who has our names straight. (Human binomial nomenclature is not absolutely precise, however. I've never met anyone else named Allen Lacy, but there may be a few, and the number of people named John Smith is huge.)

In the Linnaean system the name of the larger group, the *genus,* comes first, followed by a second name, the *species,* which sets that plant apart from the other species that combine to form the genus. (Species names, however, unlike human first names, name groups of plants, not individuals. The species is a smaller group within a larger one, the genus, and we need not bother our heads at the moment with the complication that there can be a genus with only one species.)

As its language, the Linnaean system uses Latin—not the Latin of the Caesars, but the Latin of European scholars in the late Renaissance. The Latin of the Caesars, still studied in some high schools today, is a dead language, meaning not just that no one speaks it anymore but also that it is fixed, unchanging, and not capable of growth. Botanical Latin is able to grow, since it is able to add words taken from other languages, including Oriental ones and native American ones. (*Catalpa* is the name of a genus of woody plants, and the name is Amerindian, even though there are some species of catalpa native not to North America but to China.)

In naming plants in Latin, the genus name is always a noun, and it comes first and is capitalized. The species name, which comes second, is an adjective. Both genus and species are generally underlined or italicized—e.g., *Lilium superbum.* Like Spanish and German, but unlike English, Latin nouns have gender, and the gender is indicated by the final syllable. Latin nouns are either masculine or feminine or neuter. Masculine nouns generally end in *-us,* feminine nouns in *-a* or *-es,* and neuters in *-um* or *-n* or *-ma.* Botanical grammar, based on Latin grammar, requires that the adjectives (the species names) accompanying or modifying nouns (the genus names) agree with them in gender. Thus the Latin word for dwarf is *nanus* with a masculine noun, *nana* with a feminine one, and *nanum* with a neuter. (Often in languages where nouns have gender, the gender they have doesn't make much sense. The German word for maiden is neuter, not feminine.)

Where does the name for a genus (plural, genera) come from? The sources are many and diverse. It may come from literature or mythology, as with the genus *Achillea,* named for the Homeric hero Achilles, who legend has it used these plants to stop his soldiers' wounds from bleeding on the battlefields of Troy. It may describe some perceived or imagined resemblance of the plant to something else: *Delphinium* because someone once saw something dolphinlike in it, just as the common name for some species in this genus— larkspur—indicates that someone else thought that one of the parts of the flower resembled a part of a lark's foot. The genus name may honor a human being: *Jeffersonia* for Thomas Jefferson, *Franklinia* for Benjamin Franklin. It may describe some habit of growth characteristic of or common to at least some species in a genus: the ordinary houseplants called by the genus name *Philodendron* are called this from the Greek words, *phileo* ("love") and *dendron* ("tree"), because in the tropics where these plants originate, many species do cling tightly to the trunks of trees as they scramble up toward the light.

The origins or original meanings of specific names (the names of species) are also diverse. They may be adjectives describing the geographical places where the plants came from, or were thought to come from. (In all of what follows, for the sake of economy only, I will simply give the masculine form of the adjective.) Sometimes the meaning of the adjective is clear: *chinensis* (from China); *japonicus* (from Japan); *mongolicus* (from Mongolia). Sometimes it isn't so clear. *Atlanticus* can mean either from somewhere near the Atlantic Ocean (a huge tract!) or it can mean from the Atlas Mountains in northern Africa. *Americanus* means from somewhere in the New World. *Canadensis* means from North America. *Novi-belgii* means from New York. *Novae-caesarea* means, of all things, from New Jersey.

Species names may indicate the habitats where the plants they describe are found. Thus: *arenarius* (likes sandy soil); *rupestris* or *saxatilis* (both mean a plant likes a rocky location); *muralis* (on walls); and *pratensis* (in meadows).

Other names may refer to some peculiar feature of a plant's habit of growth, such as *acaulis* (has no stems); *angustifolius* (has narrow foliage or leaves); *arachnoideus* (seems to be covered with cobwebs); *campanulatus* (shaped like a bell); *cernuus* (drooping); *dentatus* (toothed); *horridus* (very spiny); *procumbens* (creeping); or *scandens* (climbing). Or to leaf texture or appearance: *frimbriatus* (fringed); *glabrus* (smooth); *lanatus* (woolly); *tomentosus* (woolly and hairy).

Specific names may indicate color, especially the color of flowers: *albus* (white); *aurantiacus* (orange); *atrorubens* (dark red); *coccineus* (scarlet); *flavus* (yellow). Or the size of the plant: *giganteus* (an easy guess!); *humilis* (low); *minimus* (very small); and *minutissimus* (really tiny).

Sometimes a species name commemorates a person, often the person who first discovered it growing wild in a remote part of the world. One example is *Gentiana farreri*, a gentian named for the English plant-explorer Reginald Farrer. Or a species name can point out an accidental resemblance between one plant and another; as a species name, *aquilegifolius* means that a plant has foliage that looks like the leaves of the columbine *(Aquilegia)*.

Scientific names do change, for several reasons having to do with botanical science. Sometimes botanists decide that plants that had been classified as belonging to the same genus really belong to different genera. Or vice versa—they decide that plants previously in different genera belong in the same genus. These nomenclatural pastimes are known as "splitting" and "lumping," respectively, and sometimes are the stuff of controversy. In any case, the result is that the annual Madagascar periwinkle, once *Vinca rosea*, becomes *Catharanthus roseus*, changing not only its name but also the gender of its name. A scientific name can also change as a result of a better grasp of history. The rule is that the earliest published name given to a plant ought to be the name by which it is known. If it turns out that name B, given to a plant in 1910, was preceded, in 1890, by name A, then name B, no matter how much it has been used, must be abandoned (by botanists, but not always by gardeners and nurserymen, who dislike changes of this kind). The Oriental poppy, *Papaver orientale,* is now *P. bracteatum,* but I'll stick with the old name.

One term not introduced yet in this discussion is *variety* (abbreviated *var.*). In the past, it has been ambiguous. One meaning was a naturally occurring variation within a species, some noticeable difference that was not "different enough" to turn one species into two. (An example would be an eastern dogwood that has rose-pink flowers instead of the typical white ones.) Another meaning was variation produced not in the course of nature but as a result of human intervention, such as hybridization and selective breeding for changes like larger flowers or more interesting foliage or a wider range of colors. The resulting varieties were called horticultural varieties (varieties originating in a garden) or cultivated varieties. *Variety* is now generally used for the differences that naturally arise in a species, *cultivated variety* for those humans have had a hand in producing. The latter term has now been shortened to *cultivar* (abbreviated *cv.*). Furthermore, the general rule is that cultivar names are not in Latin but in English, German, French, etc.; they are not italicized or underlined, but are capitalized and put within single quotation marks, sometimes but not often preceded by *cv.* Thus if I write to a friend about the daylilies (hybrids of various species of *Hemerocallis*) in my garden, I may tell her about 'Stella de Oro', 'Prides Crossing', and 'Little Bugger'. And some astilbes I grow have German names, such as 'Straussenfeder' and 'Fanal'.

How does a nice daylily get saddled with a name like 'Little Bugger'? The hybridizer liked the name, or the nursery that introduced it, or *somebody.* A walk around a daylily patch can be a giddy experience. 'Bible Story' grows near 'Cute Trick', 'Lusty Leland' consorts with 'Child Bride', and 'Heavenly Harp' follows right after 'Buzz Bomb'.

An Eye for
the Gaudy

IT'S ONLY A HUNCH, based on anecdotal evidence, not sober research using questionnaires and carefully constructed polls of people with horticultural inclinations, but I suspect that there are some notable differences between those of us who started gardening when we were children and our brothers and sisters of the spade who came to the pursuit later in life—the late bloomers, so to speak.

I have nothing but admiration for people whose love of gardening develops in their middle years, or even later. They commit themselves to the art and craft of digging in the earth with complete passion. They are avid readers of books on horticulture, for they need to make up for their late start by learning all that they can in as short a time as possible. They want to learn all the rules, to get things right at the very outset, including proper botanical nomenclature. They are keen supporters of the plant societies and horticultural organizations that work to improve gardening in America, offering both time and money to serve their cause. They quickly develop good taste in gardening and a keen sense for design and for plant combinations to delight the eye, rather than offend it. They know better than to grow golden-orange rudbeckias alongside bright red bee balm.

My hunch is that the major difference between those of us who started early and our tardier friends is that we have a long-standing affection for plants that they would resolutely exclude, with perfect justice, from their gardens. They would never plant an amaranthus, for example, and certainly not a celosia, especially the cockscomb sort, whose flower heads are misshapen and generally an unattractive shade of red, uncomfortably close to fresh calves' liver. They have subtle eyes and small taste for the gaudy, for plants too flamboyant to be really decent.

My tasteful fellow travelers believe in planning, in knowing what they are doing before they do it, so that they will achieve the outcome they wish. They are serious gardeners, because they started out as grown-ups, and therefore serious people. As for the rest of us, we started out as children, and something of the child remains in us. Gardening may be work, but it begins as play—something spontaneous, with no restrictive rules.

Every spring, the child in me pops out when I look through the racks of seed packets in a grocery or a hardware store and find a packet marked "mixed annuals." A moment's reflection is sufficient to realize that packages of mixed seed are not a royal road to gardening, since larkspur and zinnias, two of several plants common in such mixtures, have entirely different cultural requirements. Larkspurs, like annual poppies, need to be planted when the soil is still cold; when hot weather comes, they generally vanish. Zinnias germinate poorly and may even rot unless the soil has taken a turn toward summer. Mixtures are thus exercises in plant incompatibility. Still, I remember with great pleasure days in childhood when I bought and planted such seed packets. The experience offered a dual pleasure of surprise and wonder. I never knew what would come up—and sometimes once things came up I wasn't sure what they were. Sometimes, the grown-up gardeners around me would pass on the bad news. The plant I was tending so carefully, watering and protecting from weeds, was itself a weed.

Another remnant of childhood to which I confess is a yen for plants that serious gardeners hold in low account, especially gaudy ones that lack a shred of pretence to modesty, to taking their place in an ensemble of plants that work together in a harmonious whole. I like cockscombs, though I don't plant them. But occasionally I sneak a few plants of amaranthus into our garden. I refer here not to the old-fashioned amaranthus commonly known as love-lies-bleeding, whose drooping stalks of flowers are, again, somewhat the color of liver, but to a strain called 'Illumination', whose foliage turns ferocious shades of crimson and gold in late summer. The catalog of Park Seed Company describes it as resembling "a lighted Chinese lantern." Here's a rare case of understatement in a seed catalog, for this particular amaranthus is more like volcanic magma than a mere lantern. Its rich, deep glow shines forth from a block away, as unmistakable as ego.

The child in me still loves skyrockets on the Fourth of July, believes that there's a place far brighter than Kansas, called Oz, and revels in amaranthus 'Illumination' without a whole lot of worry that some people think my planting it is evidence of questionable taste.

CLOSELY

WATCHED

PLANTS

Claytonia:
"So Pretty,
So Ashamed"

IN RECENT YEARS many American gardeners have shown increasing interest in meadows. They eye their lawns, consider the expenditure of time and money and energy they require, and flirt with the notion of replacing them with summer wildflowers like black-eyed Susans, Queen Anne's lace, and chicory. For some, the idea of a meadow goes beyond mere flirtation. They plow up their lawns, in part or in whole, and they broadcast the seeds of one of the many wildflower mixes on the market today.

But having a summer meadow, and replacing weekly mowing with an annual one in late winter, isn't possible for everyone. Neighbors who think Queen Anne's lace is a weed pure and simple may frown on someone next door who wants to sport it in his front lawn. Local ordinances often require that a lawn be kept tidy and well mowed, and if it gets too overgrown the municipal authorities may have it cut and send the owners the bill.

Another sort of meadow, however, is easy on the neighbors and not forbidden by law, as well as being a great source of pleasure—a spring meadow that coexists with the lawn instead of replacing it.

The rules for establishing such a spring meadow are simple, amounting to benign neglect and the thoughtful introduction of suitable plants in the turf. The lawn is mowed, yes, but two or three weeks later than usual. The use of selective herbicides against broad-leafed plants is abandoned, since such chemicals will kill everything except grasses.

Under these conditions, there will be weeds, of course, but the gardener can minimize them by contriving to plant in the once-unblemished turf an ample number of low, spring-blooming flowers that go dormant or that can be mowed back in May, when the weather warms up and the grass takes over. Violets generally work well, as do clumps of grape hyacinths and wild crocuses. Dande-lions—well, it's possible to learn to love them and even to eat their leaves in salads or braised with a little garlic.

But one plant is especially wonderful in a spring meadow—*Claytonia virginica,* a native American wildflower in the purslane family that is little praised today, although our nineteenth-century ancestors thought very highly of it. In *The Song of Hiawatha,* Henry Wadsworth Longfellow celebrated it as the miskodeed, its name in one of the native American languages. (Claytonia's tubers were com-monly eaten by some Indians, but white settlers who gratefully added maize and squash to their diets failed to follow suit with claytonia.) William Cullen Bryant was another enthusiast, although he used its more common name, spring beauty. It is probably the flower Emily Dickinson described as "so pretty, so ashamed," "ashamed" referring to its habit of closing at night or on overcast days and of wilting immediately when picked. Even on sunny days, claytonia is a sluga-bed, not opening until midmorning. In her classic book *How to Know the Wild Flowers* (1893), Mrs. William Starr Dana wrote ecstatically about claytonias growing in great sheets of bloom in Central Park to uplift the spirits of city-bred children. "One is always glad to discover these children of the country within our city limits," said Mrs. Dana, "where they can be known and loved by those other children who are so unfortunate as to be denied the knowledge of them in their usual haunts."

Spring beauty grows in Central Park no longer, I hear, but it does grow, and in great sheets, in my mother-in-law's neighborhood in Manchester, Tennessee. Many years ago, a neighbor planted a small clump at the edge of her lawn. Since then it has spread by self-sowing until it now carpets the entire block with an abundance of starry, five-petaled blossoms on plants only three inches tall. Typically the flowers are white, lightly striped with pink, but an occasional clump is deep rose or light lavender. En masse, a colony of spring beauties is so stunning that I have no doubt that if the plant were native to Europe rather than North America, painters in the Middle Ages would have depicted it growing at the feet of the Virgin Mary.

In *Nature's Garden* (1900), Neltje Blanchan joined Emily Dickinson in calling attention to this plant's shy ways, speculating that its practice of opening only in sunny and warm weather was a matter of saving itself for the insects that pollinate it. "At night and during cloudy, stormy weather, when their benefactors are not flying," she wrote, "the claytonias economically close their petals to protect nectar and pollen from rain and pilferers. Pick them, the whole plant droops, and the blossoms close with indignation; nor will any coaxing but a combination of hot water and sunshine induce them to open again. Theirs is a long beauty sleep. They are supersensitive exquisites, however hardy." Claytonia's habit of not opening on dreary days means that it seems to disappear altogether, then spring forth in an almost miraculous way when the sun comes out. But even when the buds are tightly closed, they prove delightful when looked at through a hand lens. The egg-shaped olive-green buds, as many as thirty borne on light bronze stems that seem varnished, grow in loose coils in strict order of bloom, with the tiniest buds closest to the stem. The grasslike foliage has deep tints of maroon. A hand lens also shows that the flowers, when open, are intricately colored. The blossoms are white, with lilac veins running from their centers to the edges of the petals. The intensity of the veining varies considerably. In some flowers, there is so much lilac that they look pink to the naked eye. Each petal shows a blotch of greenish gold at its base, and the very heart of the flower, where the petals join the ovary, is green.

Spring beauty has no faults that I know of. It is hardy from Nova Scotia to Georgia. A perennial that grows from a tuber the size of a pea, it goes dormant in late spring, putting up in December the new growth of beet-red leaves that some wildflower fanciers consider the first real harbinger of spring. Its native habitat is moist and shady woodlands, especially along steep stream banks, but it seems to tolerate partial and even full sun.

One year I came back from a March visit to my parents-in-law with some clumps of spring beauty dug from their turf. They have begun to spread, and in due course I hope to have an entire lawn starred with them all through April.

The Little
Daffodils

THE MOST FOOLISH and also the wisest thing I did when my family moved into our house many summers ago was to order far more daffodils than we could really afford. Since I wanted a great splash of color the following April, I didn't give the slightest consideration to daffodils with modest names like 'Minnow' and 'Little Witch', whose heights were listed at under ten inches. I wanted big daffodils, seventeen inches or higher, with bold cups or huge trumpets and forceful names like 'Bravura' and 'Spellbinder'.

It was foolish, because the budget allowed a couple of dozen bulbs and I ordered a couple of hundred. It was wise because the April splash the next year was worth the money, not only brightening up the garden with an unmistakable announcement of spring, but also providing cut flowers for the house. It was also wise because daffodils are sturdy and prolific, multiplying rapidly until in a few years one bulb becomes a dozen or more.

I still enjoy the splendor of those big daffodils, for the same reason that I enjoy a production of *Aida,* complete with extras carrying fans of peacock feathers and a few elephants onstage during the triumphal march. I have ordered a few dozen more each fall every year to enlarge both the size of the April display and increase its diversity. But lately my heart has been won by some little daffodils, for the same reason that I like Mozart's string quartets.

Some of the little daffodils that are listed in the bulb catalogs are those that grow wild in their native habitats, mostly around the Mediterranean basin northward to the British Isles. One, which botanists call *Narcissus asturiensis* because it occurs naturally in the mountains of northern Spain, used to be called *N. minimus,* which seems more fitting, seeing that its leaves top out at three inches or less and that its trumpet blossom is half the size of a thimble, if that big. Another, *N. cyclamineus,* so called because the petals behind its narrow tubular trumpet flare back sharply, like those of a cyclamen, grows only four inches tall. A third, *N. jonquilla,* which can vary in height from eight to twelve inches and in blooming time from early to late spring, depending on the strain, is notable for the intense, delectable fragrance of its small bright yellow blossoms, often borne two or three to the stem.

Except for *N. jonquilla,* which British gardeners imported from Spain in the days of Elizabeth I and which since colonial times has grown so lustily in the South that southerners have a tendency to call all narcissus "jonquils" (although in some places they call them "buttercups" instead), the wild species of daffodils are not especially reliable performers in the garden. And even if they were easier garden subjects, the possibility that they have been collected in the wild, causing us to run the risk of contributing to their extinction, lays on us a responsibility not to buy them. Far better bets are the small named hybrids developed from them by breeders in Ireland, Great Britain, Holland, and the United States since the late nineteenth century. If there's anyone who's seen only one small daffodil, it's almost certain to be 'Tête à Tête', a yellow trumpet that most catalogs list as six inches tall, and which has *N. cyclamineus* in its ancestry. Bred by Alex Gray of Cornwall, who specialized in the smaller narcissi, and first introduced in 1949, 'Tête à Tête' forces so easily that it is the daffodil most in evidence at the major spring flower shows in early March and in florist shops starting in January. It also frequently shows up in the flower and plant sections of supermarkets. It typically bears two and sometimes three blossoms on the same stem, hence its name. Less common, but even more desirable, is 'Jumblie'. Somewhat shorter, with more strongly swept-back petals, it came from the same seedpod that produced 'Tête à Tête'. An older *cyclamineus* hybrid, 'February Gold', bred in Holland, is of a more intermediate size, reaching ten or twelve inches. Its trumpets are long and patrician looking, but its name stretches toward hype, since in my garden at least it would be more properly called 'Late March Gold'.

Other hybrids in the *cyclamineus* group worth mentioning are 'Charity May', 'Dove Wings', and 'Jenny', each ten inches high with, respectively, yellow, bicolor yellow and white, and white trumpets. Again, all three are reported to have been grown from seed collected from a single pod, from a cross made in the 1940s by the British breeder C. F. Coleman—luck, against all genetic odds, equivalent to winning the Irish sweepstakes and two state lotteries in a single day.

N. jonquilla also has its notable hybrids. 'Lintie' grows to eight inches—spreading like a weed where it is truly happy—and produces two red-banded blossoms per stem. 'Sugarbush', somewhat larger at twelve inches, bears attractive white and yellow blossoms that are unusually fragrant, even for a jonquil. And I must confess to a special affection for 'Suzy', which naturalizes well and produces several vibrant and sunproof red and yellow blossoms on each stem.

I owe a humble apology to 'Minnow' for not having planted it in our garden the very first season. Only six inches high, it owes its clusters of four or five lemon-yellow blossoms per stem to another species, *N. tazetta*, which in its wild state is hardy only in the Deep South and southern California, although 'Minnow' will perform swimmingly where winters are harsh. And I shouldn't overlook 'Hawera', a hybrid of *N. jonquilla* and another Iberian native, *N. triandrus*, which for two weeks in late spring produces creamy blossoms that have a fragrance reminiscent of Grand Marnier.

I'm not especially fond of double daffodils, which often remind me in an odd way of a serving of scrambled eggs, but I make an exception for a selected form of *N. pumila plena*, which is generally listed in catalogs as 'Rip Van Winkle', for reasons difficult to fathom. The somewhat greenish yellow petals of this small charmer open to form a rounded starburst about one and one-half inches across at the base of the flower. Just one blossom in a tiny vase cheers the heart.

The world of the smaller daffodils is very large. One catalog on my desk lists over eighty-five different cultivars. According to a recent president of the American Daffodil Society, the interest in daffodils is on the rise in America, and the little ones have especially passionate aficionados. Sorry 'Bravura' and 'Spellbinder' and your splashy brothers, but I'm one of them. Fickleness, in gardeners, is no sin.

Tulips:
Public or Private?

WHEN I THINK about tulips, either in the fall when it's time to plant them, or in the spring when they are before my eyes in all their splendor, two images collide in my mind. One is of what we might call the civic tulip or the public tulip, by which I mean an overpowering display of tulips en masse, a succession of rectangular beds, each given to one cultivar only. Such a spectacle—and there's probably not an example in America seen by more people than the tulip plantings in the middle of New York's Park Avenue—testifies with enormous force to the achievements wrought by hybridizers in Holland since the early sixteenth century.

As Martin Rix tells it in his fascinating book, *Growing Bulbs* (1983), when Suleiman the Magnificent reigned in Turkey, his ambassador to the court of Ferdinand I in Vienna, Ogier Ghiselin de Busbecq, introduced to the West the wild tulips and other bulbs that grew in the gardens of Istanbul. Interest in these flamboyant early spring flowers grew to great heights. After the strange horticultural phenomenon in the 1630s known as tulipomania, when whole fortunes could be won or lost on just one bulb, the speculative bubble broke. The Dutch then got down to more sensible transactions with tulips, growing them in quantity and breeding them to increase the height of their stems, the size of their flowers, and the range of their radiant colors.

The result is the modern hybrid tulip. There are many classes—Darwin hybrids, cottage tulips, peony-flowered tulips, and so on. So many hundreds of named cultivars are available that browsing through a bulb catalog, with its many pictures of tulips in full and sometimes accurate color, can lead to paralysis of choice. But the choice almost doesn't matter. Who has ever seen a really ugly tulip (except for those monstrosities touted for their supposed resemblance to parrots)?

Public or civic tulips, to put it succinctly, are best treated as annuals—allowed to flower once and then discarded, to be replaced with their like the following fall. Each bulb contains in embryo all that it needs for a single season of bloom. Thereafter, its future is unpromising. Its leaves seem to take forever to die as it goes dormant, and they are public eyesores. In large plantings, tulips are best allowed to have a merry life, but a very short one.

But there's also the private tulip, by which I mean not huge masses of flowers like regiments displaying their colors and the symmetry of their drillwork, but tulips in the home garden, used with restraint in perennial borders as accents of color. The standard practical advice about using these tulips, the same ones that will brighten Park Avenue next spring, is that they are also best treated as annuals. Again, there's the problem of unsightly yellowing foliage. But if the bulbs are planted in small groups, not in a battalion, it is easy to contrive that the agony of their leaves in June may be concealed by nearby daylilies, hostas, or other summer perennials.

It is also said that hybrid tulips bloom poorly after their first season, when they have exhausted the nutrients they stored up when they were residents of the vast bulb fields in the Netherlands. And indeed, most gardeners have some experience of this quick decline of tulips, even if we rely on the advice that we may be able to gain some small repeat bloom for the next season or two if we remove the spent blossoms and fertilize the plants as they move into dormancy.

But there's some good news, based on the research of Professor Paul Nelson of North Carolina State University, and it's especially good news considering how expensive tulips are nowadays. Tulips can often bloom well for several years in a row, provided that they are given the kind of culture Professor Nelson recommends. They should be planted deeply, and watered well, to help them initiate root growth. And they should be fed at planting time, not in late spring. The fertilizer should be a slow-acting, slow-release kind—one with a 9-9-9 ratio of nitrogen, phosphorus, and potassium. One called Bulb-Booster is dandy.

I always want a few of the more spectacular tulip hybrids in my garden, but I confess that my deepest affections lie with the more modest and charming species or botanical tulips, many of which have persisted in my garden over many years, even before the new information came out about proper fertilization in the fall with the right stuff. These are tulips as nature made them, not as gussied up by the hand of man. *Tulipa tarda* is a little wonder, low growing, with white petals and a large yellow eye. The blossoms open flat, like shallow saucers, and each stem bears as many as six flowers. *Tulipa clusiana,* the lady tulip, has been in cultivation since 1607. Thomas Jefferson grew it at Monticello, and for good reason. Its small red and white blossoms are elegant and graceful, and in a good location—a well-drained hillside that's dry in the summer—it may spread eventually into a large colony. *Tulipa saxatilis,* like *T. tarda,* produces multiple blossoms on each stem—lilac, with a yellow center. There are many, many other botanical tulips, but one that must be mentioned is *T. sylvestris.* It has yellow flowers, grows twelve inches high, and has a quality nature neglected in most other tulips—sweet fragrance.

But of all wild tulips, I am most partial to *T. turkestanica,* even if I had to grow it for several years before it captured my affections so strongly. It bears small, starry flowers, under the size of a dime even on sunny days when it is fully open. The somewhat off-white petals, with a golden blotch at their base, show a greenish tint on their backs. The considerable flurry of wide leaves is a soft gray-green that is highly attractive, making a mound about six inches high. Each stem carries six or more flowers that stay in bloom for about two weeks in late March. The flowers, on first sight, look somewhat like those of star of Bethlehem, although they appear much earlier. What makes *T. turkestanica* especially valuable is that it is a superb increaser, forming substantial clumps two or three years after it is planted and also seeding itself around the garden, if it's happy.

Allen, Spare That Paulownia!

ONLY A FEW YEARS AGO in the gift shop at Winterthur in Delaware, I bought a small potted seedling of *Paulownia tomentosa*, a tree native to China and named in honor of Anna Paulowna (1795–1865), a Dutch princess noted for her passion for botany. The tree was only one year old, and it had been pruned back to the ground to give it a root system capable of supporting the rapid vegetative growth that was sure to follow that summer. The following September I grabbed an ax and headed for the tree, bent on its eradication. It had grown twelve feet in a single season, and its trunk was three inches in diameter. It had a gross, rank, and weedy look, and I figured I'd get rid of it while it was still easy to do. But Hella stayed my hand. She had seen the tree in bloom not only at Winterthur, but also in nearby Longwood Gardens, where they grow in a long double *allée*. She dissuaded me from getting rid of our paulownia.

My doubts continued to grow, however. Someone told me that under the right conditions, paulownias are prodigious self-seeders, almost as successful in reproducing their kind as catalpas and ailanthus, both rank and weedy trees. The evidence of my own eyes was that this tree was out of scale in our garden of modest size. The immense and very coarse leaves blacken at the slightest hint of frost in the autumn, falling immediately to the ground, where they can smother smaller plants that are still in bloom.

The tree has grown faster than my doubts about it. It now stands thirty-five feet tall, and its long branches, curiously tilted upward at their tips, cast a twenty-foot circle of deep shade from the first unfolding of the leaves in late May until that blackening frost arrives.

I've learned to live with our paulownia and even to love it. Against the background of two white dogwoods nearby, its heavy clusters of pale purple flowers are a pleasant sight, if not exactly spectacular.

But my younger son, Michael, gave me a lesson about the true merits of this tree. He and his wife were still living in an apartment, and our garden provided them with cut flowers from March to October. He dropped by the house one day during that lull in midspring when not much is blooming.

The paulownia, however, was at its peak. The lowest branches were out of reach by now, but Michael fetched a ladder and pruning shears and brought down half a dozen clusters of flowers. What was merely a pleasant sight at a distance turned out to be so lovely close up that I am ready to abandon all fear of overstatement or hyperbole: the blossoms of *P. tomentosa* are more beautiful than those of any other tree.

Each cluster of blooms bears small rounded buds at the top. Farther down, these elongate into velvety purple-blue tubes two inches long. Near the bottom of the cluster, the flowers look like elegant ballroom dresses of a century ago, pleated from the waist to half their length, then flaring out, as if ready to waltz. When fully open, their deep purple changes to pale lilac suffused with creamy yellow. The calyx enclosing bud or flower is also very beautiful, a light tan with the look and feel of suede.

Paulownia delights the nose as well as the eye. The fragrance is honeyed, with suggestions of lemon and apricot, and it is so pervasive that a single spike of flowers in a vase indoors sweetens the air a room or two away.

Paulownia is a source of great sensual pleasure all during the winter after the leaves drop, when the attractive form of the branches, like arms raised high in benediction, is revealed. The tightly closed fruits formed after bloom the preceding spring hang in great clusters, like enormous yellow-green grapes. The seedpods of the previous year have by now dropped their seeds, but they still persist, half-open, a pale mahogany in color. They clatter like castanets in a strong breeze or when a squirrel chases through the barren branches. The erect spikes of buds for spring bloom, which have a velvety texture, form in early autumn, to lend additional grace in winter.

As for self-seeding, it does happen, but the seedlings, which have large downy leaves, are easy to identify and pull up.

A final curious fact about paulownias is their attractiveness to an odd element of the criminal underworld, paulownia rustlers. The wood is in huge demand in Japan, where it is used in making little ceremonial boxes for jewelry and other treasures. The tree has as a result become uncommon there, and here a source of profit to thieves with chain saws and good connections to the international black market in this timber. Several of these trees were lost on Riverside Drive in New York City a few years back, and the population of paulownias at Winterthur, where I got my plant, has also been reduced by theft.

A Garland
of Irises

A COUPLE OF MILES from my house, there's a garden I usually contrive to drive by in late May. I don't know the owners, but the character of their horticultural passion is clear, even from a car at thirty-five miles an hour. These people love irises. More specifically, they love the tall bearded hybrids—bearded because the falls or lower petals bear prominent bands of short yellow hair near their tops, hybrids because many breeders in Europe and America have worked on bearded irises for many decades to transform them according to their wishes.

The breeders have given us an extended range of colors that Iris herself, the Greek goddess of the rainbow whose name the genus bears, would be proud of. Blues of every shade, yellows, purples (some so deep that they seem black), pinks, coppers and bronzes, whites— all of these are present in the iris palette today, as well as bitones, blends of several colors, and stipples of one color outlining the edges of a flower of a contrasting hue. The breeders have also increased both the size and the number of the blossoms to a dramatic degree, and they have added flounces and waves and ruffles to the petals.

In a good year, I understand why the owners of this garden of tall bearded irises and only tall bearded irises have specialized to the point of monomania. On a clear May morning, the interplay of shimmering color is hard to resist—and of course I've already said that it was just such a sight of color in an iris field in Texas that made gardening a seduction not to be resisted, although in the course of years my affections have strayed down other paths.

I say in a good year, because in a bad one—when there are heavy rains or winds more substantial than a light breeze—a garden composed of tall bearded hybrid irises is almost a graveyard of dashed dreams and spoiled hopes. Immense flowers wet with rain and raked by wind fall over altogether or assume odd, seemingly inebriated angles of growth. These overbred plants are so liable to wind damage that several years ago, with some reluctance, I got rid of mine.

I still have irises, however, including bearded ones. The dwarf bearded forms, which grow anywhere from six to fifteen inches tall and which bloom in mid-April, not late May, are splendid little creatures, if not as magnificent as their taller cousins in a good year. They offer the same wide range of color, and their smaller blossoms and shorter stems enable them to come through a windy rainstorm with pluck.

There are some other bearded irises I cherish. Some are the old-fashioned flags of the past, grown for many centuries and long before hybridizers appeared on the scene. The colors are limited, purple and slate blue being the most common. These irises are seldom found in nursery catalogs, but they travel from one garden to another as gifts between neighbors.

The very best of the bearded irises, however, is the wild species *Iris pallida dalmatica*, in its variegated forms. The flowers are pale lavender, small, and produced rather stingily. But they are sweetly fragrant, and this iris has such handsome foliage that I would gladly grow it even if it never bloomed. The fan of swordlike spiky leaves contrasts nicely with more mounded perennials nearby. There are two forms. One (*I. pallida dalmatica* 'Alba-marginata') has leaves banded with pale green and silvery white; the other (*I. pallida dalmatica* 'Aurea-marginata') with soft yellow and green. I firmly believe that to deserve fully a place in a garden a plant should be of interest in several seasons. *Iris pallida* looks wonderful nine months of the year. The foliage of both forms seems to capture sunlight and radiate it all around it from the onset of growth in early April well into autumn, so that these irises have persistent value before and after their brief season of bloom. If I had to choose between them, I would select 'Aurea-marginata' because of the intricate shadows it casts on itself in strong sunshine. The gold tissue is half-translucent, in such a way that the outline of one blade of foliage can be seen on another. This plant is especially fine underplanted with golden moneywort or creeping Jenny (*Lysimachia nummularia* 'Aurea') and with another creeper, *Veronica rupestris*, which blooms in late May. The gold parts of the iris leaves play off well against the more chartreuse tones of the moneywort, and the blue-purple flowers of the veronica lend a contrasting note.

The world of irises extends far beyond the bearded ones, and the season of bloom among those without the tufts of hair on their falls is very long. The iris season in my garden begins in midwinter, when the Algerian iris, *I. unguicularis*, gets underway. Some years it starts blooming in very late autumn, producing an occasional blue-violet blossom whenever there are a few mild days. It is slightly tender, so I grow it in a protected spot on the south side of our house, close to the stone foundation and with a mulch of oak leaves. If the little flowers are picked before they open and then brought into a warm room, they develop a sweet perfume.

Other winter irises commonly found in catalogs are *I. reticulata* and *I. danfordiae*. The first is bright yellow, the second blue-violet, and they both bloom close to the ground in early March.

In April these are followed by the native American *I. cristata*, a very low grower with flowers ranging from violet through pale blue to white. When it is given a suitable location—beneath deciduous trees, where it will have winter sunlight and dry shade in summer—its rhizomes spread rapidly to form colonies that make it an excellent ground cover.

Just as the tall bearded irises near the end of their bloom, the Siberian irises—*I. sibirica* and its cultivars—take over. The colors include white, a winy shade of purple, and blue-violet. The falls are often peacock marked with strange and gleaming, almost metallic, swirls of greenish gold. The stems are wiry enough that when the plants are in flower they give with the wind without flopping over or breaking. The tall, narrow, and sharply pointed foliage is attractive long after bloom has ceased.

In late June come perhaps the most glorious of all the irises, the Japanese irises (*I. ensata*, formerly *I. kaempferi* and still found under that name in some catalogs). Blooming in late June, they are spectacular for their huge, rather flattened flowers in shades of blue, white, purple, and pink, as well as combinations or blends. I confess to not having yet gotten round to growing Japanese irises (nor the spuria and the Louisiana irises that are on my list to explore in the future), but I love them for their names—sometimes in Japanese, such as 'Gekke Ikan', sometimes semitranslated in English, as 'Cry of Rejoice'.

I also love and grow an iris called 'Aichi', possibly a hybrid between *I. ensata* and *I. pseudacorus*, the European yellow flag, which prefers very damp soil. 'Aichi' has yellow flowers in mid-June, but I grow it for its pale chartreuse foliage. It combines well with ferns, dwarf cattails, and marsh marigolds in our little bog, and its leaves have a fine glowing quality, as if they were producing light themselves, not just reflecting the sun.

Something of a rarity, but ending the iris year is the Gladwin iris, *I. foetidissima*. The flowers in June are passable enough, but modest in their appeal. The seeds are the real attraction, and a spectacular one at that. In the fall, the ripe pods open, revealing polished large round orange seeds, fully a match for the berries of holly or other bright autumn fruits. The species name warns that this is a plant of great stench. But the bad smell comes only if the leaves are crushed, so all gardeners who have never developed a penchant for crushing leaves at every opportunity can grow the Gladwin iris without olfactory distress.

Finally, there's a new iris, still rare though worth waiting for, that blooms in May but, once seen, stays forever in the memory—*I. x* 'Paltec'. Said to be a hybrid between *I. pallida* and *I. tectorum,* the Japanese roof iris, it grows to about fifteen inches. The attractive foliage makes it a promising ground cover. But the flowers of this plant, which does best in light shade, are what make it so stunning. They are a pure, crystalline, radiant blue, close to the color of 'Heavenly Blue' morning glories. I wouldn't kill to get this plant for my garden, but a crime of lesser gravity is not unthinkable.

The Dance of Columbines

THE MIDDLE OF MAY is the time of the greatest profusion of bloom in my garden. Spring is at its peak. The dominant color, besides the fresh new tide of greens in the lawn and the shrub border, is white. Our native dogwoods are still in bloom at the back of the garden, spangled with white flowers or bracts of pristine purity. A rampant colony of lily-of-the-valley offers its own sea of white in the multitude of little bell-like, sweetly fragrant flowers nodding gracefully on each stem. When a strong breeze touches the lilies-of-the-valley, the flowers tremble so in unison that I almost expect to hear the sound of tiny chimes.

Many of the plants of May are like children begging for attention. Here I am, many of them say. Look at me, for I am purely wonderful. And so they are. But the deepest pleasures of the garden in this season lie in those plants that make more modest claims for recognition, that wait to be noticed and admired.

High on my list of such plants are the columbines or aquilegias, with many species and cultivars, some hailing from Europe, some from the Orient, and others from North America. The great number of common names they have accumulated over the centuries testifies to the affection that they have called forth. Columbine, from the Latin word for dove, is one such name. Others include doves-round-a-dish, boots-and-shoes, and Jack-in-trousers. It would be pleasant to think that the genus name *Aquilegia* comes from the Latin word for eagle, so that the flower is named for two birds of very different character, but a colleague who teaches Latin says it derives instead from *aquilegus,* meaning "a water carrier"—a puzzling etymology, because it bears no conceivable resemblance either to a vessel or to a fellow hauling pails of water. But then columbines don't look much like eagles, anyway.

The columbine season gets underway in early April, with the first flowers on the Japanese species *Aquilegia flabellata* 'Nana'. The plants make low mounds of fetching blue-green foliage about eight inches high. The flowers rise about four inches higher. The blossoms face downward, so that seen from above they are little circles of five petals, each with a spur rising to clasp the stem. Some are entirely of one color, an odd but appealing grayish white that reminds me of skim milk. Others look blue from a distance, but turn out on close inspection to be suffused with a slight rosy tint. The corolla of the flower (you have to lie on the ground to see it, or pluck a blossom and turn it so you can look it in the eye) is that same ambiguous rosy blue, banded milky white at its tip.

This lovely columbine—the one I would choose, if I could have just one species—blooms over a long season starting in late April. But in mid-May another species, *A. canadensis,* an American native, joins it. It is considerably taller, to twenty inches or higher, and the flowers are built to an entirely different model. The pale scarlet petals and spurs are fused into conical tubes pointing upward. They termi-nate with little globes at the top, so that the comparison to a jester's cap is irresistible. The corolla faces downward and is pale lemon.

Aquilegia canadensis is highly variable in color and in the size of its flowers. A dwarf plant just popped up in my garden one year, from no certain source. It probably came in a shipment from a nursery that arrived on a day when I was too busy to make proper labels, or it may have hitchhiked as a seed in the soil of another potted perennial. Wherever it came from, I like it, for its abundance of small, buttery yellow blossoms, which so dance in the wind that from a distance it seems to be attended by tiny butterflies.

Finally, among the species, late in May comes another native North American, *A. chrysantha,* which grows to thirty inches and produces large flowers—typically yellow, as the species name indicates, but sometimes a brilliant white.

Then there are the myriad cultivated strains—McKana's giants, the Music series, and others. For over a century, hybridizers have been at work, taking what nature offers and transforming it by artifice. The palette of columbine colors now embraces mauve, lavender, lilac, Tyrian purple, yellows of many hues, pinks, whites, and many combinations of two or more colors.

Almost any columbine is delightful in the late spring garden, but I make a strong exception for an old-fashioned one called 'Nora Barlow'. I don't know who Ms. Barlow was, but whoever named this plant in her honor rendered her a dubious favor. The double flowers, with many petals combining pink and green and white, look like little mops. The grace and delicacy typical of the genus have departed altogether. And I do not stand alone in this firm opinion. The English critic William Morris once wrote, "Be very shy of double flowers; choose the old Columbine where the clustering doves are unmistakable and distinct, not the double one, where they run into mere tatters."

I haven't bought columbine seed in years, although I occasionally buy in full bloom from a local nursery a plant that is especially pleasing. The fascination of columbines lies in never knowing what will turn up. They are short-lived perennials that interbreed among themselves most promiscuously. They seed themselves with blithe abandon, but not in a particularly troublesome way. New plants keep popping up every year in unexpected places, often with flowers whose exact color I've never quite seen before.

The three-lobed, deeply scalloped foliage of columbines remains attractive after the flowers have quit appearing, except that it is often attacked by leaf miners, tiny insects that bore twisting and unsightly tunnels inside the leaves as they feast themselves on one of their favorite foods. The remedy is simple and nonchemical. In early June, all the leaves can be cut back to the ground and put in a microwave oven for a few seconds to make them fit for the compost heap. The plants will make new leaves, which generally get through the rest of the year without further infestation.

Geraniums
by Fischer

ABOUT GERANIUMS, some serious gardeners can get bossy, even rude. If they discover that when you say "geranium" you mean the plants that go in window boxes or tubs on the deck, bloom from Memorial Day until the first hard freeze, and have pungent foliage and clusters of pink or red or white flowers, they will correct you. What you are talking about isn't a geranium at all, but a pelargonium. Real geraniums are woodland perennials, commonly called cranesbills, that produce a mass of white or pink or electric-blue flowers in late spring or early summer and then call it quits until next year.

It doesn't matter, really. I still call pelargoniums geraniums, like almost everybody else I know, and will undoubtedly still be doing so around the time I draw my last breath.

A few years ago on a trip to Switzerland I had a depressing experience with geraniums, which I thought grew pretty well in my own tubs on the deck in southern New Jersey. It was late summer, in Zurich, where it seemed that every chalet and apartment balcony was adorned with geraniums—and such geraniums they were! They were perky upright ones, and others that cascaded in sheets of pure white, glowing pink, and flamboyant scarlet from planter boxes or down sloping banks. I could not name all the variations of color, and the flowers were so abundant as to almost obscure the foliage, making me wonder how photosynthesis could take place.

Switzerland, not New Jersey, I concluded, was the place to grow geraniums because of some trick of altitude or climate. My own were paltry by comparison. The following year I considered not planting any geraniums, for the same reason that you can't keep 'em down on the farm after they've seen Paris. But for decades I've planted geraniums late each spring, and it's gotten to be a tradition, so I kept it up. What would a summer be without a geranium or two to lend some fairly carefree color?

Last year, however, I discovered that it wasn't New Jersey after all, but my geraniums that were at fault. One of the garden centers in my neighborhood had the usual geraniums I had been planting, but it also had some new ones, which a sign identified as Fischer geraniums. In health and vigor, they outdid all the competition. They had at least twice the number of blossoms and buds that the others had. And they were labeled, bearing German names like 'Schöne Helena' and 'Grenchen', as well as more English-sounding ones, like 'Snow Queen' or 'Mars'. They were precisely the geraniums I had so admired and envied in Switzerland.

As with almost everything that happens in a garden, there is a story here. It seems that many of the geraniums I'd been growing for years were not in very sound health, plagued by viral and bacterial diseases picked up over the years and transmitted by propagation that inhibit bloom. And it seems further that a German geranium lover, Gerhard Fischer of Hillscheid in Germany, established a company called Pelargonien Fischer and began efforts not only to breed new geraniums but also to get rid of the baleful viruses and bacteria, by propagating them by tissue culture.

Europeans seem to love geraniums more than any other flower.

Pelargonien Fischer as well as Fischer's pelargoniums were great successes, both horticulturally and financially. The company now grows millions of the plants in the Canary Islands, producing small rooted cuttings, which then go to wholesale growers in Europe, and finally reach retail customers in late spring, already blooming their heads off and ready to keep it up for months without stint.

These superior geraniums are now widely available at garden centers in the United States. They have a great deal to offer. 'Mars' is a fine bright red that will not fade in the hottest sun. 'Schöne Helena' is a glorious shade of salmon pink. There are several others, including the so-called ivy types, which cascade rather than stand erect. My favorite is a very deep pink that is marked with blotches of white and deeper rose and that for some unfathomable reason is called 'Blues'.

Like all geraniums, the Fischers are easy to care for. They like a deep drenching but enough time between waterings that the soil can dry out slightly. I suppose cutting off the spent blossoms keeps the flowers coming, but with these terrific bloomers I haven't noticed much difference when the task of deadheading is neglected. There is some strange insect, on my deck at least, that loves to eat the flowers while still in tight bud, but a little pyrethrum dust or a dousing with soapy water seems to keep it in check.

The dissemination of basic information among part-time clerks at garden centers is sometimes less than complete, so a customer who comes in to ask for Fischer geraniums may get a shrug or an uncomprehending stare. But if a garden center has them—and the best ones surely will—they're easy to find. For one thing, they outshine any others in sight. For another, they're marked with a tag with the name of the plant on it and the company's logo, a geranium peeking out from underneath a black rectangle and the words "Pelfi by Fischer."

New Horizons
for the Bastard
Pellitory

I CAN THINK of no plant as rich in associations, or as promising for the future, as the yarrow. I give here only one of its common names in English, for it is also known as bastard pellitory, calico border plant, carpenter's grass, devil's plaything, nosebleed, old man's pepper, seven year's love, sweet maudlin, thousand-leafed clover, and woundwort. Its scientific name, *Achillea*, goes back to Homeric times and to the legend that the centaur Chiron taught Achilles its medicinal uses in cleansing the wounds of his soldiers in the Trojan War. A decoction made from its leaves was put to the same use during our own Civil War. The British herbalist John Gerard claimed in the seventeenth century that chewing its leaves was an infallible cure for toothache. In European folk medicine, yarrow tea was believed to remedy depression and halt the onset of baldness.

One of America's best writers on wildflowers, Neltje Blanchan, thought it provided wisdom, as well as healing properties. Of one species, *Achillea millefolium,* introduced by the earliest English settlers and now a common roadside weed in much of North America, she wrote in *Nature's Garden* (1900), "By contenting itself with neglected corners of the earth, the yarrow gives us many valuable lessons on how to succeed."

The yarrow also has a place in Chinese culture, as its dried stems are used to cast the hexagrams of the I Ching and thus to foretell the shape of things to come.

I don't happen to believe that plants teach us the way to success or that they have prophetic powers. And I'm wary of folk medicine and of the yarrow in particular, which can cause a nasty dermatitis when combined with exposure to sunlight. But I value one of these achilleas very highly indeed as a garden plant. The cultivar 'Coronation Gold' is sturdy and imposing, eventually forming a clump three feet high and four feet across, with slightly rounded flower clusters that are not only attractive in midsummer bloom but also are handsome when dried for winter arrangements.

Until now, I have contented myself with 'Coronation Gold', leaving the other and weedier sorts of yarrow to bloom by the roadside, since in rich soil they sprawl and look untidy. But 'Coronation Gold' has lost its preeminence in my garden as the sole representative of the genus, thanks to Herr Heinze Klose, a hybridizer in Stuttgart, Germany, who has taken these perennials in hand and gussied them up considerably.

The news about these achilleas is that they are sturdy, standing upright rather than flopping under the weight of their blossoms. Furthermore, they offer a new range of good colors. One, which is called 'Hope', is a soft and creamy yellow. Four others now on the market—'Fanal', 'Paprika', 'Salmon Beauty', and 'Weser River Sandstone'—vary from light pink to ruby red. They bloom over a long season in the summer, and they lend a new note to bouquets for the house.

Worthy
Hypericums

ACCORDING TO *Hortus Third*, the genus *Hypericum* is a large one, made up of over three hundred species of both woody shrubs and herbaceous perennials from Asia, Europe, and North America. These plants have some history to them, as well as a good bit of mythology and theology. The etymology of the genus name is confused. Some authorities assert confidently that it was named for the Titan Hyperion, father of the sun god Helios, and of the sun itself, as well as the moon and the dawn. Other authorities claim with equal confidence that the name derives from Greek roots meaning "over the icon," because of ancient Orthodox Christian practices of decorating religious icons with its blossoms.

I have no way of judging between these contrary claims, but I lean toward the theory about Hyperion as the father of Helios, for all the hypericums I have ever seen are just about the sunniest flowers imaginable. They range in size from fairly tiny (about the size of a dime) to fairly large (bigger than a silver dollar—the old kind), but most of them are built to a common pattern. Their single flowers, often borne in clusters, have five petals of a very sunny and pleasant shade of buttery yellow. From the throat of each flower explode long stamens, even more attractive than the petals for their sunburst effect.

Except in the coldest and the warmest regions of the country, hypericums are so easy and undemanding in their culture that I wonder why they are not planted much more widely. They come into bloom in mid-June, and many kinds keep it up well into early fall. They can tolerate a bit of drought, and a hot and sunny location is to their liking. Insects don't seem to bother them, and they are generally free of disease, although in a muggy climate some kinds may be susceptible to a disfiguring blight.

I have some old favorites, and some new ones, too.

One old favorite is *Hypericum calycinum*, a Eurasian species, which in exception to the rule prefers a fairly shady location. It is a low and spreading woody ground cover. In a harsh winter it may die back to the roots, but it doesn't matter, since hypericums bloom on new wood. It grows about fifteen inches tall. *Hypericum reptans*, from western China, is a true creeper, only reaching four inches in height. I also like *H. olympicum*, although it has only a brief season of bloom in early summer. The tiny oval foliage, which grows on stems that encircle or spiral outward from the plant, remains green and handsome in my New Jersey garden throughout the winter. I am also partial to *H. buckleyi*, another low shrub suitable as a ground cover, which is native to the southern Appalachians. And anyone who likes hypericums—and who could not?—will decide that the English cultivar 'Hidcote', a hybrid of uncertain parentage, is indispensable in a summer border or grown as a hedge some three feet tall or even taller. It is extraordinarily vigorous and doesn't seem to know the meaning of the words *stop blooming*.

Two of my recent discoveries among hypericums are *H. x inodorum* 'Elstead' and hypericum 'Albury Purple'. I saw 'Elstead' in late summer in Seattle and was bowled over by its fruits as well as its flowers. The ripening fruits of hypericums are generally green, but 'Elstead' produces a heavy crop of large berrylike fruits the color of Queen Anne cherries even when it is still in bloom. I have one small plant of 'Albury Purple', and it is an exciting addition to the garden for its burgundy-toned foliage and red fruits that turn black as they mature.

As for the mythology and the theology, in pagan times hypericums were strongly associated with the bonfires common all over Europe on Midsummer Eve. Because of their sunny color and their wheel-like shape, they were worn in garlands, chaplets, and wreaths at the summer solstice, the longest day of the year, but also the day that marked the turning back toward darkness and winter.

Christians adapted this pagan practice to their own uses. Believing that John the Baptist was born on June 24, they transformed the old midsummer ritual bonfires into the Feast of Saint John, meanwhile continuing the practice of wearing hypericum blossoms and of weaving them into garlands to cast into the huge fires still set on the Eve of Saint John. The English common name for hypericum is Saint-John's-wort.

Hypericum plays no role in modern medicine, as far as I know, but in earlier times it was highly regarded as a cure for several ailments and maladies. The English herbalist John Gerard in the 1633 edition of *The Herball, or General Historie of Plants* wrote that "S. Iohns wort with his floures and seed boyled and drunken, provoketh urine, and is right good against the stone in the bladder . . . The leaves stamped are good to be layd upon burnings, scaldings, and all wounds; and also for rotten and filthy ulcers." He recommended an infusion made by allowing olive oil mixed with hypericum leaves and flowers to stand in the sun as a fine remedy for "any wound made with a venomed weapon." And he quoted approvingly the claim of the ancient Greek herbalist Dioscorides that ingesting the seeds of this plant for forty days "cureth the sciatica, and all aches that happen in the hips."

Like most gardeners, I know full well those "aches that happen in the hips," plus a few other places. But I think I'll just enjoy the sight of hypericums in their cheering bloom, meanwhile sticking to aspirin.

Lantanas:
The Bane and
the Boon

BEFORE SAYING a single good word about some hybrid lantanas of exceptional merit, I need to point out that in some parts of the world they represent an ecological disaster of high magnitude; another example of the unintentional bad outcome of a seemingly harmless desire to add new and lovely plants to gardens.

Early in the eighteenth century, several species of lantana arrived in Europe from their native habitats in the West Indies, Central and South America, and southern Africa. Complicated crosses were made among them, resulting in hybrid forms with splendid colors: scarlet, yellow, rose, lavender, white, plus those with two or more colors in the individual florets arranged in clusters of bloom. Some were upright and shrubby; others pendant or creeping. Even though they were perennials too tender to survive European winters, they could be overwintered inside and then propagated by cuttings taken in February, which by May made substantial plants, with all the vigor that is often associated with hybridization.

Within a few decades, hundreds of cultivated varieties had been named and were widely used in gardens in France, Italy, and Spain, where they were highly valued for their bright colors, their quick growth, and their nonstop bloom over the entire growing season.

If the story of the hybrid lantanas stopped here, it would have a happy ending, but unfortunately it didn't stop here, for the new lantanas were exported to European colonies in tropical and subtropical regions. Without freezing weather to halt their growth, they spread unchecked. Birds feasted on their glossy black fruits and excreted the seeds to sprout everywhere that birds could fly. Eventually the seed-grown lantanas that escaped from gardens lost their interesting range of colors, tending instead to muddy shades of orange, but they retained all their hybrid vigor.

A new weed had been created, a highly invasive plant with chemical properties that inhibited the growth of many potential rivals native to the habitats lantanas began to take over. In South America, Madagascar, Australia, Hawaii, and similar frost-free regions, the descendants of these hybrid lantanas have become a menace to indigenous plants. Their toxic fruits have also been responsible for the deaths of both humans, especially children, and livestock.

Having recited this tale of horror, I can now go on to say that I have long had much affection for lantanas. They have their faults, of course. They are so attractive to white flies that if I brush against a plant in midsummer, a little cloud of the things swarms up in momentary protest before resuming their lantana feast. Their foliage has a rank odor, and touching it causes a rash in some people.

But lantanas are colorful and undemanding, and they bring a long season of good cheer to a deck or a patio when grown in hanging baskets or pots. I never bother to bring them inside for the winter (since I would bring with them an infestation of white flies that would attack other houseplants). I just let them die when winter comes and then replace them the following spring with rooted cuttings from a nearby garden center.

Some new things have happened to lantanas lately, as I learned when I wandered into the greenhouse of a little nursery near McMinnville, Tennessee, not long ago. The greenhouse was bright with bloom, but one thing stood out above everything else: a spot of glowing, fire-engine red on a bench in the distance. It turned out to be a lantana called 'Dallas Red'. It was a knockout, blooming on a mere rooted cutting about three inches tall, with four clusters of blooms made up of florets twice the usual size.

'Dallas Red' lured me to the bench where it was blooming so lustily, but it turned out to have company in the form of several other named lantanas I had not seen before, and of clear superiority to the ones I had seen. I picked out several to bring home to New Jersey. 'Golden Plume' is a rich deep yellow, 'Lady Olivia' a blend of lavender and pink, 'Irene' a multicolor, with individual florets of yellow, red, and fuchsia. These are upright, shrubby cultivars, but there are others with a more trailing habit. 'Silver Mound' is sparkling white with a touch of cream at the center, 'Samantha' a clear yellow with variegated green and gold foliage, and 'Lavender' (no surprise here) is lavender.

The owner of the nursery knew nothing of the history of these splendid new lantanas and could tell me only that she had bought the plants from a wholesale nursery called Colorado Cuttings in Lafayette, Colorado. I called the company, but the owner had no information to impart beyond the fact that he liked lantanas and had been collecting unusually good ones here and there, but he couldn't quite remember where, or tell me why it was 'Dallas Red' and not 'Duluth Red'. He doesn't sell retail and knew of no mail-order retail nurseries that carry these fine new lantanas. I cannot imagine, however, that it will be long before they become widely available.

Lilies:
An Ancient
Affection
Renewed

THE LILY HAS LOOMED larger in the human imagination for a greater stretch of history than any other flower, except for the rose. One species, the Madonna lily *(Lilium candidum)*, is depicted in frescoes in Crete dating back to about 1500 B.C. The fairly small flowers of this plant are so dazzling in their whiteness that it is hardly surprising that they should become laden down with legend, becoming the stuff of myth and of theology. An ancient Greek tradition holds that this lily originated when Juno suckled the infant Hercules. Where drops of her milk fell to earth, lilies sprang up.

Christians were quick to adopt *L. candidum* as their own, giving it a range of meanings extending from the virtue of chastity to the bliss of heaven to the toil-free life of Adam and Eve before they ate of forbidden fruit and were driven out of Eden. But the Madonna lily, as its common name suggests, was preeminently the symbol of the Virgin Mary. In late medieval and Renaissance paintings, the iconography of this lily was extremely rich. It betokened Mary's

Immaculate Conception, whereby she was conceived without original sin. Paintings of the Annunciation often show the archangel Gabriel presenting white lilies to Mary as he proclaims that she will give birth to a savior while yet remaining a virgin. And at her death and assumption into Heaven, she was sometimes represented as being greeted by throngs of angels and martyrs bearing lilies and red roses.

I like to think that the Madonna lilies I grow, which bloom in June and then race toward their summer dormancy, bring some ancient testimony to my garden, linking it with the history of human religion, with Juno and Hercules, as well as with Mary and Christ. But Madonna lilies only initiate a long parade of lilies, blooming in succession from early summer until late August. Most of the lilies in my garden span geography rather than long stretches of time into the distant past.

There are lilies native to North America as well as Europe, but the treasure trove of the lily world is Asia. British and European plant-explorers began collecting species in China, Japan, Korea, and Tibet early in the nineteenth century. It was not long before gardeners, not content with the riches nature provided, began to create hybrids of two or more species. The first hybrid of record was bred in 1830 by an Englishman named Henry Groom, who crossed two Asian species, *L. dauricum* and *L. bulbiferum*, to produce a varied group of cultivars, which were grown in the United States by Charles Mason Hovey. Mr. Hovey, a nurseryman from Boston, soon began his own breeding program, crossing Groom's hybrids with the lovely Japanese species, *L. speciosum*. The evolution of modern garden lilies of extraordinarily complicated genetic ancestry was underway, in a process that continues today, as new varieties are introduced to the market each year.

These garden lilies fall into three main groups. First to bloom, just as Madonna lilies cease, are the Asiatic hybrids. All by themselves, these are mainstays of the early summer garden and they are wonderfully diverse. Some start blooming in mid-June, others in mid-July, so their season is long. Some bear open, slightly flattened bossoms, others are cupped, and still others have petals that are strongly reflexed or swept back. The flowers of some are nodding and pendant, so that to look them in the face it may be necessary to kneel. Others face outward, and the rest face upward. The range of color is huge: white, yellow, orange, red, lavender, and winy purple are just a few colors to choose from. Some are spotted with brownish purple for a freckled look, while others have clear complexions.

The names of the Asiatic hybrids are legion. The most famous and the most widely grown, as a cut flower for the florist trade as well as in the home garden, is 'Enchantment', a spotted, upward-facing, glowing orange-red bred in the 1940s by Jan de Graaff, then the owner of Oregon Bulb Farms, a leading source of new lilies since World War II. I've never seen an Asiatic lily I didn't like; in fact, the unnamed seedlings, hybridizers' rejects, that are sold as mixtures by nurseries such as White Flower Farm and Wayside Gardens make a good way of furnishing a garden with an abundance of lilies at little cost. I do have, however, a personal favorite: 'Red Velvet', which was introduced a few years ago by B and D Lilies. It is easily the most magnificent plant in my garden in July. It stands six feet high, bearing dramatic trusses of as many as twenty-five outfacing flowers to a stalk. The red is intense, and, somewhat to my surprise, the plants look wonderful in combination with deep pink achilleas.

In late July, the Aurelian hybrids begin. These are tall plants, typically bearing large trumpet-shaped flowers in a somewhat narrower range of color than the Asiatics. 'Moonlight', 'Pink Perfection', 'Copper King', and 'Black Dragon' are widely available. The Aurelians are irresistible to hummingbirds, who add their vibrant color and their darting movement to a garden where these lilies are planted.

The lily season reaches its climax in August with the Oriental hybrids, largely derived from crosses among several Japanese species, including *L. auratum* and *L. rubellum*. A few are pure in color, all white or all pink, but most are like floral tapestries, mixing red, white, yellow, and pink in every imaginable combination. The Orientals often bear strange raised markings called papillae on their waxy and elegant petals. Even at night, when they cannot be seen, these lilies make their presence known by a fragrance matched in its powerful sweetness only by gardenias and southern magnolias. A single blossom can perfume a room, although some people find the scent overpowering and funereal at close range.

All lilies have some things in common. They are easy to grow, provided that they are given moisture and good drainage. They also take up very little room in a garden, considering the great show they make. They perform best when the ground is covered with other plants, such as vinca or other low-growing perennials. They thus provide a tiered look to plantings that otherwise might be dull and uninspiring. And they bring over the years many a surprise, in the form of seedlings cropping up in unexpected places. These seedlings are seldom inferior to their parents, and may even be superior.

No Chauvinism
Intended, But...

I DON'T ENTIRELY share the views of my fellow gardening writer, the late Caroline Dorman, who wrote a book called *Natives Preferred* and who resolutely chose to landscape her country place in Louisiana entirely with plants native to North America. Such a thing is entirely possible; indeed, many of our finest garden plants, such as phloxes and perennial asters, are American wildflowers that were exported to Great Britain, taken in hand by hybridizers, and then repatriated. But it still strikes me that the lives of American gardeners would be impoverished by the kind of horticultural chauvinism that would bar plants of European or Asian origin. Spring would be bleak indeed without daffodils and tulips and other common bulbs, not to mention peonies. In the summer we would have to do without daylilies and hostas. We could have lilies, yes, but not the glorious Aurelian and Oriental hybrids bred by American hybridizers from Asian species. In the fall, there wouldn't be a chrysanthemum in sight.

To my mind, a garden ought to be a polyglot affair, a floral

United Nations. It should be a place where plants from all the temperate zones mix and mingle in tribute to the plant-explorers of our century and centuries past. These adventurers went to enormous trouble, sometimes risking and even losing their lives, to give us diversity and choice in a gardening year that begins, here in New Jersey, in late January when the heaths (from northern Europe), the hellebores (from Asia Minor and southern Europe), and the Chinese witch hazels all come into their welcome bloom.

Having taken a stand in favor of an open-door policy in the garden, however, I must go on to state one of the plainer facts about gardening in America. We are too neglectful of many native plants, especially shrubs and small trees, that deserve a place in our gardens. Dogwoods, yes—we have dogwoods (although they are now imperiled by blight), but we overlook equally rewarding plants.

One such is surely the beach plum *(Prunus maritima)*, whose name indicates that it will survive near the shore but does not imply that it will not thrive in inland areas. A small tree, generally six feet high or under at maturity, it flowers profusely in very early spring. Some people describe its blossoms as a dirty shade of white, but they are attractive nonetheless, to honeybees as well as humans. Even though it is shallow rooted, the beach plum is tough and virtually immune to drought. The small fruits produced in the summer are edible and make an especially delicious jam. Somewhat gnarled and twisted, its black limbs and trunk have a fascinating silhouette in winter.

Another plant, this one a shrub, is also associated with the northeastern coastal areas but may perfectly well be planted elsewhere. I refer to the common northern bayberry *(Myrica pennsylvanica)*. A fast grower, it makes an ideal informal hedge—informal because it does not take well to the clipping that yews and boxwoods can easily stand. Its ultimate height is ten feet, but it can be kept lower by light pruning. In mild winters the foliage, which takes on a purplish tint in the fall, may persist until early spring. The profusion of small round fruits on the female plants is not only highly attractive, with a pewter gleam, but also wonderfully fragrant, as our earliest colonists, who used the fruits as an ingredient in candles, knew quite well.

Fragrance is also a major attraction in two of our best native plants. The clove currant *(Ribes odoratum),* a favorite in nineteenth-century American gardens, is hard to find nowadays and should probably not be grown in areas where there are large stands of white pines, since it is the alternate host of a rust disease inimical to this species of pine. Nevertheless, it is one of the glories of the spring garden, bursting into bloom ahead of forsythias, with primrose-yellow flowers somewhat resembling those of the winter jasmine. Their sweet and heady aroma is unmistakable from fifteen or twenty feet away. And sweet fern *(Comptonia peregrina),* which is not a fern at all but a low semi-evergreen shrub, fills the air with an astringent aroma from its leaves, a smell somewhat resembling that of witch hazel lotion.

As for the common yucca *(Yucca filamentosa),* I think Congress made a terrible mistake in not choosing it as our national floral emblem, selecting the rose instead. This stalwart American native, which grows from Florida to New Hampshire, is a plant of many uses. Native Americans made sandals and rope from its fiber. Soap has been made from its roots. The flowers are said to be edible, though I haven't tried them. A clump of four or five yucca plants in a garden setting is appealing throughout the year, for the sculptural quality of their sharply pointed swordlike evergreen leaves, and in June for the tall steeples of dozens upon dozens of creamy-ivory fragrant blossoms, which are as lovely a sight as one could wish. It's not at all difficult to understand why the American yucca was among Gertrude Jekyll's favorite plants.

In its own way, the oak-leafed hydrangea *(Hydrangea quercifolia)* is just as handsome as the yucca. A medium-sized shrub with large leaves, whose shape is adequately described in both its common name and its Latin specific name, this plant produces large panicles of white bracts and inconspicuous flowers in midsummer, which fade to pink and then to parchment tan. The bloom stalks may be cut for dried arrangements indoors, or left on the plant to lend interest in winter. Although I generally prefer plants with single flowers to those with doubles, I gladly make an exception for 'Snowflake', a double cultivar of oak-leafed hydrangea that has enormous pendant spikes of green and white bracts in a hose-in-hose double arrangement.

Clethra alnifolia richly deserves its common name, sweet pepperbush, for it announces its presence first to the nose and then to the eye. The spikes of small ivory-colored blossoms are abundant and pretty, but their spicy fragrance is one of the most characteristic smells of late summer along roadsides, beside the damp woodlands where clethras generally grow in great numbers. (This shrub will live on dry ground also, but it may be subject to infestation by spider mites.) The mahogany-colored seed clusters are pretty to behold in winter. A pink variety, *C. alnifolia rosea,* exists, although it's rare and hard to find.

Need I even bother to mention our native mountain laurel *(Kalmia latifolia)*? This mound of a shrub, which grows thickly in the understory of New Jersey's Pinelands as well as in other regions, has glossy evergreen leaves that stay bright throughout the winter, unlike the mournful ones of the rhododendron, which turn a gloomy blackish green and on really cold days fold up, looking something like limp cigars. The mountain laurel is a year-round shrub, but it comes into true splendor in late May and early June, when it is smothered with clusters of waxy deep rose buds that open into blossoms of pink so pale they verge on white.

It's impossible for me to understand why only a handful of home gardeners have discovered the merits of the cultivated varieties of the native blueberry. Like bayberries, they make a fine informal hedge. The pink-tinged creamy white blossoms that appear in the spring, often before the leaves, are attractive small bells somewhat like the flowers of lily-of-the-valley. The dense foliage is pleasing. If two or more varieties are planted for proper cross-pollination, the homeowner can have fruit for pies and muffins and eating out of the hand, without making a trip to the grocery store or roadside stand. Finally, blueberries would be worth planting if only for the sake of their beauty in late winter, when their stems are a warm shade of red with golden overtones. One of the most dazzlingly beautiful sights in my part of New Jersey is the blueberry fields near Hammonton, especially early in the morning or late in the afternoon, when they are backlit by the low rays of the February sun. Had he seen these fields, Wordsworth would have ditched his daffodils in a nanosecond.

New Periwinkles
Add Glory
to Virtue

ONE OF MY FAVORITE annuals has always been the Madagascar periwinkle. It used to go around under the name *Vinca rosea,* until the taxonomists, who are always meddling in these things, decided that it was *Catharanthus roseus.* Whatever the name, it has every solid virtue that one could ask for, plus another unsuspected one that gives it importance far beyond the confines of the garden.

These periwinkles have dark green foliage so glossy that it fairly shines, as if sprayed with furniture polish. Their single flowers are deep pink or pristine white, sometimes with a darker rosy eye. They bloom nonstop from early June, when the soil warms to their equatorial preferences, until a hard freeze cuts them down in the fall. Although I've never seen one rot during periods of heavy summer rainfall, they thrive on heat and tolerate drought that leaves many other annuals wilted and thirsty looking. For some years now I've grown a large drift of white periwinkles in a very sunny spot next to a driveway of black asphalt whose surface can reach 120 degrees on an August day, but I have seldom had to water them.

Mildew may attack zinnias and leave them looking ratty by midsummer, and petunias are often prey to botrytis blight, but I've never seen a diseased periwinkle in many years of gardening.

Insects leave *C. roseus* out of their diets. So, for that matter, do deer. The reason is that the plants are loaded with alkaloids so potent that they are the source of vincristine and vinblastine. These drugs are important in routines of chemotherapy for treating Hodgkin's disease and certain forms of leukemia, this being the plant's unsuspected virtue.

Now, however, there's been an improvement on excellence. Several mail-order nurseries are offering three new varieties of periwinkles, with names that sound like they're right out of the opening scenes of *Gone With the Wind*, with the swirl of crinolines and petticoats. There's 'Pretty in Pink', 'Pretty in Rose', and 'Parasol'. They are distinguished from previous periwinkles by flower petals that overlap, and by larger blossoms. 'Parasol', a white with a dark rose eye, has especially big flowers, about the size of a fifty-cent piece. All three are 1991 winners of the All American Selection Award, meaning that they have performed exceptionally well in test gardens in most parts of the country.

It is possible to grow these new periwinkles from seed, but they require the warmth of a greenhouse to germinate and spurt into growth. Good garden centers offer the plants in early May, already well established and ready to grow. The easiest route to get the new periwinkles is from one of these local nurseries.

Some fourteen years in the making, the new strains are the first fruits of an ambitious program of breeding by Ronald Parker, an associate professor of horticulture and plant science at the University of Connecticut. Professor Parker went to considerable trouble to acquire rare species such as *C. trichophyllus* and others, hybridizing them among themselves and with *C. roseus* to produce inbred strains whose progeny were predictable and stable.

When I talked with Professor Parker about periwinkles, he confirmed their advantages for gardeners plagued by deer. In his trial fields he has seen huge numbers of deer tracks left by herds, with not a single nibbled leaf on twenty-two thousand plants. He also spoke guardedly and off the record about future introductions from his breeding program. Hybridizers are of necessity tight-lipped about what they are working on, for the good reason that the seed business is highly competitive, and their projects must be protected by strong security measures.

Parker's greenhouse and fields are not open to visitors, and he's not willing yet to say what he's up to or talk about the kinds of new catharanthus to come. But I can say this. Thirty years ago, the impatiens was not an exciting annual. The plants came only in mixed colors, and they were tall and leggy. Then breeders like Claude Hope in Costa Rica took them in hand. Impatiens are now much more tailored and much more floriferous over a long season, and they come in a wide range of colors. Periwinkles now seem destined for similar transformation. 'Pretty in Pink', 'Pretty in Rose', and 'Parasol' are just a peek into the future. It is to be hoped, however, that the seed companies who give names to the wonders that breeders create will investigate alphabetical possibilities beyond the letter *P*.

Mary's Phlox

MY FRIEND MARY FINCH'S GARDEN grows very well indeed, and Mary herself is not the least bit contrary. But her large garden a few blocks from my own does go counter to the conventional wisdom about perennial phlox.

The reference books agree that it is a dangerous thing to allow named varieties of *Phlox paniculata* to seed themselves. According to this advice, the large trusses of flowers should be deadheaded immediately after bloom, and a vigilant eye kept out for any unwanted progeny that escaped early detection. The seedlings will be magenta, for one thing, and magenta is a color fit only for loathing. These illegitimate children, moreover, will be very vigorous and utterly lacking in filial piety. Within no time at all, they will shove aside their more polite and highly bred parents. The garden where they are permitted to grow will scream with magenta, revealing in the act the ignorance of the people who tend the plot.

There are a couple of things wrong with this sensible-sounding piece of advice.

First, I'm not at all convinced that magenta is dreadful. It doesn't look especially good near the hot orange of marigolds, butterfly weed, or tiger lilies, but then little else does. And to my eye, magenta combines elegantly with gray-leafed plants such as artemisias. I have, incidentally, good company in not just tolerating but also fancying magenta. Louise Beebe Wilder's classic book *Color in My Garden* rejects the conventional wisdom and champions this color. Admitting that it is almost "universally shunned and despised," she demurs, calling it a "tender, hushed" color that comports itself well not only with gray but also with the blues and purples of monkshoods and many perennial salvias.

For another thing, allowing phlox to seed themselves does not condemn a garden to a flood of magenta hence and forevermore. The evidence is in Mary's garden, and it is incontrovertible.

Mary inherited from her mother the original garden she has added to over the years. More than forty years ago her mother planted it, laying out its beds of daylilies, bee balm, foxgloves, and phloxes. Mary's mother never heard the advice about extirpating phlox seedlings. Or she didn't heed it, possibly because she shared Mrs. Wilder's relish for magenta.

On the basis of my own experience, self-sown phloxes do deck themselves out in this color, but only in the first generation. Later generations show a much broader spectrum of shades and hues. Magenta is always present, but it does not dominate.

There must be over a thousand different phloxes in Mary's garden. My vocabulary is grossly inadequate to name more than a fraction of their colors. They range from glistening white to rich and sullen purple, with countless intermediate shades of mauve, lavender, lilac, peachy pink, salmon pink, and so on. Some blossoms are selfs, all of the same color, but many of them have contrasting eyes or overlays of other colors. Adding to their beauty in August are the host of swallowtails and other butterflies that pause in their busy flights to sip the nectar of these lightly fragrant blossoms, fanning their wings lightly as they drink. This large patch of seedling phloxes, the great-great-grandchildren of those that Mary's mother planted, buzzes with bees in late summer, adding to the delight.

Mary's garden has taught me some new lessons about phloxes. Breeders, most of them British, have in the twentieth century held some strong opinions about what a phlox ought to be. The individual florets ought to be large (no smaller than a nickel, ideally almost the size of a quarter). The panicles they combine to form should be immense and as billowy as a cumulus cloud in summer. The plants should be of modest stature. Twelve inches is acceptable, but the norm lies between twenty-four and thirty-six inches.

Mary's phloxes are contrary and conform to no such standards. Many of them are very tall—shoulder high, head high, or even higher—and it is an agreeable sight to look up at the heavens through their haze of pastel color.

These may not be named varieties, but many of them are so desirable that the exchange of plants between Mary's garden and my own has been heavy. Her phloxes have some virtues missing from some of the fancy ones I've gotten from nurseries over the years. The florets are often smaller and the panicles less than immense. The result is that they don't have to be staked to keep them from toppling into the mud during a summer cloudburst and windstorm. Left unstaked, the stems still move with the breeze in a graceful way. These plants also show considerable resistance to the mildew that can make phloxes in late summer such a sorry sight.

I quickly tagged a few, selecting for height, late bloom, absence of mildew, pleasant fragrance, attractive color, and that impossible-to-describe quality, distinctiveness. One plant shows distinctiveness beyond all possible doubt. The florets are quite tiny, and their petals stand apart from one another, instead of overlapping. The admirable result is that the florets are starry looking, rather than having the rounded appearance that is so common. The whole panicle suggests tiny firecrackers exploding in a blaze of the palest pink.

I do not mean to discard my pedigreed phlox. I will keep 'Dresden China', 'Sir John Falstaff', 'Starfire', and all the rest. But some of Mary's seedlings now grow alongside them, their noble stature lending variety to my garden. In time, I will certainly share a few with friends who don't look down on phloxes they have to look up to.

I will even let the plants seed themselves, unafraid of magenta and curious about the surprises that lie ahead.

The Wildflowers
of August

EARLY AUGUST brings a pause to the garden. It is a time of already over and not yet begun. The vegetative rush that began in the spring has come to a halt. Except for crabgrass and poke, even my weeds have lowered their metabolisms, moderating their ambitions to conquer the earth I tend. The daylilies that came in on a tide of radiant colors in July have had their day and now show only tired foliage and ugly brown stalks that I would remove if I felt more like working a few hours to tidy up.

Perennial asters, colchicums and autumn crocuses, toadlilies, chrysanthemums, hardy begonias—these and a host of other autumn bloomers that make fall my favorite season will not begin to strut their stuff for weeks to come.

I do a lot of sitting in August. It is my favorite chore now. I sit on the deck underneath the pergola thickly covered with the hardy kiwi vines that this year, after five summers of waiting, are bearing fruit, perhaps half a bushel of shiny green fruits the size of grapes.

I admire the perennials that are still blooming in beds sufficiently distant that the damage slugs have done is hardly visible. I wait for hummingbirds. Sometimes they come to the pots of blue plumbago on the steps of the deck, but their favorite haunt is clearly the trumpet vine that has climbed seventy-five feet into the top branches of an old juniper, which it adorns with myriad deep-throated and waxy blossoms of exuberant orange.

I also do a lot of driving at this time of year, but I never get very far from home. I live in a surburban neighborhood in New Jersey, but close at hand are the farms and roadside markets that provide fresh zucchini and corn and tomatoes in high summer.

Country roads are never more enjoyable than at this time of year, especially the verges of the little lanes the county crews have not yet gotten round to mowing. If they don't qualify as gardens, they come close in their reflection of the human influences on some plants that grow there.

Although they have become wildflowers, some of the most beautiful plants of the roadside are immigrants from Europe, brought here by accident in ship ballast or by intention for use in gardens, from which they soon escaped to assume the role of amiable tramps.

The pink or white perennial sweet peas that sprawl on the ground when they must, or clamber up fence posts when they can, aren't Americans, although they have made themselves so much at home that they can be considered naturalized citizens. So can bouncing Bet, with its fluffy pale pink blossoms and its sweet clovelike fragrance. *Saponaria,* the Latin name of this plant, as well as the seldom-used alternate common name, soapwort, testify that it was once an ingredient in a cleansing compound. Chicory, whose ragged cerulean flowers lend brilliance to the landscape before they close at noon, is another escapee. In hard times, its roots were once roasted as an inexpensive substitute for coffee. Chicory is still added to coffee in Louisiana, where its slightly bitter note is relished.

I don't know how Queen Anne's lace came to North America,

but its hold on life is tenacious. Left unmowed, this relative of carrots and parsley will grow six feet high, covering itself with cluster after cluster of tiny off-white florets that are the very image of graceful insouciance. Mowed to the ground, it moderates its habit, blooming at only one foot or so. It self-seeds generously, to understate the matter: one plant this summer will be one thousand the next. It is best not given even a toehold in the garden.

The roadside is the true American melting pot, where common American native wildflowers thrive alongside the happy immigrants. One can't drive far now without seeing the earliest species of golden-rod, or *Solidago*, a handsome and varied genus of flowering plants that bring pleasure to the eye without the least distress to the nose. (The true culprit in the hayfever attributed to goldenrod is rag-weed—a plant with no redeeming feature whatsoever except that it looks good dead and dried for winter arrangements.)

At this time of year, other wonderful plants are much in evidence. Butterfly weed is glorious for its rich and glowing orange, as well as for the monarchs that haunt it for its nectar and give it its common name. Sneezeweed or helenium, with its bright single daisies of yellow or gold, is another roadside jewel.

American gardeners have been slow in following the example of our British and European cousins in giving goldenrod, heleniums, and butterfly weed places in our gardens. Perhaps we will never do so to any great extent. A case can be made for this reluctance: why grant valuable and limited space in a garden to plants so easily enjoyed in vacant lots and on the verges of country roads?

But there is one American native plant that is highly popular across the Atlantic Ocean that I have invited into my own garden, to what I consider a smashing outcome. It is *Eupatorium purpureum* or Joe Pye weed. Privately I call it Eliza Doolittle plant, in that while fairly unprepossessing in its native habitat, it transforms itself into a true aristocrat with a little help from Professor Henry Higgins. (I paid court to this plant in *The Garden in Autumn*, but praising it only once is less than it deserves.)

Left to itself, this plant is pleasant enough—a late summer bloomer growing anywhere from two to ten feet tall with pearly pink buds that open into frothy clusters of smoky light purple flowers.

Given fertile soil and generous moisture from the time it starts growth in spring until it blooms, Joe Pye weed becomes the star of the garden, a diva of Wagnerian proportions. My colony of plants stands over ten feet tall. The flower clusters are almost two feet across, and they are surrounded by an adoring and constantly moving retinue of bees and wasps and other admiring insects paying their court.

I can't imagine a garden at this time of year without Joe Pye's magnificence.

Surprised
by Cotton

THE ROCKWOOD FILLIN' STATION, a restaurant at a busy highway intersection in Durham, North Carolina, whose name records its former uses as a place to buy gasoline, check the oil, and have your car's windshield washed, looks like, and is, a good place to have a no-nonsense breakfast of bacon and scrambled eggs, plus the grits inevitable in this part of the country. It also delivers a powerful dose of nostalgia. A red gas pump, circa 1940, next to the cash register brings back memories and serves as sculpture. The jukebox, from the late 1940s, offers Glenn Miller, Judy Garland, Kate Smith, and Frank Sinatra, from back when he was billed as a crooner.

But the Fillin' Station is the last place on earth you would expect to find horticultural inspiration. Filling stations seldom offer anything of the sort. If they have flowers growing, they usually are red salvias next to orange marigolds, in gruesome juxtaposition. They may just settle for plastic shrubbery. I am accordingly delighted to report that in dropping by this restaurant, in a building once devoted to dispensing petroleum to the driving public, for a spot of late breakfast (no grits, please) I saw something growing in half a whiskey barrel so wonderful that it went right to the top of my list of gardening copycat ideas.

It was a cotton plant, certainly not something I'd have thought of on my own to plant as an ornamental, not even if I had many lifetimes to live. But in the autumn, a single cotton plant is purely marvelous. It has a pleasingly rounded form, growing four feet wide. The leaves have withered and dropped away, leaving a skeletal structure of branches and stems bearing dozens and dozens of bolls of cotton that almost look as if they've come from the pharmacy. The bolls have opened by this time of year to the size of golf balls, packed with glistening white fiber, dazzling in the light of early morning.

Each boll invites you to touch it, and the tactile rewards are as substantial as the visual ones. The cotton fiber is soft and springy, but the finger detects within it the hard nubs of seeds for the next generation.

I wanted to plant some cotton the next chance I got, and I had my reasons. When I first saw the one growing by the old gasoline station, our granddaughter, Samantha, was old enough at five months to laugh and roll over and make her first efforts to crawl. I want her to know where things come from, besides department and grocery stores, and a cotton plant is a good place to start the instruction. It gives us fabric for comfortable and long-lasting clothing. Its seeds, so hidden in the bolls, provide the raw materials for some salad oils and vegetable margarines. The seeds also are ground into a powdery aromatic meal that is a terrific fertilizer for azaleas and other acid-loving plants. And the seeds happen to be part of my family history, for my own father and his father before him were commodity brokers, much more involved with cottonseed oil than with pork bellies.

But a cotton plant or two in a northeastern suburban garden teaches other historical lessons as well. The desirable things that cotton has brought have a tragic dimension not to be ignored. The pursuit of profit through growing cotton has its dark side. Planted almost exclusively on southern plantations after the invention of the cotton gin, cotton impoverished the earth and many human lives. Slavery was fed on it before the Civil War. Once slavery ended, the sharecropper system brought misery to white and black farmers alike, meanwhile enriching a few. Textile mills, in both America and Britain, kept clothed people who never reckoned the human cost of the fabric they wore.

Cotton's beauty in late autumn cannot be ignored, but its history has a way of intruding. I remember as a boy, growing up in the South, the miles and miles of country highway with patches of scrub pine separating the acres of cotton fields. In the houses, crude wooden shacks with sagging front porches and rusty tin roofs and privies out back, economic injustice and poverty were made plain.

I hardly looked at the cotton itself, barely enough to know that the pinkish white flowers were as simple and beautiful as those of their kin, hollyhocks and hibiscus, barely enough to see the pristine white of the bolls when they first opened.

Early the next year I decided to order some cotton seeds. I spent an entire morning calling seed companies from Texas to Georgia. They all advised me to go down to the nearest cotton gin for seeds, but warned that I wouldn't be able to buy in quantities less than fifty pounds. I didn't know where the nearest cotton gin was exactly, but it was bound to be many hundreds of miles from my front door. After searching further through the piles of seed catalogs on my shelves, I finally found a source. Cotton is listed as an ornamental plant in the spring catalog (free) of the Henry Field Seed and Nursery Company in Shenandoah, Iowa. The seed should be started indoors in late March and transplanted outside once the soil has warmed up and all danger of frost is past.

Carex

IN LATE WINTER most ornamental grasses enter their sorry season. The seed plumes of miscanthuses, pampas grass, and Ravenna grass, which stood proudly all through December into January, finally defeated by snow and insistent winds, melt into a heap, signaling the time for them to be chopped off near the ground to await new growth.

But two little ornamental grasses—sedges, to be exact—remain beautiful throughout the year, especially in late winter, when so little else competes for attention. One, which is fairly common, is *Carex morrowii* 'Variegata'. A native of Japan, it is a little rounded mop of swirling golden foliage edged in green. It should be planted, I think, in a part of the garden where it can be seen every day, for it somehow asks to be visited. I have mine next to the driveway, so I can pay my respects to it mornings when I go to work and late afternoons when I return. It is especially lovely when there has been a freezing rain and the leaves are encased in glistening ice.

The other sedge, *C. buchananii*, has a much more subtle beauty, so subtle, in fact, that I almost dug it up in its first summer and hauled it to the compost heap. It came as a gift sent along with a shipment of perennials from a mail-order nursery early that spring. Its leaves were brown, a coppery shade of palomino, and I waited and waited for new green shoots to appear. They never did, and in late June, when a friend who's a demon gardener came visiting, I pointed it out and mentioned my intention to throw it away, since it was so obviously dead.

"Allen, that's the way it's supposed to look," she informed me. "Look more closely and you'll see. It's alive—and it also happens to be a really wonderful plant." I was dubious but nevertheless looked more closely. I also felt the leaves. They were plump and resilient with life, not wizened and dry as they would have been if this carex had been a goner.

It was alive, yes, but I wasn't so sure about its being really wonderful. What good is a plant that looks dead? This carex inspired in me no affection whatsoever, especially against the background of a mulch of salt hay.

My friend suggested that when autumn arrived I should transplant *C. buchananii* to a spot where it would get winter morning light. She went on to add that she thought it would be fine in a bed near a sidewalk, where there was an evergreen cover of creeping golden moss sedum to offer a contrast of color.

This carex turned out to be everything my friend claimed, once I rid myself of the prejudice that basic brown is not the right color for a grasslike plant, and once I transplanted it to a location already covered with the sedum. It grows upright to about a foot high, then weeps down from the top, like a little fountain. The winter color is a strange metallic shade of beige, with an overlay of garnet and cranberry. In the morning light, it fairly gleams, as if waxed and polished. It is one of the small pleasures of the winter garden, but a pleasure nonetheless.

Yews

EARLY EVERY SPRING, when it's time to trim back the yews that a previous owner of my house planted to corset its foundations, I rejoice that years ago I ripped many of them out and lament not having exterminated more of them. One of the most basic and most neglected principles of gardening is that no garden should have more than one yew, and that it should be placed at a considerable distance from the house and allowed to grow into the handsome tree that any yew will eventually become. Yews planted in great numbers as a hedge near windows require regular trimming—twice a year at least. If the chore is neglected too long, downstairs rooms will soon be plunged into twilight gloom all day long during every season. And the chore can be nasty. Sometimes a ladder is needed. There is always the risk of disturbing a nest of wasps or hornets.

My hometown has not, to my knowledge, adopted an official plant, but if it did, it would probably be the yew. Yews—English yews, Japanese yews, and a multitude of hybrids between them—

grow in throngs all through the neighborhood. In the spring, more yews arrive at the garden center by the truckload from wholesale nurseries in California. The yew seems to be the emblem of the American suburb, certainly in the northeast part of the country.

It's an odd emblem indeed, for the yew has some curious associations, detailed in William Dallimore's *Holly, Yew, and Box,* a fascinating book that is hard to come by. Published in 1908 and reissued in 1978 in a facsimile edition of only 250 copies, it devotes over fifty pages to the yew, especially *Taxus baccata,* the common English or European yew.

Yews, for one thing, have a long association with death, which comes as no surprise, considering their somber greenish black color in winter and the fact that every part of the yew, except the pulpy berries that turn red in the autumn, is extremely poisonous to both humans and beasts. The ancient Egyptians regarded it as a symbol of mourning. The Greeks and Romans used its wood for funeral pyres; in Virgil's *Aeneid,* Queen Dido immolated herself on a bed of yew. The Druids venerated the yew, and when England was Christianized, the yew became the graveyard tree of choice, continuing the pagan tradition. Medieval English plant lore held that yews fed on corpses and that after sunset the trees gave off poisonous vapors. Some British herbal writers in the seventeenth century reported that persons who fell asleep under a yew would sicken and possibly die. Hilderic Friend's fascinating book, *Plant Lore,* however, passes on the news that if someone dreams about a yew, a wealthy friend or relative will die, leaving the dreamer a large inheritance.

These morbid associations of *T. baccata* were not left untouched by the English poets. Shakespeare wrote in *Titus Andronicus* of "a dismal yew," and a meeting by a yew tree plays its part in the tragedy of *Romeo and Juliet.* If William Wordsworth had his hosts of daffodils to cheer his soul, he also had his yews, which symbolized for him solitude and "gloom profound."

Paradoxically, yews are symbolic of immortal life and resurrection as well as sorrow and mourning. As evergreens, they defy the death that winter represents. And they are also extremely long-lived plants, easily surviving for a thousand years, an age attained by a number of historic specimens in British churchyards and monastery cloisters.

According to Mr. Dallimore, the yew (which has been spelled various ways in English, including "ugh" and "eugh") also has military associations. Its fine-grained, tough but flexible wood made it ideal for use in archery. William the Conqueror's soldiers fought and won the Battle of Hastings with bows of yew. Much later, in 1307, according to legend, William Tell used a bow of yew to shoot the apple off his son's head, thereby helping Switzerland secure freedom from Austrian domination. The American Revolution was fought with guns, not bows and arrows, but the yew still had a small part to play in our history, inasmuch as George Washington is alleged to have proposed to Martha Custis beneath a yew.

For a plant so associated with the inevitability of death and with the exercise of military power, the yew is uncommonly docile. It is the poodle of the tree world, offering virtually no resistance to our desire to refashion it to our intent, to clip it and trim it to realize some pattern we have in mind. At Versailles and other formal French gardens of the old regime, where power was symbolized by geometry, the landscape was dotted with obedient yews sheared into cones. At Hampton Court, hedges of yew formed a maze. In other British gardens, such as Sissinghurst, tall hedges of clipped yew both form a backdrop for other plantings and separate one area from another. Those with a taste for topiary can turn yews into dour green elephants and other shapes they would not assume of their own accord. I have, however, already announced my own preference, and it's a minority opinion. If there must be a yew in a garden, let there be but one, grown freestanding and unclipped, allowed in its own good time (as it may last for hundreds of years after I'm gone) to become the tree it is its nature to be.

PEOPLE
AND
PLACES

Middleton Place

TO REACH MIDDLETON PLACE, twenty minutes from the historic district of Charleston, South Carolina, I first had to drive through territory that was familiar, even though I had never been there. The highway that eventually becomes Ashley River Road passes through a commercial suburban landscape that could be anywhere in America where people live to the rhythms of the automobile. Shopping centers and malls, convenience stores and gasoline stations, fast-food franchises—this landscape bears a litany of names everyone knows: McDonald's, Burger King, Radio Shack. It is everywhere, and it is nowhere. It has no history. It is anonymous. It knows nothing of tragedy, and it embodies no dreams of either past or future.

Then the shopping centers and the residential subdivisions thinned out. Ashley River Road on this, my first (but surely not my last) visit to Middleton Place, bore witness to the fury of Hurricane Hugo, which had slammed into Charleston eight months earlier, on September 21 and 22, 1989. Downed trees and broken branches were piled up along the roadside, but many live oaks survived to form a cool tunnel of green en route to Middleton.

Middleton Place—both words name it with precision. Since Henry Middleton began to work on its gardens in 1741, it has been in the loving care of the Middleton family, some bearing other surnames as the property passed down through the female line. All that remains of the original house—built circa 1735—is a pile of rubble. The house and one flanking building to the north, a library containing twelve thousand volumes, were looted and torched by Union troops in 1865, at the very end of the Civil War. The great Charleston earthquake of 1886, whose epicenter was probably on the Middleton property—with tremors estimated at seven or even higher on the Richter scale—completed the destruction of these two buildings. Left standing is a two-story south flanker of reddish brown brick, built around 1755 as gentleman's guest quarters.

The gardens fell into neglect at the end of the Civil War and languished until the 1920s, when Middleton heir J. J. Pringle Smith and his wife, Heningham Ellet Smith, began their life's work of bringing back the plantation's former splendor. Today the hand and mind of Henry Middleton are still evident. These are very much gardens of the eighteenth century, designed according to what Blaise Pascal called "the spirit of geometry." Middleton's design was a strong one, basically a right triangle. One side runs eastward from a point on the main drive, on through the center of the ruins of the main house to a lawn overlooking a series of grassy terraces above the Butterfly Lakes, Middleton's unique contribution to the history of the formal garden. The base of the triangle bisects a long rectangular reflection pool. The hypotenuse bisects a series of garden rooms with their own geometry of square, circle, and octagon.

These Euclidean forms are imposed on a natural landscape of surpassing beauty: a bluff overlooking tidal marshes teaming with life, and a long and graceful curve of the Ashley River twenty miles upriver from Charleston, where local tradition holds that the Ashley combines with the Cooper River to form the Atlantic Ocean. In the far distance across the river from Middleton lie woods as dark and deep as those Robert Frost pondered.

The gardens of Middleton Place were not designed once and for all in their final form. They evolved over the first century of their history, reflecting changing tastes. When formal gardens went out of fashion in England in the late eighteenth and early nineteenth centuries, old gardens were often scrapped to make way for new ones in the English landscape style. At Middleton, beyond the formal bones of the original plan, there was ample space to accommodate the new desire for naturalistic planting.

The gardens also evolved to make use of new plants from Asia. The glory of old Middleton lies in its live oaks, especially in one called simply the Middleton Oak, which, if the most extreme claims are true, may well have germinated a thousand years ago, well before the Magna Carta was signed. But Middleton is also notable for its camellias and its crape myrtles, some reputedly dating back to 1786, gifts from André Michaux, the botanist who introduced these Asian plants in the early days of the republic. And I must not forget the azaleas, which first came here in the 1840s; thirty-five thousand of these shrubs burst into flame every April on the hillside overlooking Rice Mill Pond.

Middleton Place has long been a point of horticultural pilgrimage for Americans and visitors from overseas alike. When Harold Nicolson was lecturing in Charleston in 1933, he visited Middleton with the South Carolina writer DuBose Heyward. In a letter to his wife, Vita Sackville-West, then in Ohio, Nicolson approvingly described the tall camellias, the grassy terraces, and the vista of marsh and river. "It is as romantic in its way," he wrote, "as Sissinghurst."

That April, Vita Sackville-West made her own visit to the low country during the height of the azalea season, when Middleton Place moved her to poetry. "Stand I indeed in England? Do I dream?" she asked in the opening line of "Middleton Place, South Carolina." Her answer finally was no, that in England's glades there was no flash of scarlet wings, no flame of azaleas, no "greybeard moss bewitching ancient trees." But there were still affinities, still connections, between this stately American garden and the English gardens she knew and loved. Here, she concluded, she found "a heart still mindful of the English way."

Her husband's comparison of Middleton with Sissinghurst is a charming example of British horticultural chauvinism. The year 1991 marked the 250th anniversary of the gardens at Middleton Place, the oldest surviving formal landscape in America, now tended through a nonprofit educational foundation by Charles Duell, the tenth direct heir of Henry Middleton. It also marks the sixty-first anniversary of the year that Nicolson and Sackville-West acquired Sissinghurst and began to make a garden there—a garden now under the care of the National Trust.

My own visit to this stately garden on the Ashley took place weeks after the camellias and the azaleas had stopped blooming, strewing the pathways with the radiant color of their fallen petals. The crape myrtles had not yet begun, but the roses were in full bloom. The green of the grassy terraces where peacocks paraded, the deep blue of the Butterfly Lakes, the dark waters of Rice Mill Pond where swans glided by—these all bespoke a sense of place and of almost palpable time in Middleton's long history.

Hurricane Hugo had hit hard here, destroying fences and some five hundred trees. But the live oaks, the Middleton Oak included, had ridden out the ferocious storm; only two were lost. The debris had been cleaned up. Middleton had survived, showing only a few scars from its ordeal.

On my second evening here, the Charleston Symphony Orchestra played a pops concert on the greensward between the formal gardens and the stables. A crowd of at least one thousand souls had assembled to await the music in the gathering dusk. Small children ran and chased balls. Teenagers and grown-ups hurled Frisbees against the darkening sky. "We are not Hugo-nuts" said a placard by a card table where a family spread out its corn bread and barbecue. In front of the table, they also spread out some legacies of Hugo—a limb from a fallen tree, shingles from a roof destroyed, cans of tuna fish like those that had sustained them for weeks after the great storm.

The orchestra platform was right in front of the rubble of the old house, which had been damaged beyond repair by war and destroyed by earthquake. The concert opened with "The Star-Spangled Banner." In the dawn's early light, the anthem's words proclaim, a patriot took pride. Our flag was still there. Both places and people can be survivors, and the comfort in that thought brings a lump to the throat.

The Astilbes of
Georg Arends

ONE OF THE AXIOMS of horticulture is that all plants have their histories, their roster of human names that explain their presence in our gardens. E. H. "Chinese" Wilson brought us regal lilies and many other ornamental plants from the Orient. David Fairchild gave us Japanese flowering cherry trees—and kudzu. Dr. A. B. Stout collected the many Far Eastern species of hemerocallis that were the basis of the complicated hybridization resulting in the daylilies that are the mainstay of many American perennial borders in midsummer.

Sometimes the names of the people behind the plants we treasure—or despise—are not known. I don't know what genius first discerned the horticultural merits of *Helianthus angustifolius*, a perennial sunflower native to the moist lowlands of eastern North America that can reach eight feet high and is arguably one of the most glorious of all plants in the garden in late fall (although I have friends who scoff at it as awkward and ungainly). Nor do I know who deliberately imported from Europe the two species of digitaria that American gardeners curse collectively as crabgrass. Sometimes, however, the names are known, but insufficiently known, as in the case of Georg Arends (1862–1952), who outdid even Luther Burbank in hybridizing an enormous number of ornamental perennials and shrubs over a long career at his tiny nursery of under five acres in the village of Ronsdorf, not far from Cologne, Germany.

Scarcely any genus of hardy flowering perennial seems to have escaped Arends's attention. His earliest work in hybridizing, beginning in 1890, involved bergenias, primulas, and hardy fuchsias, but he went on to breed dianthuses, achilleas, ericas, hostas, potentillas, rhododendrons, silenes, veronicas, and many other things, constituting a very long list indeed. He introduced some 343 plants, 117 of which are still sold at the Arends nursery, now being run by his granddaughter, Ursula Maubach, and are widely available in the German perennial trade. A goodly number of Arends's introductions—the sedum 'Autumn Joy', the phloxes 'Alpha' and 'Omega', and *Campanula glomerata* 'Superba', for example—are sold by American nurseries. But the plants most associated with Arends and most likely to grow in American gardens are astilbes, his special passion, as may be deduced from the fact that between 1902 and 1952 he named and introduced 74 cultivars, in a wide range of colors previously unknown. Of these, 38 are still in existence and offered in the catalog of the Arends nursery. Many of these, but by no means all, can be tracked down in the mail-order catalogs of specialized nurseries in the United States.

BEFORE GOING FURTHER with the story of Georg Arends, I want to praise his astilbes, which would be wonderful plants even if no one knew how they came into being. They are tremendous weapons in the war all gardeners must fight against rugs, dumplings, and gumdrops—plants that may be fine individually but that collectively make the garden they dominate tedious and boring, the home of the blahs and the ho-hums. The rugs are the ground covers like vinca, golden moss sedum, pachysandra, and of course the various carpet junipers—one-dimensional plants that fill up space and that's about all. The dumplings and the gumdrops are plants with mounded forms: hostas when not in bloom, hemerocallis in or out of bloom, lavender, and most composites or daisies. The garden with only such plants becomes a study in monotony. It needs the vertical pizzazz that comes from steeples and spikes and plumes—the stalks of yucca blossoms, the waving flower and seed heads of miscanthus and other tall ornamental grasses, the altitudinous but graceful and delicate stems and flowers of meadow rues. Every garden needs them—the spiky plants that aspire toward heaven.

Astilbes, it is clear, are close to the top of a list of such plants. Some, of course, don't aspire very far. *Astilbe chinensis* 'Pumila', a late-blooming variety with rosy lilac spikes, calls it quits at twelve inches. Most others are considerably taller, however, producing flower spikes ranging from two to three feet; *A. taquettii* 'Superba' can tower upwards to four or even five feet high when grown well, given the heavy feeding and constant moisture that all astilbes require to thrive.

Whatever its height, every astilbe is built to the same general form—hundreds of tiny florets arranged in feathery plumes that rise like exclamation points above attractive foliage sometimes so deeply cut as to be downright ferny. But there is so much variation among astilbes that I can conceive of a pleasing garden consisting of few perennials other than hostas (as dumplings) and astilbes (as spires). The leaves, which are bright and glossy when they first appear but grow duller as the season progresses (which is perhaps the reason that astilbes take their generic name from Greek words meaning "without luster"), are generally deep green, but some cultivars show a purple or a bronze-red cast. The flower colors range from white to pink to lilac to a glowing red that would be right at home in Hades. Since there are early, midseason, and late cultivars, their blooming season extends over a long period—from late May to the first week of August in my garden in southern New Jersey. (In Germany, under cooler conditions, the blooms last longer and the season stretches well into September.)

The flower spikes of astilbes also vary. *A. taquettii* 'Superba' has tight, dense spikes, forming something of a thin cone. 'Cattleya', a glowing pink, is more open and free. 'Ostrich Feather', which is sometimes listed under its German name, 'Straussenfeder', also a pink, cascades down from the top of the spike.

It's almost never mentioned, incidentally, but a good many astilbes are fragrant. The scent is delicate and subtle, certainly no competition for wisteria or Arabian jasmine, but it's there.

The cultural requirements of astilbes are simple and uncomplicated. Although they are often thought of only as plants for the shade, in the north they will grow perfectly well in full sun. Their best use, however, may be in light shade, since they provide a bright splash of color to banish gloom. They are, as I have mentioned, thirsty plants and heavy feeders all during the growing season. They should be planted in soil amended to incorporate a lot of organic matter, such as peat moss. Two other items about their culture deserve pointing out. To keep them vigorous, they should be divided every three or four years early in the spring, using a sharp knife to cut their woody crowns into three or four pieces, each with three or more eyes; it's a chore, but it also increases the number of these plants to enjoy in the summer garden or to share with friends. Also, some rodents such as meadow mice and voles have such a keen taste for the underground sections of astilbes as a part of their winter menu that they can destroy a planting altogether. This danger can be lessened by cutting the plants back to the ground in late fall and removing all mulch—which astilbes appreciate during the hot days of summer but which also provides a dandy place for small burrowing animals.

In Europe, astilbes are commonly forced in cool greenhouses for both cut flowers and temporary houseplants, like potted chrysanthemums. They are rarely forced here, save at Longwood Gardens in Kennett Square, Pennsylvania, where they are one of the midwinter glories of the main conservatory. In the United States, they are used almost exclusively as summer garden perennials, excellent for landscaping, since their perky foliage and flower spikes show up well at a distance. Many of my own astilbes grow at the back of my garden, among some hostas and small ornamental grasses in the light shade of a large dawn redwood tree. They look fine there, but they please me even more in another spot, a large raised wooden container running the length of our deck, in the shade of an open pergola next to the house. Here we sit most pretty mornings to drink coffee and read the newspaper. Viewed up close, astilbes are exciting plants to watch. They do not simply come into bud and then bloom; rather, they develop over a long period of time, in a process of unfolding, as they gradually lift their main spikes and their subsidiary branches and slowly take on the red or pink or white color they will eventually display. The spikes persist after the bloom is over, forming handsome dark brown seed heads that can be left on the plant (after the leaves are cut off to discourage mice) for a somewhat sculptural look, or harvested and put away for winter use in dried arrangements. And (it ought to be clear by now that I like astilbes very much indeed), we also have a large patch of astilbes in a long bed, curving around the base of a lilac hedge, where we planted them in a deep, plastic-lined trench, with a rubber soaker hose at the bottom to keep them moist in our sandy soil.

I foresee a great future for these plants. I suspect that they will grow in more and more American gardens, increasing our midsummer delight and the debt we owe to a very busy German plantsman named Georg Arends.

In a chapter called "How My Astilbes Came into Being" in the memoir of his life with plants that he published shortly before his death, Arends recalls that in his youth, "I came to know *Astilbe japonica* in my parents' nursery. It was then called *Spiraea japonica* because of its spiraea-like flowers, although as a member of the saxifrage family it had nothing whatever to do with the true spiraeas, which belong to the rose family. For many years only this species, with its rather small and meager flower spikes, was grown in Europe. Then *A. japonica* 'compacta', which had a denser set of flowers, came along, and also *A. japonica* 'aureo-reticulata', which had yellow-veined leaves, and finally there came from Holland two much more vigorous cultivars with large flower stalks, named 'Washington' and 'Gladstone'." (Both of these are still sold today, although they have no special merit.) In 1897, Arends acquired from Belgium a chance hybrid of *A. astilboides*, a species with bronze-toned leaves, with *A. japonica;* two years later he got from England a plant of a species that proved to be critical to his breeding program, *A. chinensis.* Until then, all astilbes had white flowers, and a rather dirty white at that. The flowers of *A. chinensis*, however, were a soft shade of rose. When it bloomed in his garden, Arends immediately decided to cross it with all the varieties of *A. japonica* he had on hand.

He potted up most of his astilbes and put them in a greenhouse, bringing them all into simultaneous bloom by regulating the temperature, and then making the crosses he had planned. In 1901, the seedlings went into cold frames, and Arends eagerly awaited the first blooms in July of 1902. He and his wife went out early every morning to inspect his new hybrids, and they were not disappointed. There were very few whites, to his surprise: most were pink, with a wide range between light and dark shades. There was also considerable variation in the flower stalks: some feathery and open, some upright and tight. Most of the leaves were dark green, but some tended toward bronze. The plants were more vigorous than their parent species. The modern astilbe was on its way.

But Georg Arends had a vexing problem—severely limited space in his nursery. (His memoir speaks enviously of Luther Burbank's much greater acreage in California and the hybridizing on a mass scale it made possible.) The problem was solved when the Dutch nursery company Van Waveren and Kreufft, in Sassenheim, got word of the new astilbes and dispatched a representative to purchase the entire crop, except for a few especially promising *A. japonica x A. chinensis* hybrids, which Arends retained. For three more years, the pattern persisted. Arends made his crosses, selected the best, and sold the rest to the Dutch firm. Some of these plants would seem still to be available commercially, sold only by color.

The first named astilbe hybrids made their debut in 1904, when Arends exhibited a dark pink named 'Queen Alexandra' and a light pink named 'Peach Blossom' at a meeting of the Royal Horticultural Society in London. The plants created a huge stir, earning a gold medal for their hybridizer. And Arends got more on his trip to England than honor and attention. From the British nursery Veitch and Sons he acquired a new species of astilbe just imported from China, *A. davidii*, which had very tall, sturdy, and feathery spikes of an intense rose-red. *Astilbe davidii* also bloomed much later than other astilbes, offering genetic possibilities of extending the season of bloom from June into later summer. Again, Arends resorted to forcing in a greenhouse, crossing *A. davidii* with his previous hybrids. (By way of digression, I might mention that *A. davidii* is no longer an acceptable botanical name, as will be explained further along, and that a form of it recently collected in Korea, of which only a handful of plants are now growing in the United States, has several prominent American nurserymen panting with lust to acquire it for its huge, highly colored flower spikes.)

When the seedlings bloomed, Arends recalled in his memoirs, he was overwhelmed. "The color-play was fantastic, from pure white to delicate pink to bright and glowing red. The flower plumes were as varied in form as in color—some open and feathery, others tight and compact. It was extremely difficult to select the best plants from such abundant material. Probably we discarded some that we should have kept. Everyone who could, from the head gardener down, was asked to help make the selection—even an American business friend who happened to be visiting at the time." The year was 1907. In 1908, after selecting the very best plants for future introduction as named cultivars, Arends offered to the trade for the first time, by color only, the new race of astilbes known collectively as the arendsii hybrids. The following year he introduced the named cultivars 'Ceres', 'Juno', 'Lachskönigen', 'Rosa Perle', 'Venus', and 'Vesta'.

Meanwhile, Georg Arends had some French competition. Hybridizers at the Lemoine nursery in Nancy were also working with crosses of *A. japonica* and *A. chinensis*. The competition did not worry Arends. He assessed 'Carminea', 'Rubella', and 'Rutilans', all introduced by Lemoine in 1907, as having "good color but poor flower stalks." He kept working with his own lines, introducing a Wagnerian series with names like 'Brunhilde', 'Siegfried', and 'Walküre', and into some of his breeding he incorporated two other species, *A. grandis* and *A. thunbergii*.

World War I put a temporary stop to all hybridizing in Ronsdorf, but the introduction of new cultivars in the arendsii series resumed in the early 1920s. An important color break, a plant with bronze-red leaves and fiery red blossoms, was exhibited in Berlin in 1933, under the name 'Fanal'.

Most of Arends's breeding of astilbes occurred in the lines I have described, those that constitute the arendsii hybrids—but (and this point is a little tricky) not all of Arends's hybrid astilbes are arendsii hybrids. The earliest crosses he developed, those between *A. japonica* and *A. chinensis*, those he sold to the Dutch without names (some of which may still be sold today by nurseries that list just "white astilbe," "pink astilbe," and so on), and the named cultivars 'Queen Alexandra' and 'Peach Blossom', are generally called the japonica hybrids. Crosses deriving from hybridizing the japonica hybrids with *A. davidii* make up the arendsii hybrids. But there were other lines.

In 1911, on a visit to England, Arends saw at Kew Gardens a small Japanese species, *A. simplicifolia*, in bloom in the rock garden, with flowers ranging in color from white to rose-tinged ivory. Acquiring three plants from a German-born nurseryman living in Kent, Arends brought them back to Germany, crossing them with his hybrids to produce a small number of choice plants he called the simplicifolia hybrids. Other small astilbes resulted from his work with some stray seedlings that turned up in his greenhouse with foliage that looked like parsley, from which he developed the cultivars 'Gnom', 'Perkeo', and others.

If I make the subject of astilbes sound simple, I owe someone an apology. Checking in *Hortus Third*, I discover that some things in Georg Arends's account of how his astilbes came into being don't jibe. *Astilbe astilboides*, for example, is probably not a separate species, but a varietal form of *A. japonica*, and *A. davidii* a varietal form of *A. chinensis*. To make things worse, cultivar names are often mixed up, for a variety of reasons. Arends introduced two different plants, each white and each called 'Deutschland', and two pinks called 'Rheinland'. Apparently he intended that the second would supplant the first, but in each case both cultivars are still in circulation. Furthermore, astilbes have strong tendencies toward mutation, a trait that has given rise to several new cultivars out of old ones, so that 'Montgomery' is a sport of 'Düsseldorf', and 'Ostrich Plume' of 'Betsy Cuperus', a hybrid Arends acquired from a Dutch nursery. But this same tendency to produce sports means that if a field of astilbes is not watched over with great vigilance and carefully culled or rogued, several visibly different plants may enter the nursery trade, all called 'Fanal', to name one that mutates with especial ease. Astilbes also self-seed, so that an unusually vigorous seedling may sprout in the middle of a clump and eventually muscle aside its parent, showing no filial piety whatsoever. Thus it is, for one reason or another, that I have, from two mail-order nurseries, both of them of unquestionable honesty and integrity, two different astilbes under the name 'Cattleya'. Both are extremely handsome, and both are a deep and glowing pink, but to any eye they simply aren't the same.

It matters, I suppose, that occasionally the name of the astilbe proves to be uncertain or ambiguous, but the fact remains: astilbes are wonderful, virtually indispensable garden perennials. We owe Georg Arends a lasting debt for his spires among our gumdrops.

RECOMMENDED ASTILBES

Many perennials—hemerocallis, hostas, and iris, to name just three—have attracted so much attention from people who love them with special devotion that they have plant societies created around them, organizations that tout the merits of particular cultivars that perform well across the country. Thus far, however, we have no American Astilbe Society to hand out prizes, award honors, and guide the gardener who wants to plant some astilbes but is bewildered by the prospect of choosing a few good specimens from a list of many.

But a large number of astilbes, mostly those introduced by Georg Arends, was tested for garden-worthiness in the Netherlands in 1962 and again in 1966 and 1967 by plant scientists and nurserymen, and the results were published in 1968. The rating system used a zero to indicate "can be eliminated," a single asterisk to indicate "good," a double asterisk for "very good," and a triple asterisk for "excellent." I have used the Dutch list as a basis for the following list of recommended cultivars, including for the most part only those ranked as very good or excellent. But I have eliminated certain excellent ones, such as a fine dark red named 'Spartan', where these are not generally available in the United States at the present. After some discussion with several nurserymen who make astilbes one of their specialties I have listed some that the Dutch gave only one asterisk but that seem to perform especially well in America. Except as noted, all these astilbes were bred and introduced by Arends.

'Amethyst'. Early, lilac-lavender, thirty-six inches.
A. *chinensis* 'Pumila'. A varietal form of a species native to China. Very late, raspberry pink, good stoloniferous groundcover, twelve inches.
A. *simplicifolia* 'Atrorosea'. Late dwarf, glowing pink, with a full plume, ten inches.

A. taquettii 'Superba'. Late midseason, purple-rose, forty-eight inches or more.

'Bonn'. Early, carmine-rose, twenty to twenty-four inches.

'Bridal Veil'. Midseason, white, twenty-four inches.

'Cattleya'. Late, pink, thirty-six inches.

'Deutschland'. Early, white, twenty-four inches.

'Fanal'. Early midseason, intense red, twenty-six inches.

'Fire'. Late, bright salmon red, thirty-six inches.

'Montgomery'. Midseason, red, twenty-eight inches.

'Ostrich Plume'. Midseason to late, drooping pink panicles, thirty-six inches. Not an Arends hybrid but a sport of the Dutch cultivar 'Betsy Cuperus'.

'Red Sentinel'. Midseason, scarlet, twenty-four inches.

'Rheinland'. Midseason, very prolific pink, twenty-eight inches.

Celia Thaxter
and Louise
Beebe Wilder:
Romanticism in
the Garden*

SINCE ONE OF the quintessential features of the romantic movement, whether in literature or the visual arts or in music, is a strong emphasis on individuality of expression, it is a rather messy cultural phenomenon. Its primary definitions are probably negative ones. It rejects classical formality. It rejects the idea that we should find in the past our models for the present—or at least, in certain areas, such as painting and architecture—it rejects the more ancient past of Rome and Greece in favor of models taken from medieval Europe. It favors the heart over the head, and it is impatient with rules. All good romantics consider rules to be artifices that separate us from the great gushing throb of life, and they would substitute for them more immediate, unpredictable, and presumably natural ways of behaving—and especially of feeling.

*From a lecture given at the Museum of Fine Arts, Boston, in April 1990.

My topic is American romanticism in gardening, as regards the writings of two American women especially. One is Celia Thaxter, who died in 1894, the same year that her classic book *An Island Garden* was published, illustrated with chromolithographs based on her friend Childe Hassam's paintings of her garden on Appledore, one of the Isles of Shoals off Portsmouth, New Hampshire. The other is Louise Beebe Wilder, who died in 1938. There are some incidental similarities between the two women quite lately, in that what they wrote about gardening is being rediscovered by the public. In 1988, Mrs. Thaxter's original publisher, Houghton Mifflin, brought out a very handsome slipcased edition of *An Island Garden*. Reviewers were enthusiastic, and sales were brisk. In 1990, Mrs. Wilder's works saw a great revival. Macmillan republished in paperback two of her classic books, *Adventures with Hardy Bulbs* and *The Fragrant Path*. Atlantic Monthly Press also brought out in cloth cover a handsome facsimile edition of the 1918 book, *Color in My Garden*. I see some other things that Mrs. Thaxter and Mrs. Wilder have in common, but before that I want first to tend to some of their differences.

First, the differences between these two American writers. Celia Thaxter would never have described herself as a garden writer. She was a popular New England poet, well respected by Whittier and Sarah Orne Jewett and by Childe Hassam and other painters who helped turn the parlor of her house on Appledore into America's first salon worthy of the name. Thaxter's circle of cultured friends, many of whom visited her on the island during the summer, included the painters Ross Turner and William Morris Hunt and Appleton Brown and the musicians John Knowles Paine and William Mason.

Celia Thaxter ventured only occasionally into prose, as in *An Island Garden*, which she found agonizing to write, in contrast to the verses that came to her so easily as she ironed and carried out other chores during the summer at her family's resort on the island. Her poetry, by any assessment, has not held up well. Her prose, however, is still fresh today, not only in her one garden book, but also in some of her published correspondence with family members and friends.

Louise Beebe Wilder, on the other hand, was a southerner, born in Maryland and privately educated (as was Thaxter, in fact) until she married an architect and moved to the suburbs north of New York City. She wrote only on gardening—and prolifically so, writing some ten books between 1916 and 1937 and contributing articles regularly to *House and Garden* when it was edited by Richardson Wright. She resembles Celia Thaxter strongly in that she wrote almost entirely out of her experiences in her own gardens, especially her first, a walled garden occupying a portion of the country place called Balderbrae, some two hundred acres near Suffern, New York. Here she lived with her husband, an architect, until they divorced in the early 1920s and he built for her a smaller place called Little Balderbrae. Celia Thaxter was a summer gardener only, but Wilder gardened year-round, observing the progress of the seasons and the succession of colorful bloom. Perhaps her best book, *Color in My Garden* was illustrated with twenty-four color plates made from paintings done at Balderbrae in a single year.

A further word is in order about romanticism and gardening. I am fairly sure what romanticism means in relation to fiction, poetry, philosophy, music, and the visual arts. But the term is a borrowed word when it is applied to gardening and to the garden writing of these two women. Certain elements of romanticism cannot be found in gardening. One is the idea of nature and of human fulfillment by immersion in it; gardens are artifices or contrivances, not nature in the raw. Another is the emphasis upon ego. Making gardens is more often a lesson in humility than it is the chance to make an exuberant display of self. Another difference is that in gardening, unlike the other arts tinged with romanticism, living plants are the medium, not musical sounds and not words, although I realize that this difference must be moderated when the topic is two Americans who not only made gardens but also wrote about them. Finally, romantic painters or musicians created objects of art that achieved fixity and permanence once their creation had finished. A garden goes forward in time. It is also often obliterated by time, as has not yet happened with the poems of Hölderlin or with Brahms's Alto Rhapsody. And finally, I cannot imagine Celia Thaxter passing the time of day with Goethe's tormented and fairly silly prototype of the romantic hero, young Werther. It also beggars the imagination to conceive of a conversation over tea between Jean Jacques Rousseau and Louise Beebe Wilder.

What then remains of the idea of romanticism, as applied to gardening? There are several points to make. Some would apply as equally in Great Britain as in America. Others are uniquely American. I take the romantic garden to involve several features.

The first is the rejection of formalism, with its symmetry and its solid geometry and its Cartesian rationality, and its greater interest in curves, in flow, and in unpredictability.

The second is the interest in plants as plants, not as elements of a previously conceived design, with a great emphasis on color and fragrance.

These qualities, the forsaking of formal symmetry and the emphasis on color, appear in the writings of both William Robinson and Gertrude Jekyll. And they are certainly present in the work of Louise Beebe Wilder, in her writing and gardening alike. Celia Thaxter, however, gives me pause. It is time to describe her garden. It was tiny indeed, only fifteen by fifty feet, set in front of the hop-covered front porch of her summer house on Appledore in the Isles of Shoals. Its plan was geometrical, regular, and symmetrical—entirely composed of rectangles, in fact. Straight beds surrounded the entire garden, which was fenced in, with interruptions in these beds only for the steps leading down from the porch and for gates to the west and to the south, which overlooked the rocky shore and the cold and turbulent waters surrounding the tiny island. In the center of the enclosed area, nine flower beds were arranged in groups of three, with strips of lawn separating them. Celia Thaxter awoke before dawn each morning to tend her garden and to pick flowers to arrange in the music room of her house, a place for painters to talk while music poured from the room's grand piano.

The garden was geometrical in design, yes, but only in an accidental way and in the service of convenience, much in the way that vegetable gardens tend to be rectangular and to have their plants in rows, for easy access for weeding and cultivation. Mrs. Thaxter's flower patch, to put it baldly, was not even second cousin, once removed, to Versailles.

It would be a bit pointless to tell you, secondhand, that both Thaxter and Wilder wrote vividly about color and about fragrance, when I can let them speak in their own voices by just quoting a few passages, but before that I want to say something about how I discovered Thaxter. About four years ago I was putting together an anthology of almost two centuries of American gardening writing, in part to counter the myth that we don't have any. I had several categories set up in advance. One was color, and another was fragrance. In other sections of the anthology, such as pests and what to do about them, the material sorted itself out chronologically over the entire period covered. But not color and not fragrance. A friend sent me Mrs. Thaxter's book, and as far as I have been able to discover it is the first American book to address these topics, and address them very vividly indeed. I think I know the reasons, and they mark something of a division between American and British garden romanticism.

The purposes of gardening, it was long held in America, were not the gratification of the senses. They lay rather in moral uplift, improvement, and utility. Henry Ward Beecher and his sisters Catharine Beecher and Harriet Beecher Stowe were explicit on this point. Gardening made better people of us, better Christians, even—especially so for women, as it would keep them from idleness and frivolous pursuits. As regards the benefits bestowed on women by gardening, the Reverend Henry Beecher was quite certain. It was a sure antidote to fevers, dyspepsia, neuralgic complaints, feebleness, and morbid tastes, to name only a few of the evils he catalogs. "A love of flowers," he wrote in 1859, "would beget early rising, industry, habits of close observation, and of reading." And it would also "unfold in the heart an enlarged, unstraitened, ardent piety." Beecher's views were commonplace in the American credo of the Victorian age. Horticulturist Joseph Breck of Boston wrote in his *New Book of Flowers* in 1866 that "flowers are the expression of God's love to man. . . . The more we examine flowers, especially when the eye is assisted by a microscope, the more we must adore the matchless skill of the Great Supreme." And a sterner, much more ascetic strain in American religious sensibility regards the beauty of flowers not as messages of God's love, but as satanic temptations. U. P. Hedrick's *History of Horticulture in America* quotes an account by a Shaker sister on the roses raised in Shaker communities for medicinal use in making rose water. Roses for this purpose—and they were raised for this purpose alone—must be picked without stems, lest some sister idly decorate her garment with them, in an act of idolatry. A sick person in a Shaker infirmary could bathe his head in rose water to ease his pain, but he could not have a rose or any other flower by his bed to offer him cheer and pleasure.

Celia Thaxter had her conventionally religious side, expressed in some of her poems, although I believe on the basis of some of her correspondence she carried on a fierce dispute with God and placed Him squarely in the wrong. But when she wrote her book, in prose, about flowers, it is sensual, sensuous, and even plainly erotic. On the California poppy, the Oriental poppy, on annual phlox, Mrs. Thaxter became as frank as D. H. Lawrence.

I said a moment ago that one of the hallmarks of romanticism in gardening is an interest in plants as such, and in their colors, not in their subsidiary role within a scheme of formal architectural design. Many of the best passages in *An Island Garden* are rich and glowing portraits of individual plants, where Thaxter writes with very close observation and an obvious satisfaction that is purely aesthetic.

Almost at random, I would like to quote Celia Thaxter on California poppies. "Down into the sweet plot I go," she wrote,

> and gather a few of these, bringing them to my little table and sitting down before them to admire and adore their beauty. In the slender green glass in which I put them they stand clothed in their delicate splendor. One blossom I take in a loving hand the more closely to examine it, and it breathes a glory of color into sense and spirit which is enough to kindle the dullest imagination. The stems and fine thread-like leaves are smooth and cool gray-green, as if to temper the fire of the blossoms, which are smooth also, unlike almost all other poppies, that are crumpled past endurance in their close green buds, and make one feel as if they could not wait to break out of the calyx and loosen their petals to the sun, to be soothed into even tranquility of beauty by the touches of the air. Every cool gray-green leaf is tipped with a tiny line of red, every flower-bud wears a little pale-green pointed cap like an elf. Nothing could be more picturesque than this fairy cap, and nothing more charming than to watch the blossom push it off and spread its yellow petals, slowly rounding to the perfect cup. As I hold the flower in my hand and think of trying to describe it, I realize how poor a creature I am, how impotent are words in the presence of such perfection. It is held upright upon a straight and polished stem, its petals curving upward and outward into the cup of light, pure gold with a lustrous satin sheen; a rich orange is painted on the gold, drawn in infinitely fine lines to a point in the centre of the edge of each petal, so that the effect is that of a diamond of flame in a cup of gold. It is not enough that the powdery anthers are orange bordered with gold; they are whirled about the very heart of the flower like a revolving Catharine-wheel of fire. In the centre of the anthers is a shining point of warm sea-green, a

last, consummate touch which makes the beauty of the blossom supreme.

Here, two comments are irresistible. First, for someone who speaks of the impotence of words to describe flowers, Celia Thaxter wrote with enormous power. Second, the rumor among many American publishers today is that books on gardening must be lavishly illustrated with color photographs, each worth a thousand words. In this passage, Mrs. Thaxter proves the contrary point. No color photograph could possibly give us such a sense of exploring just one flower until we have penetrated to its very center and its very essence, to that "last consummate touch," that "shining point of warm sea green."

Much of Louise Beebe Wilder's writing shows the same interest in individual plants. Most of her *Adventures with Hardy Bulbs* consists of a detailed encyclopedia, genus by genus and species by species, beginning with allium and ending with zygadenus. Although she passes along a great deal of practical, technical, and historical information, her aesthetic delight is always to the fore, especially as regards color. Of the genus *Calochortus*, for example, she wrote:

Gardeners are accustomed to thrills, not the kind with which they are confronted in the press or on the screen, but those none the less authentic stirrings of the blood caused by the recognition of uncommon beauty or by unexpected success in some field of horticultural endeavor. Amazing and lovely things happen daily in even the littlest garden. But to him who grows successfully for the first time a collection of Calochortus, may confidently be promised surprise and delight such as he has not heretofore experienced. These natives of our west country, it seems to me, stand virtually alone among flowers in their strange and fantastic beauty, their amazing diversity. I can call up no words that will give an adequate idea of their pure and brilliant hues, the exquisite brushwork on the satin petals, the startling "eyes" that ornament them, the breadths of Persian embroidery, the silken fringes, the velvet-like pile that is the embellishment of many. The doubting Thomases must see them to believe in their reality.

Color, however, is a plural thing. The romantic gardener, as Stephen Lacey has well pointed out in his book, *The Startling Jungle: Colour and Scent in the Romantic Garden* (1990), must learn early on the lessons that Gertrude Jekyll taught about combinations of colors. But we can learn these lessons just as well from Louise Beebe Wilder's *Color in My Garden,* now that it has been reprinted. Mrs. Wilder knew all about keeping orange tiger lilies away from pink phlox, about ways of taming magenta with gray-foliaged plants, and about the excitement brought on when something small and scarlet like just one annual poppy is used to punctuate a sea of blue scillas or grape hyacinths.

Mrs. Thaxter, I think, comes off poorly when compared to Mrs. Wilder in the matter of color combinations, in the garden at least. The evidence in *An Island Garden* is that what she called her "sweet plot" was a wild disarray of plants, especially the annuals that she raised in eggshells in late winter in her home in Portsmouth before making the rough crossing to Appledore. In writing of Mrs. Thaxter's garden as she remembered it in 1902, Candace Wheeler called it a place "where the flowers grew luxuriantly at their own sweet wills, or at the will of the planter, never troubling their heads at all about agreeing with their neighbors." Wheeler expressed disappointment that Thaxter had "so little thought of color effect in her garden."

But this was far from Wheeler's final word. Thaxter raised most of her plants to provide cut flowers for her music room. Here, wrote Candace Wheeler, "I have never seen such realized possibilities of color! The fine harmonic sense of the woman and artist and poet thrilled through these long chords of color, and filled the room with an atmosphere which made it seem like living in a rainbow." Wheeler recalled vividly the banks of cut flowers in arrangements, carefully placed to range from pale white poppies through ever-deepening shades of pink to "the peculiar pin-red which is found only in the poppy tribe." The arrangements were carefully orchestrated to move toward blues and clarets and purples, sweeping across the entire room. Wheeler's conclusion is that in this room she learned from Celia Thaxter more than she needed to know about colors in combination.

I have one further point about romanticism in general and about the particular form it takes in the garden. True romantics talk a great deal about personal experience, about direct confrontation with the forces of nature, and about the lessons these forces teach. But the roots of romanticism are often literary, and sometimes secondhand. Goethe's young Werther, in his delectable misery over his love for Charlotte, which could come to nothing, and in his journey toward suicide, was much inspired by the forgeries of the supposed poet Ossian. Faust's pact with Mephistopheles begins in his study. Our own feelings about great masses of daffodils in the spring probably owe much indeed to English romantic poetry, which has a very high daffodil quotient.

It seems clear that both Celia Thaxter and Louise Beebe Wilder were literary gardeners, that their perception of flowers and of gardening was informed by their close study of British literature. Wordsworth, both the Brownings, and many other poets appear in their pages. John Ruskin, in particular, seems to have been a strong influence. Wilder's knowledge of literature, however, went beyond Thaxter's, to embrace the literature of gardening, from John Parkinson and the other herbalists right through Gertrude Jekyll and E. A. Bowles—whose writings Thaxter could of course not have known. And Mrs. Wilder in this regard much resembles another great American gardening writer of the twentieth century, the late Elizabeth Lawrence of North Carolina. Miss Lawrence, who is coming to be known as much more than a regional writer, fits very easily within the romantic tradition.

Gaudì's Trees

THE TOPIC OF garden ornamentation and its underlying philosophy somewhat daunts me, both as a professional philosopher and as an amateur gardener. Statues of gods and goddesses, fountains, sundials, stone troughs, English hares made of lead, jockeys, gnomes and toadstools right out the Brothers Grimm, pink plastic flamingos, mirrored globes of blue glass, little arching bridges leading nowhere, cute little cats of terra cotta—the range of artifacts that become elements in a garden design (or the lack of one) is so vast that the general truths that might unite them are hard to come by. It strikes me furthermore that the purposes and intentions behind them are diverse. The statuary at Versailles is symbol and visible token of political power. A sundial tells time, in a crude way, but it may also tell a lesson about the temporal dimension of every human being's existence, serving to remind us that we are creatures of time, who in time will surely die. I can't quite fathom the meaning of those little arching bridges, except that probably the people who install them in their gardens like them and that surely they have the right.

And I must also here make a confession. Unless I count some wind chimes on my deck, my own garden is almost entirely devoid of ornaments. The one bona fide piece of ornamentation is a whimsical terra-cotta statue, glazed in pastel pinks and greens and ivory, an abstract sculpture by Betty Bell, an artist friend in Chapel Hill, North Carolina. Called *A Katydid Contemplates the Universe*, it lives outside, next to a small pool, three seasons of the year, but spends the winter in our living room. It makes me smile whenever I see it.

As in my mind's eye I recall other gardens than my own and the ornamentation they contain, a single image comes to mind, and it is a strange one in a strange place, a bit of land on a hilltop, intended earlier in this century to be a suburban development but now a public park—Parc Güell in Barcelona, designed by that genius of an architect, Antonì Gaudì. Parc Güell is a garden, with wisteria-clad cliffs, cool walks through groves of pines, even beds of celosias and petunias and lawns and grassy knolls. But it is also a place where nature and architecture intersect most fascinatingly. Wrought iron, concrete, broken ceramic tiles, and parts of discarded machinery mirror the world of nature and its living forms in a somewhat hallucinatory way. The gates at the entrance to the park suggest palmettos, prehistoric reptiles, the wings of monstrous insects. The gatekeeper's lodge, rusticated stone beneath a steeply swirling roof of terra cotta and ceramic tile, is a gingerbread house incorporating the forms of snails and mushrooms—the deadly fly amanita, most likely. Those wisteria vines twine around columns shaped like slanting tree trunks, which define a cool, vaulted arcade and which also support a walkway at a higher level. A staircase is split in two by a watercourse inhabited by lizards made of concrete and ceramic tile.

Here, more than any other place on earth, is the impulse toward ornamentation most forthrightly and freely expressed. But Parc Güell as a whole is too large a topic for this space. It is properly the subject of a book, one that may in fact have been written. I want instead to call attention to just one element of Gaudì's design for his Parc Güell, his trees. I write from memories of repeated visits to the park with my whole family in 1970 (my young sons were delighted, for Gaudì's enormous powers of imagination made Walt Disney a pedestrian plodder), and from memories of more visits, alone, in 1983, when I was on sabbatical. I have no notes or photographs to rely on. I don't know how many trees there are, but seventeen seems a reasonable guess. I would place their height at around fifteen feet—a scale that puts human beings in their places without dwarfing them or overawing them. Arranged in an arc around a curve in a wide path of gravel and packed earth, their trunks are constructed of cement and golden-tan stone quarried on the site. They bulge outward at about eye level, suggesting the ancient cork oaks of the Iberian Peninsula. Then they taper inward, finally flaring out into wide and open goblets, becoming containers for plants—mostly large agaves, whose forms, in this setting, are seen as no less fantastical than the "trees" whose living parts they are.

In *As You Like It* Shakespeare spoke of "tongues in trees, books in the running brooks, sermons in stones"—of nature, in short, if I have his meaning aright, as a system designed to send moral messages to the human race. The hubris and anthropomorphism of this doctrine of our place in nature is now discredited, even if it produced in its time some thrilling poetry—not only Shakespeare, but also Dante and Wordsworth—as well as some terrible stuff. Gaudì's trees, however, are the creations of a human mind, and I think they do have sermons to preach, about gardens and other things as well.

Every garden tempts us to live within an illusion, perhaps even a delusion. That illusion is that it is something natural, not the creation of artifice. We plant oaks or willows, and in time we forget that it is we who have planted them—we our own selves, or some previous inhabitant of our patch of earth. We come to believe that they have grown of their own accord. Gaudì's trees argue unmistakably that they are the product of human artifice. They are artifacts, and as such they illumine the fact that the rest of the garden—its walks through groves of pines, its pleasing grassy knolls—is also a human artifact.

But those trees of concrete and stone in the Parc Güell would be brutal and dehumanizing were they only concrete and stone. Dead, they mimic the forms of nature, of real trees. But Gaudì was too witty—and too deeply a Christian mystic as well—to let inorganic materials, mocking organic shapes, have the final say. Though dead, the trees are also in a sense alive, for they are home to living plants. A garden is a place of intersection between the natural and the artificial. It teaches us at once humility and pride in achievement, acceptance of what is the case and willingness to change things from what they are.

Here, I suspect, may be one of those elusive general truths mentioned earlier. The plastic flamingo, the concrete gnome, the majestic gods and goddesses, the images of Pan, the bronze lizards, the katydids contemplating the universe—all of these are artifices, but copies of things that live on the earth or that live in the human imagination, itself a product of the earth. They complete a garden, for they remind us what gardens are: not the gifts of nature to deserving human beings but the products of human beings cooperating with the natural order to create utility and delight.

There's one more thing about Gaudì's trees, however, and about garden ornaments in general. I'm not certain when those trees were constructed, but it was sometime between 1900, when work began on Parc Güell, and 1914, when the project was abandoned unfinished, never becoming the center of the group of private homes the architect envisioned. The trees have stayed much the same since they were built, but the gardens of the park have changed as they have matured. Palm trees, once tiny, now immense, stand guard along the perimeter of an area set aside for grown-ups to sit on benches and watch their children play ball. The grown-ups on the benches perhaps once played ball in Parc Güell, in the days of their own childhood.

Garden ornaments, especially those carved from stone or fashioned in strong clay, are fixed points in a changing landscape of both growth and decay. They endure. The artifacts that Gaudí, the mystic and the architect, created are not eternal. But they somehow stand for the eternal, something solid and real and unchanging in the flux of time.

Listening to
Miss Lawrence

SIX WEEKS BEFORE Elizabeth Lawrence died in a nursing home near Annapolis, Maryland, in June of 1985 at the age of eighty, Joanne Ferguson, an associate director of Duke University Press, asked me to spend an afternoon in her office on the Duke campus in Durham, North Carolina, to look through the materials in a large pasteboard box and offer an opinion about whether it might hold the makings of a book worth publishing. Miss Lawrence had given the box to Mrs. Ferguson a year or so earlier. It contained, among other things (including packages of seeds), a great many copies of *The Mississippi Market Bulletin* and similar periodicals published since early in the century by departments of agriculture in almost every southern state as a service to rural citizens. Here farmers could place free classified advertisements for their hay and grain, their unneeded farm machinery, their "sweet Dooley yams," and their surplus livestock. Here the farm women could sell seeds and plants by mail order for pin money. Hundreds of letters from scores of these women to Miss Lawrence were also in the box, neatly sorted by correspondent and tied with string, like old love letters—which in a sense they were. And the box also contained Miss Lawrence's unfinished manuscript about all the southern market bulletins and about her correspondence, over some twenty-five years, with these women.

The manuscript, to put it gently, was a shambles, some eight hundred pages typed on an ancient manual typewriter that seemed never to have gotten a new ribbon, with an enormous number of corrections in Lawrence's spidery, almost indecipherable hand. The pages were unnumbered. The text often came to an abrupt halt, where something was clearly missing or out of place. It seemed likely that the author had simply stopped work on her book and dumped the pages into the box in no order at all, perhaps meaning some day to get back to them.

I browsed for two hours, but ten minutes was enough to know that here was indeed a book worth publishing—a book about people and their plants that was humane, sympathetic, quietly humorous. It was deep in its erudition, ranging back to Virgil and Pliny the Younger and to Parkinson and the other great British herbalists of the Renaissance. It was also conversant with nineteenth- and twentieth-century literature, filled with intelligent understanding of Henry David Thoreau, Harriet Beecher Stowe, Lafcadio Hearn, Sarah Orne Jewett, and Eudora Welty—who had, it turned out, first called Lawrence's attention to the market bulletins that so fascinated her in the years that followed. And it was most appealing for the obvious respect its author felt for the rural southern women who sold plants to her and exchanged letters with her. Lawrence was a highly educated woman, with a degree in classics from Barnard College and a second in landscape architecture from North Carolina State College, but she wrote about the farm women who were part of her subject without a trace of condescension. Gardening and garden writing have their snobs. Elizabeth Lawrence was not among their number.

Once Joanne Ferguson heard my enthusiastic judgment, her

question was inevitable. Would I agree to edit the manuscript? I was an avid gardener, and in recent years a gardening writer. I had worked for Duke University Press as an editorial assistant back in the late 1950s, while in graduate school. I had co-translated two books by Miguel de Unamuno for Princeton University Press. My answer was equally inevitable. Although her reputation has been primarily as a regional, specifically southeastern, writer, Elizabeth Lawrence is one of the best writers we've ever had. Her three major books—*A Southern Garden* (1942), *The Little Bulbs: A Tale of Two Gardens* (1957), and *Gardens in Winter* (1971)—are horticultural classics, fully a match for anything written by such British gardening writers as Gertude Jekyll and Vita Sackville-West. Furthermore, she transcends the usual category of "gardening writer": she wrote about gardening only in the same sense that M. F. K. Fisher writes about cooking. And finally, somewhat like Dana Andrews in *Laura,* I had for years been pretty much in love with Elizabeth Lawrence, or at least the picture of her in the frontispiece of *A Southern Garden.* Taken around 1940 or so, this haunting photograph shows her poised on a short flight of steps in her first garden, in Raleigh, a radiantly beautiful woman in a flowing dress, something difficult to make out in her right hand (possibly shears, maybe a folded scarf), a large dog named Mr. Cayce peering out by her left. The combination of elements in this image is really quite mysterious.

The pasteboard box came home with me to New Jersey, but since I had a book of my own to finish, several months passed before I could edit the Lawrence manuscript. And when I started work, the task posed some insistent questions. What are one's obligations when editing a manuscript that was never completed, partly because of the author's advancing age and seriously declining health, partly for another reason I'll get round to later on? I also discovered some serious problems. There were multiple versions of the same material, with no way of determining which was the latest, and presumably the preferred, text. Parts of the manuscript, it was obvious, were missing. Some sections, admirable in themselves, didn't quite fit with the topic at hand—those market bulletins and those farm women and their letters and plants. And the number of pages had to be pruned severely to make a coherent book.

Editing a posthumous book, especially one by a writer one deeply respects, calls for fear and trembling. There's no chance of the usual interplay between editor and writer—the letters and telephone calls in which an editor can suggest that there may be a slight misfire in this paragraph, that the writer has fallen into some verbal tic of overusing "sulk" or "call it quits," that it simply will not do to say that someone is a "lifelong native of Barcelona," and the return letters and telephone calls in which the writer can accept or reject the criticism. What takes place in editing, ideally, is a conversation, a dialogue. The notion that editors, like parents and teachers, always know best ill serves the mutual and collaborative task of editor and writer—that of seeing to it that a manuscript becomes the best book it can be. So does the notion that writing is a lonely task of the soul, a precious means of self-expression whose Holy Writ can't be improved and is thus not to be touched. I had heard, from Joanne Ferguson and some of her friends, that Miss Lawrence was sometimes peckish with newspaper editors who undertook to improve her gardening columns by rewriting them without her absolute consent. It occurred to me that if there's such a place as Heaven and if I were to encounter her there, there could be a terrible ruckus between us if she thought I tampered with her book—if I "improved" it to its detriment. Two rules, I think, apply to the relations among an editor, a writer, and the manuscript. The editor should make or suggest no textual changes merely for the sake of change. And the writer shouldn't be so bullheaded as to resist every suggested change, merely because he wrote something else originally.

I don't think there's any generalization that stands up about what happens when writers edit other writers. Some fine editors don't themselves write. Some do. Some not very good editors are writers. Some aren't. The essential thing is that editors must be good listeners—must hear the writer's voice and do everything possible to assure that it sounds forth in print.

But then I recognized that although she was no longer alive, Lawrence's voice could still be heard. It was there on every page of *Gardens in Winter* and her other books. It was clear in what obviously must be the first chapter of the new book, a long essay about *The Mississippi Market Bulletin*, which was simple and alive and full of nuance. Editing became easier. Where two or more versions of the same material were in the box, I would pick the version that sounded most like Lawrence's voice. Where a question arose about whether to include a fragment of text, I would listen: did it have the right voice? The manuscript grew shorter, but I grew surer: what was emerging was Elizabeth Lawrence's book—and admittedly an unfinished one. It was not merely her health that prevented her from finishing, but her subject matter. Those southern market bulletins are still published today, but they have lost much of their peculiar flavor. Regional differences disappear with the advance of a homogenized (not homogeneous) national culture. Lawrence's book could not have been completed. She was writing about something contemporaneous with herself, not as a historian. Her subject matter was vanishing even as she kept writing. Her book, nonetheless, stands as a testimony to a fascinating southern institution.

THUS FAR, I have written about Lawrence's "voice" as something purely literary, a style, a consistency of expression. But there is also the spoken voice, the voice actually heard, its pitch and intonation, its tone of confidence or timidity, which one somehow hears when reading words written by the person who owns that voice, that real-life voice. I suppose that editors who deal with living writers and who talk to them over the telephone hear this same voice when they read the words they have written. I never knew Elizabeth Lawrence, never talked with her over the telephone, but as I edited her manuscript, entering its words into the memory of my word processor, I began to hear—not just read silently—not only what she had to say but what she had to say in what I took to be her actual voice. It was deep and melodious. It was confident and assured. The accent was southern, to be sure, but it had been altered by her years at Barnard College. If I had to find a single adjective to describe Elizabeth Lawrence's voice, it would be *sophisticated,* as this word was used when I was growing up in the 1940s to describe movie stars. The voice I heard in my mind's ear was much like that of Rosalind Russell—except that I doubt that Rosalind Russell ever had occasion to talk about *Trachelospermum jasminoides.* Or perhaps she had the low and dulcet voice of another film star, Margaret Sullavan. Or a southern version of one of the most distinctive voices of our time— musical but with an edge to it—that of Katharine Hepburn.

There's a bit more to this story, however. First, *Gardening for Love* turned out to be an instant classic, hailed by everyone as such except for a peevish review in *Horticulture* magazine. Second, it was followed in 1990 by two additional posthumous books by Miss Lawrence. One, *A Rock Garden in the South,* turned up in another pasteboard box at Duke. Wise and funny about the whole enterprise of rock gardening and the challenge it offers southerners in particular, it was revised by Nancy Goodwin to bring the concluding plant encyclopedia up to date. Again, Duke University Press was the publisher. The other, a selection of Lawrence's newspaper columns for the Charlotte *Observer,* was edited by Bill Neale for The University of North Carolina Press. And finally, I got to hear Miss Lawrence speaking, but not in some message from the beyond. After *Gardening for Love* was in production, Joanne Ferguson called to say she had run across a tape recording of a conversation with Elizabeth Lawrence made on the day that Lawrence gave her the manuscript. Would I like to hear it? Two days later I put it on my tape recorder, eager to hear the voice of the woman whose manuscript I had edited, the voice of the woman whose photograph I had fallen in love with, the voice I heard in her pages, the voice now stilled by death.

That was not the voice I heard on the tape. Lawrence was

soft-spoken. She spoke melodiously, but that melody was almost a singsong. She had nothing in her of Hepburn, Sullavan, certainly not Russell. But the voice one hears in a piece of writing sometimes bears no resemblance to the writer's human voice. Dylan Thomas spoke like Dylan Thomas wrote. Truman Capote was another matter altogether.

J. C. Raulston, Plant-Evangelist

DR. J. C. RAULSTON, professor of ornamental horticulture at North Carolina State University in Raleigh and director of the university's arboretum since it opened in 1980, is an amiable, sandy-haired man with a widespread reputation of showing malice to none. "I've never heard him say an unkind word about any other human being," says Allen Bush, who owns and operates Holbrook Farm and Nursery in Fletcher, North Carolina. But Raulston speaks his mind forthrightly when it comes to the way North Carolinians and people elsewhere in the United States plant the home properties that combine to form neighborhoods.

"Ninety percent of all home landscaping in the country today," Raulston says, "uses only some forty-odd species of woody plants, and that's a terrible thing to have to say." He offers this analysis, in the slight southwestern accent that betrays his upbringing in Oklahoma, with the tone of pained concern a parent might use in lamenting the fact that a grown-up son or daughter had never eaten anything but Jell-O for dessert.

"It would be interesting and also a little shocking to pick a couple of blocks in a neighborhood here in the Southeast and do a plant census. There would be a high quotient of forsythias, photinias, and of course dogwoods, by which I mean *Cornus florida,* the one everybody plants. The case of the dogwood is especially interesting, because virtually no one plants *Cornus controversa,* the giant or pagoda dogwood from the Far East." Having dismissed the native eastern dogwood that everyone plants, he warms with enthusiasm over the exotic one almost no one does. "It's a wonderful plant, reaching seventy feet in the wild and over thirty feet in cultivation. E. H. Wilson called it one of the finest of all ornamental plants. It grows rapidly, three or four feet a year here in our arboretum, and it's far more tolerant of our poor clay soil than the eastern dogwood. It has attractive blue-purple fruit, and the fall foliage is a good reddish purple. Considering how easy it is to propagate, it's very strange that it has never caught on in the American nursery business. And unless at least a few nurseries offer it, it might as well not exist as far as home gardeners are concerned."

In his estimation of one dogwood versus another, the basic pattern of J. C. Raulston's horticultural thinking shows clearly. He criticizes one plant that's overused and offers an alternative choice— or several, because, after all, if everyone planted pagoda dogwoods instead of eastern dogwoods, pagoda dogwoods would themselves be overused. But sometimes a plant will have worse faults. A good example, in North Carolina at least, is white pine *(Pinus strobus).* He'd like to see it disappear from the market, because it's terribly subject to root rot. "White pine will survive a few years in our heat, but of a given planting of these pines, ten years later ninety percent will be dead." In place of white pine, Raulston would like to see the native scrub pine *(Pinus virginicus)* planted instead. "It grows happily here, and it's more in scale in the home landscape. It will do well even in poor and rocky soil. It's got a good texture. But it's almost never grown commercially, so people don't realize its true merits."

Raulston has another sharp criticism of typical gardening practices in America. We are, he says, a nation of springtime gardeners. As the sap begins to rise and we begin to buy plants for our gardens, we go for the trees and shrubs that we see in bloom in April or May at our neighborhood nurseries or garden centers. The result is that our front yards are ablaze for two or three weeks with azaleas, flowering crab apples, Japanese weeping cherries, and of course eastern dogwoods in pink and red as well as white. We have already missed our chance to have the Japanese flowering apricot *(Prunus mume)* brighten our spirits in late winter—January in North Carolina—when it covers itself with delicate single or double blossoms in red or pink or white, depending on the kind. We have also missed out on the hybrid Chinese witch hazels such as 'Arnold Promise' and 'Paladin', which stay in glorious bloom for several weeks starting in January or February, and whose blossoms are so fragrant that a single branch can perfume a whole room.

Spring comes, our neighborhoods are briefly glorious, and then everything lapses into a bland and boring green. As Raulston sees it, we make too little use of shrubs that flower in late summer and autumn, extending the season of bloom by several months.

If Raulston is pained by the way too many of us approach our gardens in the United States, he is nevertheless tolerant and understanding of human motives, those of nursery owners as well as the customers who buy their plants. "Generally, if certain plants are overused, it's because they work. They make money for nurserymen. They are easy to propagate. They withstand the stress and sometimes rough treatment of being handled commercially. They are reassuringly familiar to homeowners, and they're usually easy to grow. They serve a lot of people's needs. But they're boring when they're planted in great numbers all over town. There's nothing really wrong with something like photinia, except when it's used so often that it's almost a conditioned reflex. If we planted something else the residential landscape would be much more interesting throughout the growing season."

But J. C. Raulston is no armchair critic of the American nursery trade. He's trying to change things for the better, to promote the greatest possible diversity of shrubs and small trees up and down the streets of the neighborhoods of the Southeast. And he has a powerful tool at his disposal—the arboretum he directs. It's an arboretum shaped by his own ideas, an arboretum with a different style of operation from any other in the country.

THE DICTIONARY NEAREST at hand gives as the primary meaning of *arboretum* "a place where large numbers of different kinds of shrubs and trees are grown for observation and scientific study." It offers as a secondary definition "a large and wooded public park." Neither of these definitions satisfactorily describes the North Carolina State University Arboretum, which is surely one of the most exciting horticultural institutions in the country today. Large numbers of woody plants, thousands upon thousands of genera and species native and exotic, deciduous and evergreen, do grow there, of course. And they are studied scientifically, since the arboretum is an integral part of the university's Department of Ornamental Horticulture and its educational programs at both the undergraduate and the graduate levels. If not exactly a park, this arboretum is public. People can and do visit. There are large collections of several genera of woody plants—six different vitexes, all eleven known species of *Cercis* or redbud plus such named cultivars as 'Texas White' and 'Pansy Purple' and some two hundred different magnolias. Other collections include hypericums, loniceras, hybrid witch hazels, and crape myrtles, most notably *Lagerstroemia faurei,* which has attractive red flaking bark and which is so much hardier than the much more common hybrids of *L. indica* that it virtually escaped the serious damage the latter suffered in the brutal freeze of January 1985 through much of the South.

But there's more for visitors to the arboretum to see than its collections of woody plants. The lath house contains hundreds of plants that need protection from the fierce heat and humidity of summer in the Carolina Piedmont. There's a display garden of annuals, a rock garden, a Japanese garden, and a large collection of ground covers to inspire those whose imaginations stop with English ivy and pachysandra. The perennial border, fourteen feet wide and over two hundred feet long, designed in 1982 by its volunteer curator, Edith Eddleman, is indeed quite splendid, fully deserving the attention it has gotten from horticulturists all over the country during its short history.

But the arboretum differs from a great many others in some obvious respects. It is quite small, for one thing. The Arnold Arboretum has 265 acres, the Morton Arboretum 1,525. The NCSU arboretum takes up only 5 acres of the 8-acre site set aside for it on a corner of the university's campus, right next to a busy railroad track and an even busier interstate highway. Unlike most other arboreta, this one has in evidence almost no trees that are noble in their maturity. When a tree begins to approach even the vestibule of maturity, it is moved elsewhere on the campus. (There are two reasons. One is lack of space in the arboretum itself. The other is that J. C. Raulston thinks the place should show home gardeners what they can do with woody plants on their own properties, and most of us who live in fairly new suburban developments may retire and move to Florida before our oaks and maples move much beyond a juvenile stage of growth.) Most other arboreta have resources, in both people and funds, that this one lacks. It's very much an operation on a shoestring. Raulston runs it with some student help during the year, volunteer curators for the plant collections in the lath house, the rock garden, the perennial border, and the rest. He has only a single part-time paid assistant, and in addition to directing the arboretum he teaches almost a full load in the horticulture department. The budget provided by the university and supplemented by private donations is far from lavish. There isn't even money to pay for peat moss as a soil supplement, a fact that has led to the interesting discovery that the arboretum's woody plants perform quite well—better than they would perform if the standard advice in most of the gardening books were followed about five-dollar holes for fifty-cent plants, with lots of humus added. Here in Raleigh, fifty-cent plants go in fifty-cent holes, sans peat moss, and they are then watered and fertilized and mulched with a foot of wood chips, to splendid result.

Raulston's views of the mission and goals of an arboretum—his, anyway—is unorthodox. He doesn't believe that it can in itself set an example that will work educational miracles, that people who don't know a vitex from a carpet juniper will come visit, be converted, and go home to plant some vitex. "I suspect that most visitors here come already equipped with considerable love of plants and knowledge about them. It's a case of preaching to the converted. It would be highly desirable if we could get some of the wonderful things we have here out to where the general nongardening public goes about its daily routines." He'd like to see every fast-food restaurant in North Carolina landscape with uncommon plants, and he was very happy when the city foresters in Raleigh planted hybrid witch hazels and *Prunus mume* along some stretches of highway and in a pedestrian shopping mall downtown.

Nor does Raulston think an arboretum has done its job when it has merely assembled a collection of plants, no matter how large it may be or how rare some of the specimens. He thinks of his own arboretum as a kind of horticultural way station, from which desirable but seldom-grown plants go to nursery people for evaluation and possible propagation to sell to home gardeners for their use and delight. The NCSU Arboretum is something of a missionary operation, and Raulston a kind of plant-evangelist, spreading the news that life can be richer than it is watching white pines get root rot and having eastern dogwoods out front, like everyone else on the block.

But he sees clearly that his desire for a much more varied suburban landscape—one that might itself approach the richness of

an arboretum—is a classic case of Catch-22. Why, if there are all
these wonderful trees and shrubs, are people not planting them?
Nurseries, except highly specialized ones with customers who thirst
for rarities, grow the plants that most people will buy. If the nurseries
that cater to the general public grow things people won't buy, they'll
founder in red ink. Most people, to overgeneralize a bit, buy the
plants they know. Furthermore, faced with a decision in May between buying a Japanese weeping cherry in full bloom and buying
a plant of *Prunus mume* that finished blooming three months earlier,
most people will go for the cherry, without the faintest notion in
their minds that there could be such a thing as a flowering tree that
struts its stuff in January or February.

A fainthearted person, faced with this dilemma, might just stick
to teaching, directing a dissertation from time to time, and trying to
see to it that the plants in his arboretum were well labeled and
properly tended. But J. C. Raulston, as all who know him can testify,
is anything but fainthearted. He is also a person of prodigious energy.
He sees that he must proceed on two fronts simultaneously: education of the gardening public to promote the notion that horticultural
diversity is a civic good, and encouragement of the nurserymen of
North Carolina—where the nursery business is currently burgeoning
with newcomers—to try new and unusual plants. "They can't afford
not to propagate and sell the surefire and the familiar," he says. "But
if every nursery would experiment with five or six unusual plants, and
not the same five or six as every other nursery, then we might see
something in our gardens reminiscent of the Kingdom of God."

To borrow from the title of the off-Broadway musical, Professor
J. C. Raulston clearly has his act together. He has also taken it on
the road, giving public lectures all over the state and offering short
courses, for university credit, to nurserymen.

"I'm overawed by both his energy and his sheer charisma," says
Allen Bush, whose catalog offers several plants Raulston called to his
attention, including *Lespedeza thunbergii 'albiflora,'* a fine plant for
late summer bloom. "J.C. finishes teaching a class in Raleigh, gives

a short course lasting three hours there, drives to Charlotte the next day to repeat the course, and then to Asheville to do it again. After Asheville, he drives five hours back to Raleigh, where he teaches the next day. And of course in the summer there are his presentations, at several locations in the state, where he hands out the goodies."

By "goodies," Bush means free plants. University policy forbids the arboretum to sell plants, even though that would be a good source of revenue to support its activities. But there's no objection to giving them away, and give them away to nurserymen is exactly what J. C. Raulston does. Every year he propagates from cuttings or seed some twenty to thirty plants, mostly trees and shrubs but also some herbaceous perennials, and dispenses them to some two hundred people in the nursery trade, together with extensive notes on their origins, culture, and possible commercial value. As a typical example of Raulston's "goodies," here's the list for 1985:

> *Ardisia japonica* (six different cultivars)
> *Calluna vulgaris* 'Foxhollow'
> *Chamaecyparis obtusa* 'Sanderi'
> *Cornus sericea* var. *flaviramea*
> *Corylopis pauciflora*
> *Cunninghamia konishii*
> *Fothergilla gardenii*
> *Herniaria glabra*
> *Ilex rotunda*
> *Juniperus rigida* 'Pendula'
> *Lagerstroemia indica* 'Dallas Red'
> *Ligustrum lucidum* 'Davidson Hardy'
> *Lonicera sempervirens* f. *sulphurea*
> *Passiflora incarnata* 'Alba'
> *Pinckneya pubens*
> *Pistacia chinensis*
> *Rosa spinosissima* 'Petite Pink'
> *Salix alba* f. *sericea*

Sequoia sempervirens 'Albospicata'
Thuja plicata 'Hogan'
Ulmus parvifolia 'Sempervirens'
Vitex negundo var. *heterophylla*

As a sample of his comments to the nurserymen who receive their free plants, here are Raulston's remarks about the wax-leafed ligustrum 'Davidson Hardy':

> The last two winters have been devastating to the evergreen privets in North Carolina landscapes and this year even large old trees were killed to the ground. Some people said good riddance—but the plants *are* valuable as fast-growing, cheap evergreen screening material. One plus (far outweighed by the damages) of a hard winter is that it shows hidden genetic diversity in physiological capabilities of different individuals in the population—in this case more cold-tolerant forms.
>
> This form being distributed is from an individual plant on the Davidson College campus which tolerated below $-10°$ F without *any* tip injury and *no* scorch, while all the other plants of the same species around it were killed to the ground. The parent plant (beside the science building) is 15' in diameter with very handsome foliage. It should be distributed through the industry and grown instead of propagating those coming back from root systems to insure hardier plants in the future.

The arboretum's policies permit another method of sending desirable plants out into the world, besides Raulston's packets of goodies. Nurserymen from all over the eastern and southern United States are encouraged to come to Raleigh to take hardwood or softwood cuttings of things they want to propagate for themselves. In 1987, just before Raulston took a sabbatical in Europe, where he visited 170 public gardens in nineteen countries, he estimates that ten thousand cuttings were taken from the arboretum. It isn't merely a matter of generosity, either, although the policy is certainly generous. "What if we keep something here for ourselves, trying to prevent anyone else from having it, like some of the European botanical gardens in the early nineteenth century, and then we lose it to some pest or disease? If we spread the things we have very far and very wide, then we can always have a source for something if we lose it."

How successful have Raulston's missionary activities been in promoting a wider diversity in the nursery trade and eventually in residential neighborhoods? Asked this question, he laughs and says that the single plant he's managed to promote on a very large scale indeed has beyond any doubt been the Leyland cypress *(Cupressocyperis x leylandii)*, but completely unintentionally. He had read about this plant and then admired it in Great Britain, where it originated as a bigeneric hybrid of *Chamaecyparis nootkatensis* and *Cupressus macrocarpa*. Not believing that it would do well in North Carolina, since both of its parents were Pacific-coast plants that didn't do well in the South, he nevertheless located with some difficulty a source and bought twenty-five or thirty rooted cuttings, all that the arboretum's budget could afford. Planted as a screen along a fence between the arboretum and its parking lot, they grew at a phenomenal rate, quickly reaching over twenty feet. People driving by saw it, asked their nurserymen about it, and the nurserymen were bugged so often that they asked if they could take cuttings and propagate it. Now it's so widely planted that Raulston says his tombstone will probably read "He brought us the Leyland cypress."

"We've created another weed, I'm afraid. But it's a good, serviceable plant that makes money for nurserymen and gives homeowners what they more and more want, which is, in our urban and surburban landscape, privacy. Given the increasing density of population, people want privacy and they want it yesterday. The old plants for this purpose were the Lombardy poplars, but they were deciduous and subject to disease and short-lived. This hybrid cypress is really our first fast-growing columnar evergreen that does the job, so it has just exploded in use. It's becoming the standard plant in all landscapes around here, and I kind of hate to see that. There's such a thing as too much success."

Some plants that Raulston has been keen on have been adopted in the nursery trade, of course. That white lespedeza, for one. A buddleia called 'Lochinch'. And *Vitex rotundifolia,* a shrub that grows around two feet high, with clusters of soft blue flowers in mid- to late summer and rounded olive-green leaves that are a soft shade of gray on their undersides. Collected recently on an island off the coast of South Korea, where it grew happily almost to the water's edge, this attractive shrub is being raised in huge numbers by a wholesale nursery near Wilmington, North Carolina. Raulston thinks it might have a very bright future for gardens by the sea, where the salty air afflicts many other shrubs.

But Raulston doesn't shrink from speaking about his failures, the plants that haven't caught on, despite his fervent praise for them at every opportunity. *Prunus mume* hasn't yet become a household word. And nurserymen just frown and shake their heads when he tries to persuade them to propagate sweet gum *(Liquidambar styraciflua).* "It's one of our finest shade trees," Raulston says. "It doesn't have a shallow and spreading root system, like most maples. Its leaves are fresh and attractive in the summer, and the fall foliage is truly spectacularly lovely. But sweet gum grows almost everywhere in the woods of North Carolina, and its fruits are not only messy but painful to step on barefoot." As it happens, Raulston has in the arboretum a form with slightly rounded leaves. Completely sterile, it doesn't produce the prickly seed cases that are typical of the species.

I think I know how Raulston might stir up interest in his neglected sweet gum. When those nurserymen come, about three of them a day all during the summer, to take cuttings, he should tell them that they may do so with every tree in the garden, save one, and that one they should leave completely alone. Some say that long ago, in the first garden of them all, such a prohibition proved to be an irresistible temptation. J. C. Raulston doesn't know, but perhaps it might work. Human nature, after all, is prevalent.

J. C. Raulston,
the Newsletter

YEARS BEFORE I got to visit the North Carolina State University Arboretum and meet J. C. Raulston in person, I was captivated when a friend in Hillsborough, North Carolina, sent me some issues of a mimeographed quarterly publication called *The Friends of the NCSU Arboretum.* Up to forty pages long, it is largely written by Raulston—in a style unique in American horticultural literature. Raulston, it seems, suffers frequently and painfully from writer's block. His computer sometimes disobeys him. Books and papers pile up in his office, and he can't always find what he's looking for. Furthermore, he confesses to having mastered the art of procrastination. The newsletter, as a result of all these things, is frequently late. The June issue may arrive after Labor Day. Sometimes the newsletter leads off with an account of the reasons or excuses for its tardy appearance. One Friend of the NCSU Arboretum told Raulston that the newsletter's best feature was his excuses.

Another reader, however, turned from Friend to enemy. The

story is in the issue of September 1985 (mailed in January 1986). One fellow wrote an angry letter to the president of the arboretum's board of directors, stating that he was a serious businessman who didn't tolerate lateness of any sort. He demanded that Raulston be fired. Raulston returned the businessman's membership fee of fifteen dollars, plus five dollars for the inconvenience. He reported in the newsletter that the board (consisting of himself, four volunteer curators, and two cats that lived on the premises) met, and by a narrow margin voted to keep him on. "I survived," he wrote, "to continue to keep my job, which is officially designated as an enormous 5 percent of my university job description. Even in our tiny garden, it's *never* dull."

Being an accomplished procrastinator myself, I found in Professor Raulston a kindred soul, so I promptly sent in a contribution to become a Friend and to get the newsletter, which I've been reading regularly for some four years now. Whenever it finally appears in my mailbox, I drop everything to read it.

For someone who complains about writer's block, J. C. Raulston commands respect. He doesn't write the entire newsletter, of course, and some of it is news of strictly local interest, the announcement of public lectures at the university and that kind of thing. There are usually several pages of computer printout listing new plants added to the arboretum's collections. Sometimes Edith Eddleman, the curator of the perennial border, M. K. Ramm, the curator of the lath house, or one of the other curators will report on what has been going on in their particular bailiwicks of late.

But the rest of the newsletter is pure Raulston, and it's always lively and often entertaining. Raulston writes seriously about plants, of course, giving several single-spaced pages to close observation of such things as every last redbud in his collection. He reviews books on gardening, but if he finds a book of general interest that he likes, such as Daniel Boorstin's *The Discoverers,* he will review it too. He reports on new nurseries that he likes in North Carolina and other places as well. He reports on the weather, including the disastrous freezes during the winter of 1984–85, which severely damaged or killed many crape myrtles, camellias, boxwoods, and other plants all over the Southeast. There are occasional obituaries. Sometimes Raulston pleads for volunteers to come and help weed. In one issue he tells of his plans to reorganize his desk. In another, he describes his experiences as a member of a plant-hunting expedition in South Korea. He often quotes from Lewis Carroll, and he wrote a charming essay once on the role he thinks Frances Hodgson Burnett's *The Secret Garden* has played in making children grow up to be passionate gardeners.

Professor J. C. Raulston is sometimes not at all professorial in his newsletter. He likes jokes about horticulture, some of them pretty awful.

Have you heard the one about the English vicar, a flower lover, who installed floodlights above his perennial border? He wanted, it seems, to watch over his phlox by night.

Butchart Gardens: Disgustingly Gaudy Beds? No!

"YOU WON'T LIKE the Butchart Gardens," a friend from Seattle advised me. "There are too many people there. And far too many flowers. The place is filled with disgustingly gaudy beds of tuberous begonias and things like that. It's a horticultural Disneyland, okay for children, but offering little to serious, grown-up gardeners no longer taken in by flamboyant and indiscriminate color."

I almost took the advice. It appealed to the taint of snobbery that, like most gardeners, I sometimes harbor. I prefer to visit small private gardens. I like to see how their owners have expressed themselves in choosing and combining plants. It's fun to exchange tales of woe about the ravages of slugs, moles, and root weevils. Often, a garden visit ends with a promise of some plant swapping. I will send an especially fine sedum or aster, receiving in return a terrific toadlily or a new artemisia to add to my collection.

But I still went to the Butchart Gardens, some fifty acres of velvety manicured lawns of emerald green and impeccably maintained flower beds. I'm glad I did, for I rank it with Winterthur Gardens in Delaware and Longwood Gardens in Kennett Square, Pennsylvania, as among the very best gardens open to the paying public in North America or any other continent.

My friend was right about one thing. Color is king here. Tuberous begonias are in evidence everywhere, covered with large and waxen flowers in orange, scarlet, crimson, pink, and cream. Fuchsias are equally abundant, both the familiar sorts with flaring lower petals like a ballerina's tutu and an unusual form called 'Gartenmeister Bonnstedt'. This fuchsia sports long tubular flowers of a sullen hue of dark garnet that seem to be a mecca for hummingbirds. In several long and curving beds, salmon-pink geraniums mingle on equal terms with light purple heliotropes that scent the air with the delicious aroma of hot cherry pie.

Butchart has the large rose garden that is almost inescapable in any garden that seeks to draw large numbers of tourists. As rose gardens go, this one is unusually fine, blooming unceasingly from early summer into fall, thanks to the beneficent climate of Vancouver Island, where days are sunny and mild and nights have the coolness that roses prefer. Climbing and rambling roses spill over trellises and arches and pergolas, and tea roses and floribundas grow in formal beds along walkways that permit closer inspection of any rose, such as a buff pink called 'Just Joey', that catches the eye from afar. The warm afternoon air of early autumn was fragrant with rose perfume, lent additional spice by a nearby clerodendrum or glorybower tree, whose pink and cream blossoms are redolent of cloves and nutmeg.

The dominant plants here are annuals: alyssum, celosia, nasturtiums, salvias, and many others, at least a hundred different kinds, their spent blossoms fastidiously removed, regularly and often, to keep them from going to seed and, their reproductive purpose fulfilled, giving up the ghost. But there are many fine perennials as well. I was particularly taken with a tall North American goldenrod, probably *Solidago sempervirens*, which is grown here with its lower stems thickly corseted around an invisible central stake. Ten feet above the ground, the clusters of flowers erupt into a profusion of dark lemon yellow. These goldenrods punctuate plantings of lower-growing things like marigolds and zinnias with all the emphasis of exclamation marks, to a pleasant result.

Butchart is a crowd pleaser, no doubt about it, and visitors are treated with remarkable courtesy and consideration. There are no signs admonishing people not to pick flowers or walk on the grass. Except for the roses, no plants are labeled, but in a booth near the gift shop dozens of vases display whatever may be in full bloom on a given day. The vases are tagged with names, so that the curious may identify this flower as an amaranth, that one as a penstemon, and the other as a schizostylis. Seeds of many of Butchart's plants are sold in the gift shop.

Pets are welcome here, and they have drinking fountains scattered throughout the grounds. (I do note, however, that the dogs guests bring are mostly small ones, like dachshunds and toy poodles, not more rambunctious breeds like boxers and Labrador retrievers.)

Like Longwood, established in 1906 by Pierre S. Du Pont, or Winterthur, whose woodland gardens were laid out somewhat later by Henry Francis Du Pont, Butchart came into existence as an expression of the large horticultural passions of an individual person, Jenny Foster Butchart. In 1904 she was troubled by a big hole in the ground near the house she shared with her husband, Robert Pim Butchart, on a hill above Tod Inlet on Vancouver Island.

Mr. Butchart was a manufacturer of Portland cement, whose first limestone quarry was on the 150-acre tract where he built his house. When the limestone was exhausted, Jenny Butchart saw in the resulting dismal and barren pit the opportunity to make the sunken garden that remains the centerpiece at Butchart Gardens in its finished form, decades later. Topsoil and manure were hauled in. Ivy was planted to cover the steep and forbidding quarry walls. Paths were constructed to descend into the garden at a gentle grade.

The dismal pit soon was transformed into a lovely garden, home not only to bright and common annuals but also to rare shrubs and trees and to meconopsis, the blue poppy from the Himalayas that can be grown successfully in the Pacific Northwest but almost nowhere else in North America.

Other gardens followed, including the rose garden, a Japanese garden, a formal Italian garden, and several water gardens both large and small. As word of their beauty spread, people began to beg for invitations. By the early 1920s, fifty thousand people arrived each year. They were received hospitably, stranger and friend alike. The Butcharts named their estate Benvenuto, Italian for "welcome."

Robert Butchart died in 1943, Jenny in 1950, but the garden they made so lovingly over the decades is still in the family, under the management of a grandson, R. Ian Ross. The spirit of welcome remains. It costs nine dollars and fifty cents (Canadian) to visit, but the fee is small considering the fact that eight hours is hardly enough time to spend taking in all that Butchart has to offer. Shaded benches are abundant, and no one seems to mind if a visitor lies on the lawn for a nap. There's a coffee stand, a pleasant cafeteria, and a restaurant in the former Butchart residence that serves up a splendid English afternoon tea, with scones, finger sandwiches of cucumbers and salmon pâté, and delicious jams and preserves.

Wheelchairs and baby strollers are free, as are umbrellas on a rainy day. Visitors who forget their cameras can borrow one for the asking. During the summer there are lawn concerts each night and firework displays on Saturdays right after dusk. The gardens are illuminated at night, so it's good timing to arrive in midafternoon, stroll for a while, stop for that splendid British tea, and then stroll the gardens again as night falls and they undergo a wonderful transformation under artfully designed artificial light.

Ingratiating as the lavish display of colorful flowers may be, I find that the other visitors lend additional pleasure. The paths are sufficient enough in number and wide enough that five or six thousand people at one time do not seem a crowd. The atmosphere is polyglot. A linguist who is the master of many languages could eavesdrop on conversations in Arabic, Hebrew, Japanese, Tagalog, Danish, and many another tongue. I had to limp along with basic Spanish and primitive German, but I got the drift of what I overheard: my German- and Spanish-speaking fellow visitors to this wonderful garden shared my admiration for its intelligent design, its bright play of color, and its determination to please all the senses.

The Road to Sandy Mush

THE ROAD TO Sandy Mush Herb Nursery, in a remote cove in the Newfound Range of the Blue Ridge Mountains twenty miles west of Asheville, North Carolina, is not an easy one, but it is beautiful. The narrow pavement wends its way through the Big Sandy Mush Valley past tidy farms on rolling terrain. In late October, the tobacco crop has just been harvested, using techniques unchanged since the eighteenth century. The golden-tan leaves have been cut by hand, gathered into sheaves on pointed wooden sticks, and then hauled to the two-story barns to hang and cure.

The pavement ends and a gravel road begins to ascend. The tokens of autumn are everywhere along its verges. Tall billowing clouds of native blue and white asters mingle with many species of goldenrod. The woodlands beyond the pastures where sheep and cattle graze have not yet been touched by a hard freeze. Fall color is near its peak, with sourwoods and dogwood showing their deliciously sullen and rusty tones of red.

The gravel road changes in its final mile to a tooth-jarring rubble of stones. Just before the road crosses a stream at a ford, the evidences of the final products of industrial civilization clutter its edges. Junked cars, discarded washing machines, broken-down farm machinery, and worn-out mattresses pain the eye. This seems to be the way to Dogpatch or beyond.

But when the road finally ends, it is no Daisy Mae or Li'l Abner who greets the visitor intrepid enough to have made the journey. Instead, it is Kate and Fairman Jayne, two horticulturally educated Pennsylvanians who found their way to this cove in 1978, to establish a small but very influential mail-order nursery that discerning gardeners all over America treasure for its offerings of herbs both common and rare.

Kate Jayne tells me as we walk through the fields and the complex of small greenhouses and residential buildings made of wood, in a style best described as mid-1970s nouveau commune, about the nursery's origins. She and her husband wanted to escape urban pollution and the frantic ways of cities, so they were attracted to this spot, with its old log cabin and chicken coop, to plant themselves on rural ground. They have certainly succeeded, for this country is southern Appalachia. The inhabitants may now shop in malls and snatch a hamburger from a fast-food place down on the main highway, but the old ways persist hereabouts. Folktales are still passed on to children, and the art of playing a hammered dulcimer has not been lost.

I first heard of Sandy Mush from a friend who urged me to send for their sizable catalog, which would be beautiful if only for its wonderful calligraphy and layout. It is also a catalog that spoke immediately to my heart. In the last few years, I have been consumed by a passion for salvias—the perennial species and cultivars, not the hot-red bedding salvias that so afflict the American suburban landscape for months beginning in May and not ending until a black freeze.

To my knowledge, Sandy Mush is the champion source of salvias in the country. A nursery that offers eight kinds is wealthy in them, but the Jaynes sell well over sixty sorts, including ones with foliage that smells of pineapple, honeydew melon, and grape, as well as the more musty and aromatic odors typical of the sage or salvia family. Some of these salvias are tender in the North, but it's easy to take cuttings in the fall to grow indoors in a sunny window until spring—or simply to order again each year. According to the kind, these plants range in flower color from white to red to indigo to purple. There are some yellows, though not many.

Even those who are blind to the charms of salvias (if such people exist) will find much to linger over in the Sandy Mush catalog, or at the nursery itself. There are a great many basils, including one that smells like cinnamon. Rosemary is much in evidence, several kinds, some of them immense plants grown in terra-cotta urns. Ivy fanciers can fill a large box with a variety of different kinds, including some that seem to be dusted with gold or with silver.

Spice geraniums (properly pelargoniums) are another specialty of the Jaynes'. These are the great olfactory con artists of the plant kingdom, with leaves that mock the scents of unrelated plants in a very convincing way. Some have foliage that smells of roses, others of orange, clove, lemon, lime, or apple. On my visit, I waste no time in buying a small rooted cutting of peppermint geranium; it smells exactly like peppermint candy. It also will make in time a large and very handsome plant for a hanging basket. The leaves are velvet to the touch, and they have an extremely fetching silvery sheen.

On this, as on most nursery visits, my eyes are larger than the extra suitcase I have brought along to fly back home with, bulging with new plants. I content myself with four ivies, two of those peppermint pelargoniums, and some small rosemary plants for the kitchen window, to use in cooking during the approaching winter.

I am tempted by the wealth of lovely wreaths of dried herbs and wildflowers that hang in a shed by the entranceway to the main greenhouse, but I resist. I can always order by mail anything that Sandy Mush sells.

And I will.

Arizona — and
Sedona — in Bloom

HELLA AND I came to Arizona for the month of April. I had the freedom of a sabbatical from teaching, and she took a leave of absence from nursing. We wanted to realize a dream of long standing—to see the desert blossom as the rose, as the Old Testament puts it. I did no advance research, for, based on hearsay and some old Walt Disney nature films about American southwestern deserts, I knew what we would find. The bloom season would begin in early April in the Sonoran Desert around Tucson and southward, and it would progress steadily north at intervals of a few days.

Everywhere the pattern would be the same. A torrential spring rain would awake the parched earth. Dormant seeds of wildflowers would germinate overnight and race into bloom, carpeting the ground in the brief period before the advent of summer's withering heat. Above the carpet of wildflowers, cacti would put on their own spectacular display. The fat buds of prickly pears, chollas, and majestic saguaros would swell and then burst open into waxen yet silken flowers in pastel creams and yellows, brilliant oranges, crimsons, scarlets, and wine purples. Ocotillos would wave their strange tall green stems in the breeze, each stem tipped with clusters of scarlet blossoms like flocks of tiny birds perched at its end. Roadrunners would race everywhere amidst the exuberant explosion of spring. Lizards and horned toads would bask in the sun, and we would have to keep a sharp eye out for rattlesnakes and Gila monsters.

My preconceptions about the Arizona desert in bloom were entirely wrong. Spring in the desert is not an explosion, but a slow unfolding, beginning with the annuals that germinated the previous fall and stayed tiny during the winter, biding their time. The cacti come much later, starting with opuntias or prickly pears in late April. The saguaros do not bloom until considerably later, in mid-May where they are found, so I missed them altogether. Furthermore, the desert areas in the north of the state are still in the last clutches of winter through most of April, with patches of snow on the ground. The vegetation there is also much less diverse than in the south, being dominated by sagebrush and yuccas, with far fewer cacti and no saguaros at all.

The timetable of bloom, to continue with realities instead of images from Disney films, is affected by two things. One of them— latitude as modified by altitude—is absolute. In Phoenix, more than one hundred miles north of Tucson, the desert bursts into flower earlier, because it is two thousand feet lower. The other factor—the first rains of spring—is relative, varying so much from one year to the next that no one can safely predict when the tide of color will begin to sweep the horizon.

We returned to New Jersey at the end of the month without memories or slides of giant saguaros resplendent with flowers. In the Painted Desert in the northeastern part of Arizona, we stood in half an inch of fresh snow, with nothing in bloom except one of the many species of wild verbenas that seem omnipresent there and that seem to be the first flowers to bloom, and among the last to stop.

But we were content with this visit. From Nogales, on the

Mexican border, to well above Phoenix we saw a diversity of wild-flowers exceeded in the spring only in Texas, where since the 1930s the State Highway Department has helped things along by scattering seeds along the verges of country roadsides with a lavish hand. Some plants in Arizona, like the so-called desert marigold *(Baileya mul-tiradiata)*, a brilliant lemon daisy with gray and woolly foliage, were new to me, but so stunning in the clear light of early morning under an azure sky that I covet them for my own garden. I bought desert marigold seeds from the gift shop of the Arizona-Sonora Desert Museum just west of Tucson to see if I could get them to grow in my own garden, almost a continent away. Other wildflowers were familiar old friends, or at least their close kin, for the simple reason that for both European gardeners and ones in the eastern United States, the Southwest has long been a treasure trove of highly orna-mental annuals worth inviting into the home garden. Seed catalogs are chock-full of hybrids and presumably improved forms, but a roadside in southern Arizona in mid-April gives pause to anyone who assumes that when human beings take any genus of plants in hand with the idea of gussying it up the result is an improvement. Pink and yellow evening primroses, little blue or purple lupines and lark-spurs, verbenas in many shades, gaillardias, eschscholzias or Mexican poppies (slightly smaller than the California species, but just as radiant and elegant), tidytips, penstemons—the list goes on and on.

Our stay in Arizona ended in Sedona, a small resort town south-west of Flagstaff. Situated fifty-three hundred feet above sea level, it lies at the bottom of Oak Creek Canyon amidst soaring red mesas, buttes, and pinnacles. The landscape brought on a sense of déjà vu almost instantly, since so many cowboy movies were filmed here during the heyday of the genre. Sedona is not desert, because surface water is plentiful and the aquifers are generously endowed, so far, with the Southwest's most valuable, and often scarce, natural re-source, H_2O.

A chic destination for well-heeled tourists, Sedona is better known for its restaurants and shops than for its gardens, yet the whole town is an oasis. A shopping center called Tlaquepaque, after a village near Guadalajara in the Mexican state of Jalisco, is made of ersatz adobe. It has a bell tower, but no church. Within its enclosing walls, a series of patios with balconies mimics the residential style still found in some places in Mexico, with its roots in Moorish Spain. The clear intent of Tlaquepaque's architects was by its sheer amenity to arouse the urge to shop for expensive jewelry, clothing, works of art, pottery, and rugs. But Tlaquepaque also has a welcome lesson to teach about the possibilities of a garden based on the enclosure of a space, about the play of fountains and the reflection of the sky in still pools. This is a quasi-public commercial space, but it made me long for a serious examination of what the Persians and the Arabs who lived in towns and cities knew about the purposes and pleasures of the garden and about how to find restful coolness from the sweltering sun.

The courtyards of this shopping center are bright in the spring with tiled planters containing the most magnificent pansies I have ever clapped eyes on. Yellow banksia roses spill over trellises and walls, thousands of small double flowers on each plant. They combine pleasantly with the long, pendant clusters of violet-purple wisteria, which impart to the air the delicious scent of grapes ripening in a late summer vineyard. Beds of Florentine irises give off much the same fragrance, in a deeply sensual mingling of the two similar perfumes. Beds of stocks add their note of clove and cinnamon, as fountains in the courtyards splash like soft music and quiet pools reflect the ghostly white trunks and branches of the immense sycamores that dominate the scene.

The pansies and the irises and all the other plants are natives of the temperate regions, but many of the plants of the Sonoran Desert grow here as well—including *Opuntia violacea*, a prickly pear with somber purple pads; century plants; and cholla, or jumping cactus, so named because its pads detach themselves at the slightest touch, their sharp spines being perfectly capable of piercing shoe leather to a painful result. These mingle with more plants of European origin. Rosemary cascades down walls, covered with fuzzy little flowers of Cambridge blue. *Jasminum officinale* also rules the walls and contributes its sweet scent. The few daffodils in Sedona look dispirited and far from home, and they are no match for the Mexican poppies, which seed themselves everywhere along roadsides, on rocks, and on canyon walls.

Other flowers bloom in Sedona, too, and they are the direct descendants of the flowers that bloomed with such optimism in Haight-Ashbury in the early 1960s, before Things Got Nasty. The loose systems of belief known generally as New Age philosophy have found fertile soil here. Numerous bookstores catering to adherents of these systems abound in town, to a remarkable extent considering that Sedona's resident population is about five thousand souls.

Most of the old-time Sedonans I talked to were skeptical of the metaphysical shenanigans being carried on by newcomers, some of whom seem to have more lives to live than the one that is the usual human lot. This cultural phenomenon had just attracted national attention on "48 Hours." Some people were embarrassed by the show's report on their hometown, others amused. A barber who had lived in Sedona all his life was one of the amused. "These New Age people all have just come here from other places," he told me, "and it's just amazing what they have discovered that I've missed seeing all my days, like those vortex things."

The vortices, which are variously described by those who believe in them, are springs of psychic, spiritual, or electromagnetic energy concentrated in particular areas in and around Sedona, at spots near buttes or in side canyons, although one hovers near the airport on the mesa overlooking town and another is at the post office. I couldn't see a single vortex, but I did see several people who obviously were responding to their strange and inexplicable power. The believers stood here and there, singly or in little groups, raising their arms on high, waggling their fingers, and exposing, one man explained, the darkness of their armpits to the light of the world of the spirit.

When I travel, no matter where I go, I can't just restrict myself to looking at plants. The philosopher in me comes along too, and in Sedona I could overlook all this New Age business no more than I could ignore the banksia roses or the opuntias. I needed to figure it out, although it had something terribly familiar about it, something from deep antiquity.

I visited one of those bookstores. It reminded me just a bit of a porn shop—something for every quirk and every taste, this on this wall, that on that wall, and the other thing on the one over yonder. Here be love of leather, here be . . . well, I don't need to explain. In this metaphysical boutique, some common tenets peculiar to New Age thought became clearer. One is the belief that whatever one wants to believe is serious truth. This easy tolerance permits otherwise contradictory doctrines to live together harmoniously, sometimes in a single mind. Crystal balancing sits alongside aromatherapy, Lamurian visions next to Zoosh, channeling and past-life regressions right by light-body attunements and aura readings. None of this was for me, but it sure beat people killing one another because they have different views about what anything or everything means. Besides, these were hard times, and if somebody could make a living convincing others that they get regular messages from beings in UFOs, it was probably better than some alternatives I could think of.

But I was still bothered by the familiarity of New Age. And then it came to me. As Rome was beginning to decline, being nibbled on the fringes by barbarians, there was a huge explosion of cults in the Mediterranean world. Mithraism, Gnosticism, Manicheanism—the ancient world in its final days was a smorgasbord of religious and spiritual beliefs. As a young man, Saint Augustine prayed, "Lord, give me chastity, but not yet." He carried on something more than a slight affair with Manicheanism. He was pretty sure that there were spirits in figs and that people who achieved spiritual purity, which could be done by sensual excess (maybe), eventually didn't need food to sustain themselves. He believed in astrology. He had a few doubts about what he believed, but he knew that a man was coming soon, one Faustus, who would explain it all. Augustine later, of course, rejected his early beliefs as not only wanton but silly. But when he held these beliefs, he would have felt right at home in Sedona.

The other thing common to the Sedonans of the New Age is that they think there's something very special about the place, much more than its benign climate and its spectacular red rocks of sandstone. The local fauna includes, some say, devic entities called wapekas, who came from outer space long ago. They taught native Americans how to grow crops and find water, and they send friendly messages to nice hikers, nasty messages to pushy ones. And then, again, there are the UFOs, which love Sedona as much as the people from the Northeast who come here to find sun in January. If I understand all this, it means that *Close Encounters of the Third Kind* wasn't just a movie, but the literal truth about a place much like Sedona.

I balked at that idea. But one evening, on Chapel Road, near a roadside shrine nestled among the red rocks, with architecture strongly influenced by Frank Lloyd Wright, I heard Gregorian chants being played on a tape deck in a van parked by our rented car. In a sunset that seemed never to end, but to just keep unfolding and unfolding, I watched a sandstone butte flame into magnificence like brightly lit, highly burnished copper. On the lower slopes of the butte, Mexican poppies contributed their own glow of copper orange. There were at least thirty other people, standing there, watching in silence, to the sounds of "Kyrie eleison, Christie eleison" echoing up from the parking lot below us. We all left quietly after it was over. It was like an epiphany, if not the thing itself. Few people could ever experience this drama of the departing day without being filled with a powerful sense of well-being and of being at home on this earth.

ON
HOME
GROUND

An American Cottage Garden

OVER THE YEARS, my garden has come into being by a process that my friend Linda Yang has described as an ongoing effort to cram yet one more plant into a limited patch of earth. She's right, and the planting can be frantic on those spring days when the UPS truck arrives with orders from six different nurseries. My wife has suggested that if we ever felt the need to give our place a name, Random Mess would be perfectly fitting. I've never given much thought at all to having some sense of overall design. I know what all the books on landscaping say. Plan first, then plant. That way, when some interesting new sempervivums arrive, I'd know where to put them, instead of wandering about our property with a sempervivum in one hand and a trowel in the other, looking for a blank spot.

So one fall day, when Nancy Goodwin called from a horticultural meeting in Philadelphia to say she'd like to drive over and visit my garden, I was afraid that she would be disappointed and that I would be found out. Nancy is part of a network of friends and acquaintances across the country with whom I regularly exchange plants and opinions about their merits or demerits. But none of the members of this loose and informal network had ever visited me on my home ground. She was going to be the first, and I worried that she would end up having to call on her last shred of politeness over something she would see before she even turned off the engine of her car. My garden is a hodgepodge.

Nancy is one of those rare souls who knows that praise is a precious human commodity, not to be given out carelessly. She is, I know for a fact as absolute as algebra, incapable of flattery. So I imagined that she would walk around the garden, complimenting the *Angelica gigas* and saying good things about the remarkably long season of bloom of hemerocallis 'Stella de Oro' but making no comment about the garden itself and the way nothing really fits together.

To my enormous surprise, however, she said after the first half hour, "It's delightful, Allen. Everywhere you look, there's garden. What you have done here is make a cottage garden, but an American one, not British."

Nancy Goodwin gave me a new way of looking at my garden, one in which the absence of design turned out to be a strength, not a weakness. It all came into being by pure happenstance, of course, but if I were to move to another house where there was no garden, I think I would deliberately do again what I have accidentally done over many years.

When my family and I bought our house two decades ago, we were pleased with it, since it had some history, going back to around 1810, when it was the farmhouse for a sizable tract of land that then stretched from an ocean bay a mile to the east to a tidal creek half a mile to the west. But the landscaping, if that's the word for it, was the usual suburban affair—a front yard bisected by a concrete sidewalk, a lawn open to the street, symmetrical foundation plantings of matching yew and junipers and other evergreens growing out of a dinky little flower bed where hot-red salvias and bronze-orange marigolds could fight it out.

Our new piece of real estate had some bad things going for it, however. It's on a corner lot. The street out front is the busiest thoroughfare in town. It's the main bus route and also the road used by local rescue squads to get to the regional hospital. The side street is just four doors down from our junior high school. Next door there was an unsightly old gas station, which at the time sold cold drinks and candy before and after school to urchins who thought our front lawn was the perfect repository for Milky Way wrappers and Coke cans. (I'm happy to say that the former gas station is now a tool-repair shop.) And there was a lot of visual clutter overheard, since a major electrical line runs along both streets. And our space was limited: our lot is 100 feet by 150 feet, part of it occupied by the house.

We had a small measure of privacy. There was a hedge of multiflora roses next to the side street. I would not have chosen multifloras, but at least it was a hedge. A row of Japanese black pines and white pines, then eight feet high, now forty feet, separated our backyard from our neighbor's front yard. Another hedge, some ancient lilacs, somewhat screened our view of customers buying gas from the station next door. But we were unquestionably in public view, and gradually over the first several years we instinctively began cutting back on how much of our lives people could take in at a glance from a Chevy going fifty miles an hour.

I moved some of the foundation plantings out to the street, as part of what eventually became a mixed hedge—a thicket really—of junipers, native bayberries, large cotoneasters, rugosa roses, small fruit trees, and pyracanthas. Now mature, and, frankly, a tangle of vegetation some twelve feet wide, the hedge reduces what we can see of passing automobiles and they of us and somewhat abates the sound of traffic, though not enough.

I also moved the rest of the plants by the foundation some ten feet away from the house, because I knew that those little yews would eventually become big ones (my taste doesn't run to clipped yews) and I wanted to have good light for our large collection of houseplants, mostly in hanging baskets hung at different heights in all our windows.

For several years, I was a respectable citizen of American suburbia, revving up the lawn mower every weekend to mow the front yard, the backyard, and the two side yards. My sympathies with organic gardening led me to put the clippings in a compost heap, along with kitchen waste and autumn leaves, but I must also confess to resorting to a little chemistry now and then, with the standandard commercial fertilizers and pesticides to keep things green and growing.

But the lawn, most of it anyway, was doomed by personal idiosyncrasy. I'm basically an ornamental-plant man, enamored of herbaceous perennials, flowering shrubs, and a few favorite annuals. Excess is part of my character. If three different daylilies are good, then thirty are even better, and the ideal would have to be ninety, maybe more. Furthermore, I am frequently overtaken by sudden, perhaps unpredictable, passions for particular kinds of plants, in all their diversity. Once it was sedums—not just sedum 'Autumn Joy' or *S. acre,* but also eighteen others, the most recent additions being *S. glaucophyllum* and *S. ternatum,* which Nancy Goodwin brought with her. Once it was hostas, and I confess to having thirty-two, ranging from the immense and bold cultivar 'Sum and Substance' (which gets larger with each new season and now is about the size of a wheelbarrow) down to dainty *Hosta venusta,* which forms a glossy green mound no more than three inches high and whose violet-purple flower spikes are less than a foot high. Or it was ferns (nineteen kinds). Or astilbes (twenty-two). Or heaths (twelve), so wonderful for their season of bloom stretching from October to late May. I know the names of all my artemesias—'Lambrook Silver', 'Valerie Finnis', *Artemisia versicolor, A. lactiflora.* One of these days I know I'll get round to old-fashioned shrub roses to give the couple of rugosas I already have some company. I need many more clematis, of course; who can ever have enough? The thought of huge things like gunneras and rodgersias warms my heart. For years I got by with only one hardy fuchsia, the cultivar of *Fuchsia magellanica* called 'Senorita', but one spring when I learned that a nursery in Washington State had eight others in its list, I ordered them all.

The avid plant collector needs flower beds, obviously: places to put his plants. And as the collection increases, the lawn will surely diminish. I removed the front lawn and both side lawns some years ago. There's one undeveloped patch out front, where my wife and I are now building what we call our secret garden, after the one in the book by Frances Hodgson Burnett, where a pathway leads to a kind of clearing, almost entirely enclosed by bayberries, redbud trees, and tall ornamental grasses on the outside, and by small shrubs like hypericums on the inside. But the rest of the front yard has long been pure flower bed, with a few wide pathways of woodchips and shredded bark.

The perennial border out back, which began as two tiny triangular beds at the two corners of the yard farthest from the house, has now become a wide and sweeping U. The lawn—mostly white clover, so I don't really need to fertilize it much, as it fixes its own nitrogen from the air, and so I'm not tempted to use a broad-leafed herbicide, which kills clover—is a tiny patch of green at the garden's center. I can mow it in less than half an hour, including a couple of interludes of sitting on the bottom step of our deck, watching the doves that wander among all the hostas and daylilies.

AN AMERICAN COTTAGE GARDEN? Strictly speaking, it doesn't really exist. In Great Britain, where the term and the thing itself originated, cottage gardens were, well, obviously, the gardens made by cottagers, and America's system of social class knows nothing similar. We have rich people and poor people and people in between. We have people with enormous power and people with none worth mentioning. But we don't have the landed aristocracy, the lords of the manor, and we don't have the village cottagers, who worked for them.

English cottagers have been enormously influential in the history of gardening in Great Britain, and ironically so, because they gardened in their own way for centuries, immune to the tides of fashion that had the gentry now putting in formal gardens based on French or Italian models, now removing the formal gardens for sweeping informal landscapes with long vistas and curving roadways and an occasional ha-ha, or concealed trench, to keep the cattle away from the front entrance of their houses. Meanwhile, the cottagers planted their own small gardens, generally enclosed by a low wall or a fence, in front of their doorways. They planted with no eye to design and little consideration of what they were "supposed" to plant. Profusion was characteristic of their gardens, not lawns. Often every square inch of dirt was covered with a wide range of vegetation—medicinal and culinary herbs, vegetables, small fruits, and old-fashioned perennials and biennials, including hollyhocks, foxgloves, dianthuses, sweet Williams, lupines, down through a long catalog of plants.

Gardening in Great Britain, some would hold, hit bottom among the fashionable elite in the second half of the nineteenth century, when the greenhouses of great estates and municipalities made it possible to grow ornamental annuals by the thousands. The common practice was carpet bedding, a style that meant using lobelias and alyssums and begonias in intricate formal patterns. The practice deeply offended first William Robinson and later Gertrude Jekyll. In *The English Flower Garden,* which went through fifteen editions after it first appeared in 1883, Robinson devoted an early chapter to "The Evils of Bedding and Carpet Gardening." He rejected the stiff formality of French gardens, and he advocated strongly the use of many of the old-fashioned flowers that cottagers had kept going from one generation to the next in their unpretentious front gardens. He advised choosing perennials that would together assure that something would be in bloom in almost every season of the year. Gertrude Jekyll carried his ideas further, added some of her own, and also expressed herself less cantankerously. In time, the greatest of England's gardens, including Vita Sackville-

An American Cottage Garden

West and Harold Nicolson's garden at Sissinghurst, used the traditional plants of cottage gardens, but on fine estates. (One thinks of
Eliza Doolittle here, the cockney flower seller who, thanks to improved diction and pronunciation succeeds at Ascot.)

Without cottagers, America can't have cottage gardens. The
closest thing to a cottage garden was probably the doorway garden
of New England villages. Here, within a picket fence, grew hollyhocks and dianthuses, many of the same plants the English cottagers grew. But the picket fences came down shortly after the Civil
War, partly because cattle no longer wandered village streets, partly
because our country was in the grips of a new idea of how we should
be landscaping our homes and neighborhoods. Fences were down,
and lawns were in.

The passing of the doorway garden had its mourners, people
who pointed out that the very words *garden* and *garth* and *yard*
meant in essence a place enclosed. Sarah Orne Jewett wrote in
Country Byways (1881), "There are few of us who cannot remember
a front yard garden which seemed to us a very paradise in childhood
. . . People do not know what they lose when they make way with
the reserve, the separateness, the sanctity of the front yard of their
grandmothers. It is like writing down family secrets for anyone to
read; it is like having everybody call you by your first name, or sit in
any pew in church."

But the lawn had arrived as the dominant feature of American
gardens. Most people today have never heard of Frank J. Scott, but
his book *The Art of Beautifying Suburban Home Grounds* (1870) set
forth the ideas that still rule the land. Scott believed that the walled-
off gardens of England were "selfish" and "surly" and rude-man-
nered. America's more open political principles called for an open
domestic landscape, one lawn flowing into another, and all lawns
flowing down to the street. This was, he believed, a style of planting
that was democratic, cooperative, and neighborly. By each tending
our lawns, we would together make our individual private gardens
into a great public park.

By the 1920s, Scott's advocacy of lawns as democratic had supporters whose voices were not quite so pleasant and optimistic. Not having a lawn, I have read repeatedly in garden writing of the time, was unpatriotic and un-American. (Scott himself had already called it an "unchristian" act.)

BY NOW I think it's clear where my sentiments lie. I have a lawn, but it's out back, it's definitely a minimalist kind of lawn, and I harbor thoughts of obliterating it to make more room for mulched paths and mixed plantings of perennials, annuals, summer-flowering shrubs, bulbs, herbs, and ornamental grasses, all growing in sweet profusion. I also wouldn't mind at all if my idea of a garden became a contagion in the neighborhood, which frankly is just a bit dull because everyone seems to have the same ideas, or lack thereof.

When they buy a house, they plant a lawn. Then they put in the foundation plantings, which either quickly grow so tall as to block the windows or have to be pruned back, often in geometrical forms. They plant some flowering trees, mostly flowering cherries and saucer magnolias and dogwoods. Azaleas are de rigueur, of course, as are large rhododendrons, often sited in precisely the wrong place, immediately next to the house. It is almost a suburban monoculture, in which too many people plant the same things over and over. There is a blaze of color in May. And then it all turns green, except for some marigolds, impatiens, and other bedding plants.

But there is an alternative, and we might as well call it the American cottage garden for lack of a better term. Some of its features I have already indicated. It is partially or totally enclosed from the road, so that it becomes a private and personal space not part of the public landscape. It is the gardener's garden, a place he moves through with his body, and this fact has some striking implications. Some people think of a garden as something to be seen—or photographed—from a single point of view, which implies the rule that tall plants belong at the back, low plants at the front, and medium-sized plants in the middle, so that nothing blocks anything else. But if a garden is a place to move through, to move around in, it will be seen from multiple points of view, with fine surprises when the gardener or his guests move a few paces and suddenly see something unexpected, like the bright gold flame of a kerria bush seen through the more delicate tracery of a pink honeysuckle bush in full flower amidst its somewhat open and airy blue-green foliage.

This kind of garden has most of the characteristics of a traditional English cottage garden, although it's purely American in origin. Its most striking feature is profusion and diversity. It was planted in a makeshift way over many years, with no rational planning. It is something of a jumble or a hodgepodge. I would add that it is the kind of gardening in which the only rule is that there are no rules. What design there may be is found not in grand vistas or axes either vertical or horizontal, but in smaller and more intimate matters. The emphasis is on individual plants or on small groups of plants that happen, usually by pure serendipity, to look splendid together, to be well married. I have some deep coppery orange lilies, seedlings I think, which look terrific next to the dark purple leaves of a purple smoke bush, with a large colony of lamb's ears nearby, to give an example of this sort of good marriage. Another would have to be the glorious sight one June of a sky-blue brodiaea that ended up by pure accident next to a form of feverfew with green-gold leaves.

This American cottage garden, as I conceive it, is a garden for all seasons, not just spring or summer. And since the space in any garden is finite, special attention needs to be paid to plants that earn their keep. I include here those with interesting winter silhouettes, such as the contorted hazelnut ('Harry Lauder's Walking Stick') or with winter color, like the red-twigged dogwood and *Kerria japonica* and winter jasmine, both with emerald stems. Of high importance are those that bloom over a long season. Peonies and Oriental poppies are glorious outbursts of color in the late spring garden, but their season is brief and fleeting. But coreopsis 'Moonbeam' blooms unstintingly for months. Of even higher importance are those that expand the growing season. I mean, for late fall, such plants as the native swamp sunflower, *Helianthus angustifolius* (a tall fountain of gold in late October); the Montauk daisy *(Chrysanthemum nipponicum)* and the arctic daisy *(C. arcticum)* in November; and hardy cyclamens like *Cyclamen coum* and *C. hederifolium.* For late winter, there are the hybrid Chinese witch hazels like 'Arnold Promise', which blooms for over six weeks beginning as early as January. Backlit by the slanting golden light of a winter morning or afternoon and sweetly fragrant, just one of these small trees is worth every forsythia in town. (*I know:* I do go on about 'Arnold Promise' a whole lot, in both conversation and writing, but this small tree is part of the Good News of life.) And of immense value, since single-handedly they enable the gardener to achieve what sounds impossible—365 days of bloom a year (in my coastal garden, at least)—are the *x darleyensis* heaths, hybrids of *Erica carnea,* the European winter heath, and *E. erigena,* the Mediterranean heath. I grow eight different cultivars, and they bloom nonstop from October into May—attractive low evergreen shrubs, entirely covered with little egg-shaped flowers ranging from white to pink to lilac-rose.

A cottage garden, I think, will never be finished until the gardener is at last laid to rest in his final home ground. There is always something new to try, some sad failure or some triumphant success to experience. At the moment, for example, after many years in which I planted the roots but they never bothered to come up, I have three clumps of eremurus or foxtail lily. I prefer their common name of desert candles. They don't look like they have anything to do with deserts, but they are indeed tall white spikes that look entirely right with the red foliage of a photinia behind them and the cottony gray foliage of some Scotch thistles next to them.

Even with little or no lawn to mow, my own version of a cottage garden, a pedant would say, is labor-intensive. A plain talker would just say it's lots of work. And I think it's not for everyone. I have no intention of imitating William Robinson and talking about the "evils" of lawns open to the street and in plain view. Some people, a great many in fact, simply have very little interest in gardening. It's live and let live in this matter, and if they just want to admire their azaleas and dogwoods in the spring and mow their lawns weekly during the summer, that's okay too.

Letters from
Garden to Garden

THE EVIDENCE OF SOMETHING I am far from the first to observe is plain in my mailbox every weekday. Letter writing is a dying art. Some old friends write a note from time to time, at intervals of perhaps a year. Others include with their Christmas cards a printout from their word processors, an omnibus letter to everyone and to no one about their lives since last Christmas. A son has gotten married. A daughter has made them new grandparents. Their collie died and they replaced it with a Shar-Pei. Sometimes these computerized letters have a small personal touch at the end, a question about how our own children are faring now that they're out of the house and out in the world. But even with the personal touch, they remain letters to no one in particular. It is the telephone, not the postage stamp, that keeps me bound to friends and kinfolk from Texas to Massachusetts.

But there seems to be one significant survivor of the general demise of personal correspondence. For reasons I don't profess to understand, most of my friends who are gardeners also write letters, long and chatty ones that keep me up with the course of their daily lives, while celebrating each new season in their gardens. Two or three times a week another letter arrives, and since my friends live all over the country, my mailbox is a window on the world of horticulture in the United States. In my mail in February it is simultaneously spring and winter. The first daffodils are blooming in North Carolina, one friend tells me. Another, in New Hampshire, writes that the only blossoms in sight are the frost flowers that form every night on her windowpanes. In late August, my friend in New Hampshire tells me that his tomato plants went black in last night's chilly wind, but in North Carolina the bounty will continue another six weeks at least.

Few books on horticulture have quite the precise observations, the eye for small details, that are common in the letters that come from friends who garden, and there's a reason. Books on gardening address a large audience, and they deal in generalities. Letters address an audience of one, and they deal with the day-to-day events in one small plot of earth, the heartening triumphs and the discouraging failures that take place there, to the joy or the disappointment of the gardener. If there's a prolonged drought or if the winter is so severe that supposedly hardy shrubbery dies back to the roots or perishes altogether, these things will find their place in the letters that go from one gardener to another.

My friends share their plant discoveries with me, of course, writing to say, for example, that I shouldn't let another year pass by without trying *Pyncnanthemum tenuifolium* or mountain mint, a native perennial distinguished for its strong and refreshing scent and for its cloud of lavender flowers during much of the summer. Or maybe it's *Lilium formosanum*, which blooms late in October, tall and magnificent for its white blossoms much resembling Easter lilies. I reply in kind, of course, sharing my enthusiasm for favorite plants like *Gaura lindheimeri*, a perennial from Texas that does well in the Northeast and produces pinkish white flowers like tiny butterflies nonstop from early June to the first good frost in the fall.

But more than words may be exchanged between letter-writing friends who also garden. Mountain mint and *Lilium formosanum* now grow in my garden, gifts from friends. Oftentimes the plants are not available from nurseries. New rarities finding a place in my own plot one year included *Lygodium japonicum*, a graceful fern from Japan that will climb a trellis indoors or out, and a strain of hellebore that has proved to be more beautiful than any available from commercial sources. These hellebores I treasure especially, since the stock came originally from the garden in Charlotte, North Carolina, of the late Elizabeth Lawrence, a gardening writer I admire enormously (and a prodigious letter writer herself). I have sent gaura seeds to many of my gardening friends, likewise a truly superior form of the New England aster that seems to do well from Griffin, Georgia, to Bangor, Maine.

Gardening friends who write to one another and exchange plants and information about plants are an ancient fraternity, one that Peter Collinson of London, in a letter written in 1733 to John Custis in Williamsburg, Virginia, called "the brothers of the spade," by which he meant gardeners who found in one another kindred spirits, even when an ocean separated them. This fraternity, which is also a sorority, since the love of horticulture knows no differences of gender, has some illustrious members, including Thomas Jefferson. His correspondence with friends in the United States, Great Britain, and Europe often touched on questions of gardening, as he tried, unsuccessfully, to grow oranges at Monticello, and, successfully, to introduce *Magnolia grandiflora* and other fine native American plants to his own brothers of the spade in France and England.

I claim no statesmen among my gardening correspondents, and they vary as much among themselves as the plants that grow in their gardens. Some are wealthy. Some are not. Some lean politically to the left, some to the right. Some are men, some women, some much younger than me, some considerably older. They have in common just two things. They like to write letters, and they know precisely what the British horticultural writer Gertrude Jekyll meant when she proclaimed that "the love of gardening is a seed that once sown never dies."

Critter Ridder
to the Rescue

ANYONE WHO SPEAKS of "my garden" is guilty of an act of hubris, for much more lives in gardens than gardeners and the plants that grow there. From viruses and nematodes on up, the plot I tend teams with life, some of it much more welcome than others. I love the monarchs and the swallowtails that come in summer, but not the Japanese beetles or gypsy-moth caterpillars that fortunately pay me little visit, so far. In winter I'm not keen on the starlings that throw tantrums in the bird feeders, hurling more seed to the ground than they consume with such poor table manners. But I put up with them for the sake of the purple finches, wrens, chickadees, and other birds with daintier habits, and the cardinals that are the aristocrats of the feeders. Besides, what the starlings throw to the ground will be eaten by the doves that prefer it there.

My garden also has its mammals. Some are visitors, like Cutty, the Scotch terrier belonging to a son and daughter-in-law, who likes to pull labels out of the flower bed, causing me later confusion when

I look at a hemerocallis but don't know which one it is. Some are more permanent presences. There are two feral cats, which accept food as their due but will not allow themselves to be touched. There are a few chipmunks, but not as many as there used to be before the cats turned up. Some fifteen or twenty squirrels call my garden and the garden next door home. They are fat and they seem happy, as they plant the walnuts that will sprout all through the flower beds next spring, thanks to the bad memories squirrels have for where they left things.

Then there's my raccoon. Raccoons are nocturnal, so I seldom see it. I see its evidences—dead goldfish on the lawn next to a tiny pool, garbage cans knocked over and ravaged, droppings on the roof of a low shed. I did see my raccoon at dusk last summer. I was having pizza with my wife on the deck, and the telephone in the kitchen rang, a long-distance call for us both. A few minutes later, the unwatched pizza was in the middle of the backyard, as my raccoon feasted on pepperoni, mushrooms, and extra cheese. And one night last fall I woke up during a ferocious lightning storm, just as a bolt that hit nearby illumined the form of the raccoon standing up, leaning with his front paws against the window, as if begging for sanctuary.

I prefer seeing as little of this racoon as possible, and would mourn not at all if it went elsewhere to live. Raccoons are cute, but they can carry rabies, and they are very nasty when cornered.

So I wasn't thrilled at all the other day when my neighbor from across the street telephoned with the news. There was a hole in the eave above our attic, and she had just seen an animal enter. It was, she thought, a raccoon. Every week we go to the attic several times. Filled with boxes of children's toys saved for grandchildren, boxes of books I have no other room for but do not wish to throw away, and furniture that might have use someday, it would probably strike a raccoon as a dandy home.

I called the town dog catcher. He sticks to dogs and cats. I looked in the telephone directory under Pest Exterminators and started calling such services. Most of them would gladly take care of my termites, roaches, or silverfish, if I had any, but they wanted no transactions with a creature that might bite them.

Meanwhile, my wife was delivering her reasoned assessment that whatever had made that hole in the eave and might be living there, it was not a raccoon. Our house has two stories—and the ceilings are high, so the house is quite tall. How, she asked, could a raccoon get there to begin with? It must be a squirrel, she said.

I pointed out a possible path. The pergola over the deck is latticed on one side, an easy ladder for a raccoon. The hardy kiwi vines on the pergola have also climbed a standpipe that reaches up the side of the house to the roof.

Then I found in the phone book a little ad for a company called Critter Ridders. The woman who answered was not only willing to deal with a raccoon, but also seemed knowledgeable about all sorts of unwanted mammals in attics or elsewhere. She said that she and another animal-removal technician could be over in a couple of hours. She gave me her rate schedule—$85 for a squirrel, $150 for a raccoon, $250 for a skunk. The animal would be trapped harmlessly and set free—to find a home in someone else's attic, no doubt.

She was as prompt as her promise, and she and her fellow technician were formidable in their gear and paraphernalia. My wife had to go in another room to keep from laughing; it all, she thought, looked like *Ghostbusters.* They wore heavy gloves and they carried nets. I gave them free rein in the attic. They found some evidence of powder-post beetles eating the rafters that they would gladly take care of, but no droppings or other signs of a raccoon.

The hole in the eave did not seem to lead into the attic at all, but they would investigate it. Meanwhile, just in case, they installed a large trap baited with walnuts, which they believed irresistible to raccoons, beyond even kitchen garbage or pizza. They would come back in a day or so to check the trap.

Ladders went up outside, and one of the technicians came back with a report. It was a squirrel's nest. The best procedure would be to spread repellent and seal off the hole with hardware cloth. They could do it for eighty-five dollars. And they did.

How would I deal with a raccoon in my attic, apart from Critter Ridders, if one turned up? For that matter, if there had been one there and no local business specializing in removing unwanted mammals that bite, what might I have done?

A friend has given me an answer: rock and roll. He had a raccoon, a mother with four young, who decided to live in his chimney, right above the fireplace. He got a radio, tuned it to a hard-rock music station, turned up the volume, and put it in the fireplace.

Several hours later the mother raccoon vacated, taking her cubs one by one to another, more peaceful retreat where they wouldn't have to listen to heavy metal.

The Packages
That Come in
the Spring,
Tra La

ONCE THE SPRING ORGY of azaleas and dogwoods in full bloom up and down the streets of my neighborhood is upon us, the most frantic time in a busy gardener's life is at its end. I mean the mail-order-nursery shipping season, which starts in early March, peaks in late April, and slows almost to a standstill the second week of May. Every three or four days during this time, the letter carrier or the UPS truck arrives at my gate bringing packages of plants I ordered in January or February.

Each arrival produces its flurry of activity, as I open the parcel, unpack it, check the invoice against the original order, and rush to get the plants in the ground.

In general, the contents of these packages testify to the high quality of the American nursery business today. There are some disappointments, of course. The small nursery in California from which I ordered some new hardy fuchsias was sold out. Another nursery turned out this year to sell dearly what it had bought cheaply from a supplier, charging far too much for some shrubs that were mere twigs. But there are also unexpected pleasures, inasmuch as many nurseries tuck gift plants into the parcels they send out, things they think I'd like to try, often things I wouldn't think of ordering myself. Two examples will suffice. One was a diminutive veronica called 'Waterperry', which grows only three inches tall and covers itself in early May with appealing lavender-blue blossoms like tiny open chalices. The other was *Lippia dulcis.* Used by the Aztecs to sweeten drinks, its leaves are indeed as delicious as the sugarcane I used to nibble as a child.

But what especially fascinates me during this annual shipping season is not the plants that arrive but the way they are packed. There seems to be no standardization whatsoever among nurserymen as regards getting plants to their customers with the least amount of damage in transit.

There is first of all the matter of what the order is packed in, the protective cushioning that surrounds it. Some use excelsior, some Styrofoam popcorn, and some old newspapers, either dry or slightly moist. My heart lies with the newspaper folks. Excelsior and Styrofoam popcorn are unruly materials, apt to blow about the yard and add to the chores of the spring cleanup. Styrofoam, moreover, isn't biodegradable, and ends up adding to the American garbage crisis. (It also has a somewhat indelicate nickname. Puzzled by a nursery owner's reference to these pellets as "ATs," I finally asked. The initials stand for "angel turds.") But newspapers? It can be fun to stop unpacking the order for a moment and find out what's going on in Oroville, California, or Fletcher, North Carolina.

The real originality and ingenuity, however, appears in the way the individual plants in the order are wrapped. The list of materials used is long, including plastic film, brown paper bags, plastic sandwich bags, aluminum foil, cellophane tape, rubber bands, spaghnum moss (either dry or moist), staples, paper-covered wire, and of course newspaper. The permutations among these and other materials are so vast that I've never known two nurseries to pack their plants in identical ways.

But not all the plants that arrive at my door each spring come from nurseries. Gardeners are a notoriously generous tribe, and gardeners who are friends generally give each other plants in an almost constant exchange. Sometimes the friend lives next door or across the street and just shows up one spring morning with a clump of Siberian iris in one hand and a snakeroot or cimicifuga in the other. Sometimes the friend lives in another part of the country and resorts to the mail or the parcel services.

These shipments from friends are always more fascinating than those from commercial nurseries, for several reasons. First, they generally contain personal notes. "I don't know what this is, but it blooms in August, with blue and fragrant flowers. It won't take over the place, but it does like to stroll a bit from where you put it originally." Second, they sometimes are casually packed, just thrown into a box sans newspapers or Styrofoam or excelsior. The plants generally do just fine; the fact that they survive testifies to just how tough a plant can be. And finally, commercial nurseries grow their plants in so-called planting mixes, combinations of bark and peat and vermiculite, not in real earth. Friends give us a look at their dirt when they send their plants, and together they all testify to the diversity of conditions under which Americans pursue their lives as gardeners. Some garden on a clay so heavy as to be genuine cause for despair. Some have soil so sandy that their summer water bills must be disheartening. A few lucky souls have that rare soil that's just right, light enough to be friable and easily worked, rich enough in organic matter to be properly fertile, and with just enough fine particles of clay to hold moisture well.

Into my garden I welcome all plants, once they are unpacked, those from both nurseries and friends, hoping that they will be happy on my own patch of soil.

On Helping
a Bird

WITHOUT A CENSUS of the fauna in my small garden or other hard data to back me up, I am still of the firm conviction that the population of birds that either live on my property or swoop into it on regular visits has risen sharply in recent years. Reasons aren't hard to propound. Destruction of woodlands in the county to make way for houses and shopping malls has been heavy, resulting in the loss of wildlife habitats. Birds seeking their own piece of real estate have, out of necessity, moved onto mine.

I have also been a good host, providing water and food for little finches and sparrows, for raucous blue jays, and for wrens and nuthatches and chickadees. Doves sit on the telephone wires, waiting for the seeds that smaller birds scatter to the ground from the several feeders on the premises. The thick shrubbery that surrounds the garden gives birds shelter in the summer and a good crop of fruits and berries in the fall. After twenty years, the organic content of my soil is high enough that a robin can always count on finding an earthworm with little difficulty.

The best way to enjoy birds in a garden, I believe, is just to live alongside them, recognizing that you owe them a lot. Some of them eat insects that left uneaten would eat my plants. Even if I had only vegetarian birds, they still would bring the pleasures of their songs, the interest of their constant movement, and, in the cases of blue jays and male cardinals, the brilliant colors of their plumage. They also are a constant reminder of the wild nature that humans sometimes forget, some might say to the peril of their souls.

Early summer is a crucial time for birds, often fraught with danger or tragedy. A robin's egg on the ground is one less robin in the garden. Feral cats and other animals (including, I'm sorry to report to anyone who shares Walt Disney's view of nature, birds) destroy nests and nestlings. Fledglings fall to the ground somewhat prematurely. My own garden has been an anxious place for the past two weeks, as some starling parents and one catbird have tried to herd their precocious offspring into the protection of the shrubbery.

I have made it a practice not to intervene by going to the aid of a young bird, but I made an exception one late spring night. As I was moving a hose, I heard the fluttering of wings and some distressed cheeps in a clump of phlox at my feet. Then something pecked me hard on the toe, right through my sandals.

I reached down and scooped up a young cardinal with dripping-wet feathers. It protested vigorously, but I decided that I would save it if I could, so I brought it inside to the bathroom. I called a friend who knows a lot about birds. She said to feed it tuna fish, or cooked ground beef, impaling the food on a plastic straw when I preferred it to the cardinal's gaping conical beak.

I took the bird in one hand, the straw in the other. My avian guest had a lusty appetite. It also had a fiercely independent eye, a sign of spunk. My wife was watching, and I told her that the bird would live, that I thought it could fly, and that it no longer seemed afraid of me, as its pounding heart was beginning to calm down.

On Helping a Bird

No sooner had I made this observation than I made another. I had a handful of dead bird in my hand. I also had a heavy heart. My best intentions of helping a fellow creature of the garden had resulted in a tragedy—a small one, but a tragedy nonetheless. I buried the bird and began to brood. It was clear: I had scared the cardinal to death by an act of tender mercy.

For the next day or two, I asked friends what I should have done. Their replies were fairly vague, but there were two common themes. One was that a young bird that has fallen out of its nest probably has something wrong with it and has been rejected by its parents. The other was that such birds are doomed, will always die, and are best left to their fate.

I was not happy with the crude Darwinian tone of this advice. So I brooded some more, until another friend told me about a woman named Joan Schimmelman in northern California. Ms. Schimmelman has saved many a bird and released it back into the wild. I lost no time in getting in touch with her, to ask what I had done wrong.

Her answers were reassuring. It is highly unlikely that I had scared the cardinal to death, even if, she added, birds seem to dislike making direct eye contact with humans. The bird in my flower bed might have been wounded by a cat or other animal, but the most likely cause of death was hypothermia from being drenched with cold water. Food, she said, was not the first priority, but warmth. I should have put the bird in a warm, dry place, perhaps in a small box on a heating pad turned on to low, with a towel as insulation. As for food, the best choice nowadays would be a high-protein puppy chow, slightly moistened with warm water.

Joan Schimmelman clearly knows what she is doing. Right now she is rehabilitating a heron and a nest of finches who lost their parents.

The next time I try to rescue a bird—and I probably will—I'll try to keep it warm, and then I'll call for help from someone who is trained in completing such rescue successfully.

Such help, it turns out, is not hard to find. There is an organization called the International Wildlife Rehabilitation Center, whose telephone number on weekdays from nine A.M. to four P.M. Pacific Standard Time is (707)864-1761. This center maintains a list of volunteers in most parts of the United States who have been professionally trained in rescuing baby and fledgling birds, as well as other creatures of the wild who often dwell with us in suburbs and cities.

One volunteer, I learned from the center, lives right in my own county, just a few miles away. I have put her telephone number in my address book, under Bird.

Garden Visits

THOSE GARDENERS WHO are content to take pleasure from their own gardens and only theirs, I believe, live impoverished lives. The best gardeners I know are those who practice regularly the habit of visiting other gardens. In return, they often invite people to visit their own. Much knowledge of gardening is dispensed in books and in newspaper columns, but it is too often secondhand knowledge. Gardens themselves, not words about gardening, are the best teachers.

I love Longwood Gardens, Winterthur, Wave Hill, and a good many other gardens that are open to the public, but visiting a private garden provides a different kind of pleasure. Such visits teach not only lessons about new and unfamiliar plants, but also about the personal style that is always needed to give a garden its sense of individuality, perhaps even its soul.

I visit many gardens each year, and I get a fair number of visitors myself. Most of them are delightful company, but a few are not. To put it baldly, they are boors. After discussing the matter with several friends who also receive the occasional boorish visitor, I have compiled a list of rules to follow in order to be a welcome guest and not an insensitive lout.

Rule 1. Do not show up unexpectedly. If your host has two thousand daffodils to plant in one day, company is not welcome. Furthermore, all gardens have their untidy times, and the gardener you plan to visit may wish to straighten things up a bit.

Rule 2. Do not wander into the flower beds to take a closer look at some plant that catches your eye. Plants that get crushed underfoot often stay crushed the rest of the year. An exception is grass. It's okay to walk on it unless there's a sign saying not to.

Rule 3. Ignore the weeds. The owner of the garden already knows they are there. He or she may even mention them or apologize for them.

Rule 4. This rule also has to do with weeds. Don't think you are doing the gardener a favor by pulling some up yourself. You may make things worse by pulling up a dandelion or a plantain without getting all the tap root. You may also be wrong about what's a weed and what isn't. Your host will be furious that you have just exterminated three treasured little plants of some rare perennial. It may in fact even be a dandelion or a chickweed. I have some friends who treasure a white form of dandelion and a plantain with purple leaves. Another friend has a giant variety of chickweed that she admires almost passionately.

Rule 5. Remember that you are visiting a garden, not a piece of real estate. Questions about how much people paid for their properties are out of bounds.

Rule 6. Ask permission before you take photographs. It will generally be given, but it is a courtesy to ask first. And if you use a tripod, be very careful. Tripods are often injurious to the health of plants.

Rule 7. Show interest in what you are seeing. Don't talk at length about your own garden, and above all, don't tell your host that earlier in the day you visited another garden that was really good.

Rule 8. If you are visiting a garden with a group of friends, do not act as if your host is hearing-impaired. A friend just told me that she had two women visit her garden last week. The visitors gave a running commentary about what they didn't like. "Why do you think she's growing this ugly thing?" "Look at the color clash between those two roses." "The greenhouse is too small to do anything with, and it's in the wrong place anyway." After ten minutes, my friend excused herself and asked her pair of boors to shut the gate, please, when they left.

Rule 9. If a plant is labeled, do not remove the label from the ground to read it more easily. It is easy to stick a label back in the wrong spot, creating for the gardener a mystery to come. Ask your host what the plant is instead. If he or she removes the label and puts it back where it shouldn't be, you carry no guilt.

Rule 10. This rule is already covered neatly in one of the Ten Commandments. Thou shalt not steal. Take no cuttings. Remove no seeds. Dig up no little plants from around big clumps and put them in your pocket. You may, however, if you feel special lust for some plant or other, ask which nurseries sell it. You may even comment, "Now there's a plant I would almost kill for." Such enthusiasm will often send the gardener off to the shed to get a trowel and a pot to fulfill your heart's desire.

There may be many rules for hosts, too. But I can think of only two.

Rule 1. Never say "You should have come next week. Everything will look much better then." It may be true, but the "should" implies a deficiency or failing on the part of visitors. It's really not their fault that they came too early to catch the early fall spectacle of the lablab beans or to see dog fennel in flower.

Rule 2. Unless the visitors are bona fide boors, show some generosity of spirit. Send them home with a clump of violets or an especially nice sempervivum, something that they can grow as a memento of their visit. These gifts from one gardener to another have a powerful cumulative effect in increasing the diversity of plants in our nation's gardens.

Middle Ground Between the Phile and the Phobe?

SOONER OR LATER, every dedicated American gardener must make up his or her mind on an inescapable question: what is the proper attitude to adopt toward the British and their horticulture?

There are two opposing camps among us.

One is made up of the great number of us who are Anglophiles. If we belong to this group with true orthodox fervor, the signs are obvious on our bookshelves and in our toolsheds. We read and reread the classic British horticultural texts by Gertrude Jekyll, William Robinson, E. A. Bowles, and, a bit closer to our own day, by Vita Sackville-West. We try to keep afloat in the great tide of contemporary British gardening books that washes up in our bookstores each year.

We, if we be real Anglophiles, will subscribe to the English weekly *Country Life,* and we may not spend much time reading *Horticulture,* an American magazine (which itself displays some considerable deference to All Things British).

We cherish our British-forged secateurs—and have learned to call them that, instead of pruning shears. We are likely to own wooden Sussex trugs for carrying the secateurs and newly harvested cut flowers or marrows about the garden. We eagerly browse the pages of such upscale mail-order hardware dealers as Smith and Hawken, which despite selling some products of Japanese or German manufacture appears so quintessentially British that it seems almost an aberration in the cosmos that it should be located in Mill Valley, California.

In May our hearts yearn to be in London at the Chelsea Flower Show. Our ideal summer vacation would be spent motoring from Kew to Wisley, from Hidcote to Sissinghurst, and from Mottisfont Abbey to Great Dixter.

Our attitudes toward ourselves, meanwhile, are tinged with feelings of inferiority. We feel, to put it gently, just a bit shabby about having to garden in America. In horticulture, if not in the political order, the American Revolution might just as well never have happened. Great Britain remains the mother country of gardeners, and we are mere colonials.

Our respective climates, of course, foster this view. England is blessed with a gentle and benign maritime climate, and further blessed with the Gulf Stream, a gift from the New World to the Old. We are, in much of this country, cursed with a continental climate, characterized by frigid and nasty winters, fleeting and unstable springs, and long, sweltering, humid summers. It is not difficult to understand the appeal of the refrain "O to be in England" during nine months of the year at least.

The other camp one might take to be our Anglophobes of gardening, except for one thing. Such people may exist, but I have yet to run into a genuine case of horticultural Anglophobia—someone who hates anything that is British purely because it is British. I have never heard anyone seriously express the longing to divert the Gulf Stream, so that Great Britain's flora would be reduced to a tundra of mosses and lichens. There is no enthusiastic lobby in this country for an embargo on British garden writing, although I have heard some mutterings of late that a fair number of books originating there have a me-too similarity and are long on toothsome pictures and short on readable and useful text.

These mutterings come from the people who are really in the opposite camp—not Anglophobes, but Anglophilophobes, to coin a word that may not exist but ought to.

Anglophilophobes often start out as Anglophiles, until it suddenly hits them that in fawning over the glories of the British garden they may be neglecting equally glorious possibilities of their own. I can name the exact moment when I became a convinced Anglophilophobe. It was the day I heard that in my native city of Dallas, Texas, money was being raised to put in a summer border of herbaceous perennials, designed according to the color principles set forth early in this century by Gertrude Jekyll. The border, if I have it right, was to be accompanied by an English woodland garden, filled with magnificent rhododendrons.

I think I may have giggled when I heard about this scheme. To begin with, Dallas is so torrid in the summer, with days and days on end of temperatures in the upper nineties or higher, that any sensible inhabitant contrives to be outdoors no longer than absolutely necessary. The temperature is just about as hard on plants as on people. The soil there, furthermore, is generally a degraded chalk—black gumbo clay over limestone and thus alkaline. Most rhododendrons are unhappy except in acid soil.

One good principle of gardening in Britain is to "consult the genius of the place," as Alexander Pope put it. Trying to make an English border à la Miss Jekyll or an English woodland garden in north-central Texas is to try to emulate the example, while ignoring the principle. The British equivalent would be to watch "Dallas" on television and then to hope to plant a scrub forest of mesquite trees on the grounds of Windsor Castle.

There are other routes to becoming an Anglophilophobe. I hear rumors of friends who get annoyed when British garden designers are imported here to impart their inspiration to new gardens, out of the assumption that no one in America can be trusted with the assignment. Some people get grumpy over the superstition that Vita Sackville-West invented the idea of a garden primarily of white plants, considering that the American historian Alice Morse Earle described just such a garden, remembered from her childhood, in *Old Time Gardens* (1903). Louise Beebe Wilder also wrote about a white garden she had admired, in Wales, in 1929, before Harold Nicolson and Sackville-West acquired Sissinghurst, where there was no garden at all when they started out.

I enjoy reading British books on gardening. Canon Ellacombe's *In a Glouchestershire Garden* is as fresh as it was a century ago. Vita Sackville-West's lapidary essays deserve respect, not only for their infectious enthusiasm for a wide range of plants worth growing, but also for the lessons they can teach a writer about how much can be done with so few words. Margery Fish's books instruct and inspire beginning gardeners and experienced ones as well, no matter which side of the Atlantic Ocean they call home, because she was so utterly free of the snobbery, toward plants as well as people, that is not unknown among the tribe of gardeners in England. Among writers more nearly my contemporaries, I admire Rosemary Verey, Beth Chatto, and Penelope Hobhouse. I find Christopher Lloyd often amusing.

And yet, it is a patent fact that on many a matter the British have nothing to teach us, for far too much that is good counsel in England is a recipe for failure in much of the United States. Picking up the nearest British book at hand, almost at random, I find within a couple of paragraphs enthusiastic words for two vines, *Clematis armandii* and *C. cirrhosa.* I have never seen *C. armandii* in flower, but purely for its dark green leaves it is one of the loveliest vines imaginable. It's not winter-hardy much north of Charlotte, North Carolina, however, and even there some years it's killed back to the roots. *Clematis cirrhosa,* native to virtually frost-free areas of the Mediterranean basin, is even more tender: when a friend of mine in

Durham, North Carolina, got it through the winter and coaxed it into bloom, she sent out invitations to see it. In the same book, a few pages farther, I find a discussion of *Magnolia grandiflora* and instructions on how to grow it espaliered on a south-facing wall. In England, it is apparently a frail, rather spindly thing, worth nursing along, however, for the small crop it bears in summer of immense white flowers with a lemony spice. But the solid American truth about our native *M. grandiflora,* in its natural range in the Southeast, is that it is a tree of immense proportions, scarcely suitable for anything less than a very large garden. It also is best used at the edge of a garden, away from other plants, for it will swamp them. It produces extraordinarily dense shade beneath its branches all year round. It also litters the earth with large, waxy leaves so thick that they decompose very slowly, smothering anything in the vicinity, except possibly poison ivy and Japanese honeysuckle. And I've never seen any British book even mention the most wonderful thing of all about this magnolia: its fruits. In late summer or early autumn, the slightly fuzzy but also slightly armored seed cases, which look like hand grenades and are about the same size, begin to open, revealing glistening, varnished-looking large seeds reminiscent of watermelon seeds, except bright scarlet. The seeds also hold a great surprise: crushed slightly, they have a strong scent of bay rum that is every bit as sensually delightful as the lemon of its flowers. It takes an American to know the true problems and the true glories of our southern magnolia. Anglophilia is no help at all.

The British themselves, of course, are not to be held responsible for anglophilia. They are British, and love themselves no more than any other people love themselves. Anglophilia is *our* problem, and to the extent that it pertains to horticulture, it rests on an optical illusion, a misperception of American and British social history. We go on pilgrimage to Sissinghurst and other splendid British gardens. We justly admire what we see there, and we come home dissatisfied with Dallas or Nashville or Boston, and with our private gardens. What we forget is that when the great British gardens were laid out they were the possessions of the aristocracy or the landed gentry, private gardens open only to family and friends and invited house-guests. The realities of taxation in Britain since World War II have put many houses and their gardens into the care of the National Trust, which maintains them not just as the evidences of the history of privilege, but also as tourist attractions, for Britain's own citizens and for visitors from other countries as well. Other splendid gardens not in the National Trust are on view only because their owners have put a tin cup outside the gates, charging admission to people who wish to visit.

The gardens in England that I really would like to see are the small and personal gardens, owned by people who plant and tend them themselves, because labor is no cheaper or easier to come by there than it is in the United States.

Adventures
in Teaching
Horticulture

FOR SOME TIME now, my professional life has been divided into two separate compartments. I teach philosophy at Stockton State College in Pomona, New Jersey, initiating the uninitiated into the thought of Plato, Saint Augustine, Descartes, and other influential Western philosophers. That's one compartment, and it has little to do with the other, which is writing about gardening for the general public, using my experience in my own backyard and my observations of the gardens other people have made.

Stockton is a fairly unusual college in that it encourages its professors not only to teach well within their own disciplines but also to cross disciplinary boundaries, sometimes in partnership with colleagues in other departments. (But we call departments "programs," partly to discourage departmentalization.) Thus a professor of poetry and a professor of mathematics may combine efforts to teach a course on the nature and purposes of education.

Given Stockton's interdisciplinary character, it's not particularly surprising that some of my colleagues have for a long time urged me to offer a course on horticulture. But until the spring of 1988, I resisted, for a number of reasons.

First, I have no systematic training in the subject. From experience, I know a good bit about some horticultural topics. But I know nothing whatsoever about others. Shrubs and ornamental perennials I'm fairly sound on, but I'd be badly over my head trying to teach someone about propagating ferns or about bud-grafting techniques or basic plant chemistry. Writing is a pick-and-choose matter, where some subjects can be avoided altogether, but a course in horticulture seems to require covering all the bases.

Second, gardening is my hobby, and I have philosophical reservations about people teaching their hobbies.

Third, I feared that I might fail. Failure is always one consequence of teaching. I'm virtually certain that for some students the outcome of taking a course in philosophy is the discovery that they don't like it. (Others, of course, make a contrary discovery.) But failure, somehow, would be worse when the topic is horticulture, which deals with the relations between human beings and the plant kingdom, ultimately a far more important matter than Plato's Allegory of the Cave or Descartes's ontological proof of the existence of God. (I know that this observation may sound heretical to at least a few philosophers.)

But I finally gave in, in large part because a botanist, Professor Sandra Bierbrauer, agreed to teach the course with me. Sandy is sound in areas where I'm shaky.

I don't think I succeeded, not according to my hopes or expectations.

Here's what I hoped. We would have some thirty students, none of whom knew a lick about gardening at the outset, all of whom, however, were passionate to learn. By semester's end, they would have mastered the vocabulary that goes with basic horticulture and a bit of botany. They would talk knowingly of "etiolation" and "espalier." They would know the difference between *Cornus florida* and *C. mas*—and understand why the Latin names as well as the common names of dogwood and Cornelian cherry are essential. They would, above all, be discriminating gardeners, meaning that they would have a very wide knowledge of the plants sold commercially and that they would be choosy in populating their own gardens.

At Stockton, and almost everywhere in American higher education during the last gasp of the twentieth century, one of the buzzwords is *outcomes*. Public officials and trustees expect that educators will be able to articulate the intended outcomes of their activities among their students, and there's some fond hope of being able to measure the achievements of students (to see if we're doing what we say we're doing, or just wasting time and money). I distrust this notion of measurable outcomes for a couple of reasons. One is that the outcomes may be decades in surfacing. The other is that they are highly idiosyncratic and unpredictable. (I'm still puzzled by the student who appeared in my office one day, a devout Lutheran when I had known him eight years earlier, to tell me that he was abandoning a career in medical research, moving to Jerusalem, converting to Orthodox Judaism, and then studying to become a rabbi. He attributed all of these changes in his life to taking my seminar on Søren Kierkegaard.)

Nevertheless, Sandy and I got together in the college cafeteria, brainstormed a bit with a legal pad, and put together for our students the following handout for the first day of class.

Some Outcomes of Studying Horticulture

1. Grow plants from seed.

2. Grow plants from cuttings (stem, root, leaf).

3. Divide an overgrown clump of a perennial.

4. Know which perennials need regular and frequent division, and which can be left untouched for years.

5. Know the names of and be able to recognize ten common annuals likely to be found in a garden center in the spring.

6. Know the names of ten not-so-common annuals you probably will have to raise from seed if you want to grow them.

7. Know the names of ten common perennials.

8. Know, among these ten common perennials, the cultivar names of those that are superior in some respect.

9. Know what *cultivar* means.

10. Be able to make a list of plants that will be interesting in the winter landscape.

11. Be able to identify ten deciduous trees or shrubs and ten evergreen ones in late winter.

12. Make an inventory or census of the trees and shrubs growing in a two-block area in a suburban neighborhood, assessing which ones are most frequently found, which least frequently, and determining what their place of origin is.

13. Be able, in time, to plan a garden in which no shrub or tree that grows there also grows anywhere within a two-mile radius of your home.

14. Know where to look for reliable information when you are ignorant or confused or uncertain.

15. Be able, if a friend of yours buys a new house in a former cornfield and asks for advice, to give informed and intelligent recommendations about native trees and shrubs and perennials.

16. Be able to identify, on sight and by name, ten troublesome weeds.

17. Develop a fair grasp of the history of styles of gardening in western Europe, Great Britain, and the United States over the last several centuries.

18. Understand the basic similarities and differences between western European and Oriental styles of gardening.

19. Come to know your own mind, develop your own taste, acquire enthusiasms for plants you like especially.

20. Display bravery with Latin names.

21. Know what plants, both garden plants and houseplants, are sufficiently toxic that they shouldn't be grown by parents whose children are small.

22. Know what plants have some toxic parts and other edible ones.

23. Know what roadside and meadow plants you might safely feed on in an emergency.

24. Know where the wild ancestors of all the plants in a supermarket produce department originally grew.

25. Take pleasure in gardening, above all else.

Sandy and I thought of a great many other outcomes, but we thought that these twenty-five were quite a full plate for a lifetime, much less a single course.

Our students turned out to be not at all the horticultural blank slates we had expected. Some were. But others enrolled in the course already equipped with considerable knowledge. One student, when I talked about the insect problems that plagued the white birch in southern New Jersey, corrected me immediately: the trees that garden centers label as white birches are really gray birches. Another student, an art major a few years older than I, came in with photographs of her own garden, testifying that there was little that I or anyone else could teach her.

The course was somewhat chaotic. We didn't have a proper classroom, just a little area curtained off from a large laboratory. We never got round to making out a syllabus. We could use the college greenhouse with only a handful of students at one time, because it had been designed to look pretty at night from the outside, not to function as a place to grow plants and teach in. But we covered a fair amount of territory. We had the students start plants from seeds and root them from cuttings. Sandy talked about plant anatomy, chemistry, and physiology. I showed slides of favorite plants and favorite gardens I had visited. The two of us preached about species loss, the devastation of the tropical rain forests, the urgency of holding onto genetic diversity against some powerful odds. We urged students to read the Tuesday "Science" section of *The New York Times,* clipping any story that seemed to bear on the class.

The semester raced to its end, until the only things remaining were the last lecture, the filling out of the student teacher- and course-evaluation forms that Stockton demands, and the final exams.

I don't know what I said exactly on the last day of teaching, since it's my custom to write out each lecture before it is given and then to keep it in my notebook and speak extemporaneously. But here's what the notes in my computer have for that day:

> You'll have to come to your own conclusions about your experience in this class. I can only say that this has probably turned out to be my most pleasant adventure in teaching thus far. And I have hopes for you, especially those of you who had never sown a seed or rooted a cutting before. I hope that our course will be the beginning of something that will change your life, giving it a depth and an enrichment that it would otherwise not have. If so, Sandy and I can't really take the credit. It's the plant kingdom that we have to thank, for every breath we draw, every morsel of food we eat, for almost everything that makes life a possibility on this planet. Certainly one of the lessons of the course is the interconnectedness of all that is on earth.
>
> There's one special form of interconnectedness to ad-

dress. When you begin to be a gardener, you enter into a rich communion of fellowship. You will never, in the presence of other gardeners, be at a loss for topics of conversation. Once you carry things beyond mowing your lawn and planting a few geraniums, you have entered a world in which there is always something new to learn. You look down one day and there's a mutation in the middle of a clump of daylilies. Or you learn that a prolonged dry wind can lift newly set bedding plants out of window boxes and cause tulips and tiarellas to lean at a forty-five-degree angle, like wind socks. And you also become sooner or later a teacher. Nongardeners may ignore gardeners for years, maybe all their lives, but as soon as someone begins to have an interest, they start asking questions.

Freud said that there are only two things that make life worth living: love and work. Both are at the center of a gardener's life. Here love takes many forms. There is love of plants, love of working with them to produce something that is beautiful or useful or in some other way a source of satisfaction. There is also the love of other people who love plants. Gardeners, for the most part, are neat folks to know. In the whole tribe, there's a very low level of human nastiness and a very high level of generosity.

As for work, there's obviously a lot of it involved in horticulture. I won't dwell on this point here, because I want to make another point altogether. I worry—and Sandy may also—about the current generation of college students and the values they profess. Many of them see college as a practical vehicle to a job after college is over and are very shortsighted about how things really work. What someone majors in is generally irrelevant to what they end up doing in life. Someone can major in some presumably useless subject like art history and end up being very successful in some very practical kind of business. But the point I want to make is that a basic knowledge of horticulture is an extraordinarily useful meal ticket nowadays. Gardening is very hot. Mail-order nurseries that were small-scale operations five or six years ago are now bursting at the seams and in desperate need of personnel who know what they are doing. Chances are that if you've ordered plants this spring, your order hasn't come yet.

There's something highly artificial about the way this course comes to its conclusion. We have only scratched the surface, and we have left a huge number of important topics untouched. Tools (buy the best). Garden design and garden style. The history of gardening in the West and in the Orient. Plant exploration. But we hope that for those of you already interested in gardening, you have found encouragement, and that for those of you who are newcomers, it will prove to have been a good beginning.

Some students, perhaps 20 percent of the class, learned precious little, judging from the final examination. One question, ridiculously simple I thought, called for the common names of four native American shrubs suitable for home landscaping. Some answers I got included Japanese black pine, Chinese dogwood, and Scotch thistle. I concluded that some of the students, as is always the case, took the course not because they had much interest in the topic but because it met Tuesdays and Thursdays at twelve-thirty P.M., a popular hour.

Stockton has another institutional feature, already mentioned, besides its encouragement of interdisciplinary teaching. Students, near the end of the term, evaluate each course and each professor, on a numerical scale from one (lousy) to seven (verging on divinity). I came out at five and a half, which is okay. But the evaluation form also allows students to make comments about the course and its instructors, and one comment that appeared on several of these forms bothered me. In its rudest expression, it came out as "Who gives a [word deleted] about your prejudices?" A gentler student said, "Lacy is sometimes a little unfair to some plants."

Teaching always requires taking into account the ideas, often unexamined ones, that inhabit the minds of students, so if I teach this course again, I'll have to adjust the way I present my "prejudices." But I won't give them up, and I think they are both proper and justified. Prejudice, which I prefer to call discrimination, is a bad thing when it's directed toward people. But it's almost essential to gardeners, as directed toward plants. Every gardener's space and time and budget are finite. The number of different plants he or she can grow is vast, and there are some worthy principles to help in making choices.

One principle is that plants should earn their keep. Something that is beautiful only briefly may reasonably be excluded from the garden. I have for this reason made little effort at growing either Oriental poppies or peonies. Both have a very short period of bloom, but if I had to grow one or the other, it would be peonies, because they have handsome dark green foliage. The foliage of the Oriental poppy, however, looks like a hairy weed, and it is especially ugly in the prolonged agony it suffers in going dormant after flowering.

But there's another principle to consider. Any plant that arouses a gardener's passion is something that not only may but also should have a place in the garden. If someone says that Oriental poppies may bloom briefly, but that nonetheless they are so spectacularly beautiful in their brief bloom that a garden wouldn't be a garden without them, well, that's okay too.

One thing I found very appealing about teaching a course in horticulture, as a change from teaching philosophy, is that in philosophy there are some very good questions, most of which don't have acceptable answers. Horticulture has answers as well as questions. If someone asks, "Do gardenias make good hedges?" the answer is that south of Virginia, except in mountainous regions, they do, but that in New Jersey they aren't winter-hardy. Horticulture is filled with definite facts, unlike philosophy, which has almost no factual content.

But the next time I teach a course in horticulture, I think I'll probably start off with some philosophical points. Egalitarianism, in matters of social arrangements, is one value among many, but there are good reasons for choosing it over its rivals. Egalitarianism, however, is completely out of place in other areas of human life. Music, for instance. Samuel Ramey sings better than I do, and no matter how deeply I might want to sing in his place on the concert stage, I have no right to do so. And it's the same with gardening. 'Pardon Me' and 'Peach Fairy' are far better daylilies than 'Hyperion' and 'Mikado'. To be a real gardener means to be an elitist, not a democrat.

But of course the very best students in the class knew that already, a long, long time ago.

The others? The nongardeners, who started that way and ended that way, to the extent that they could still believe that Scotch thistle was a reasonable guess as a native American shrub (when it isn't a shrub and would be very oddly named were it American)? I hope that a few of them at least may one day catch the horticultural passion all on their own, entering the exciting and absorbing world that is the world of gardening.

Green Invaders

WHEN WE FIRST pick up our trowels and begin to garden, we plant with the hope that what we plant will do well, that it will not only survive but also prosper and thrive. But the lesson comes swiftly: we need also hope that no plant will do so well that it romps everywhere through the garden, showing no regard whatsoever of our wills and wishes. We soon learn that "invasive plants" are dirty words, if not four-letter ones. And we come to read with suspicion any description of a particular plant in a nursery catalog as "vigorous," often a polite way of describing a thug.

Invasive plants may be defined as those that have bad manners. Unlike weeds, which arrive in gardens with no intent on the part of the people who tend them, the invaders arrive by invitation. They are attractive enough to seem desirable, but once they arrive, they take over, much like Sheridan Whiteside in *The Man Who Came to Dinner.* They self-sow, or spread by underground runners, or, in the worst case, by both strategies. The upshot is that they pop up where they are not wanted, often muscling aside more desirable plants with far better manners.

Invasiveness is not an absolute quality. Some plants that misbehave under certain conditions of soil or climate will be model citizens under other conditions. Among the worst plagues in my garden are the descendants of three hybrid tradescantias that have self-sown everywhere in my sandy loam. I would have nothing but tradescantias, except for constant work all during the growing season in missions of search and destroy. But friends who garden on clay don't comprehend my complaint; for them, tradescantias stay put where they are originally placed. Another of my bad actors is the so-called hardy ageratum or *Eupatorium coelestinum.* The people across the street, who aren't gardeners to speak of, have it growing in a long row beside a rail fence. They never water or add compost to the soil, and their eupatoriums bloom beautifully in the fall, producing abundant flowers like a soft blue mist, but never straying from their spot. Mine, in much richer soil that is regularly watered during the summer, roam everywhere. And I may curse my eupatorium in summer, but I always forgive it when autumn comes and it lends a misty blue haze where it has resisted my efforts to grub it out.

I have a sizable list of other plants lovely to behold that I wish nonetheless I had never introduced into my garden. Some of these came with warnings, which I ignored. When I saw pink evening primroses *(Oenothera speciosa)* in a friend's garden, I immediately had to have them. They reminded me of Texas, and the marvelous sight of them growing with bluebonnets in great sheets stretching all the way to the horizon. My friend said I would rue the day, and I did. They are incredibly lovely, soft pink cups veined in olive on low-growing plants that look entirely innocent. But they also spread with almost lightning speed by underground runners and also by seed. Rooting them out is no easy task—nor I think a possible one, since the least bit left in the ground will soon sprout into a vigorous new plant. God meant for these particular evening primroses to grow with bluebonnets in open fields dotted with mesquite trees, not in gardens.

I was also warned about the plume poppy (*Macleaya cordata*, sometimes listed in catalogs as bocconia). I mentioned in a telephone conversation to someone that I had just put it in one of my perennial borders and that I hoped it would survive, since the little pot of it I got from a local garden center was decidedly puny. "Hang up this minute, Allen," she said, "and go right outside and rip it up."

I ignored the advice, and I can now report that the plume poppy, which isn't a poppy at all, is entirely handsome and bold, easily reaching nine feet when in flower. The lower leaves are lobed and immense, like maple leaves on steroids. Their top side is a luscious soft green, with raspberry-colored veins. The lower side is ghostly gray. When the leaves turn and twist in the breeze, the whole plant seems to shimmer and quake, much like aspens in the Rocky Mountains. But in just two growing seasons, the plume poppy has spread about eighteen feet. It is very happy where it is, and I'm afraid that where it will be, before long, will be everywhere in my garden.

Then there's the staghorn sumac (*Rhus typhina* 'Laciniata') I bought many years ago from Wayside Gardens. In certain ways, it is a marvelous shrub or small tree. The large, deeply dissected leaves look like the tree ferns that the less bloodthirsty sorts of dinosaurs may have nibbled on in their heyday. They are a pleasant light green in the summer, and their autumn color is a glowing apricot, with a pinkish cast. But a year or so after a staghorn sumac is planted, it starts to colonize the earth, with new shoots coming up many feet from the original plant. Soon after I got my own sumac, I decided to get rid of it by ripping up every last piece, but a sizable chunk of it took refuge under a huge and venerable yew, where it continues to terrorize my garden with new sprouts.

I have learned my lesson, however. Someone offered me a start of the so-called winter heliotrope *(Petasites fragrans),* telling me that Louise Beebe Wilder had sung the praises of its sweet-smelling blossoms in *The Fragrant Path*, first published in 1932, reprinted in 1990, and still the best book in English on the topic of fragrance. A little bell went off in my head, so I decided to see if Mrs. Wilder had anything else to say about it. Indeed she did. "The questing nose takes pleasure in it on a cold day in early spring," she wrote. But she also said, "Weed it undoubtedly is, and not a retiring one, for the great leaves though they stay close to the ground take up a great deal of room."

I declined the kind offer of winter heliotrope, and I was glad I did, after seeing the way it romps through the woods at the Minnesota Landscape Arboretum near Minneapolis. It is one of the true steamrollers of the plant kingdom.

But there's one invasive plant growing in my garden that I love, although visitors look at it with horror and look at me as if I'm demented. It's a tall bamboo, species unknown, that occupies one corner of the yard. It was polite and well behaved for eight years or so, but now it has made a colony or grove that left to itself would spread everywhere.

We don't leave it to itself. In the spring, when new shoots first break ground where they're not wanted, we cut them off six inches below the surface of the soil with an asparagus knife. After peeling off the outermost layers, we wrap the shoots in moist paper towels and microwave them for ten minutes. Then we eat them like artichokes, squeezing them to separate the tender core from the tougher outer parts. The sweet and nutty flavor is so delicious a treat that our bamboo will never outstep its bounds. Maybe.

Mowing:
A Whir,
Not a Roar

SINCE I DON'T at all trust gardeners who say that they enjoy every last chore that goes with the horticultural life, I gladly make a public confession. For most of my life since the very early teens I have found, until only a month ago, no pleasure whatsoever in mowing a lawn. I would not in fact even have a lawn, except that my wife vetoes any idea of ripping out all the grass and putting in a soft mulch of pine needles among our many flower borders. I have, however, managed over the years to reduce the area of our lawn from around ten thousand square feet to a patch of grass behind the house roughly the size of a putting green.

Many of my neighbors use lawn-mowing services, contracting with one of several companies that own a few trucks and much machinery and have a good supply of college students to do the work. Some of us, however, are holdouts, including me. We mow our own lawns.

I know my reasons. First, it costs a lot of money to hire others to do the mowing—money I'd rather spend on plants, which offer less ephemeral pleasure than having neatly trimmed turf for a day or two. Second, it strikes me that people shouldn't have lawns if they aren't willing to care for them personally, any more than they should have children that they neglect. So every Saturday morning I join in the ritual carried out at the same time by the other holdouts. All up and down the block, there are the same sounds: the clatter of metal against cement as the mowers are taken from the garage; the slight whine of the starters; and then the roar of the gasoline engines as the mowing gets underway.

It may be a ritual, but not all rituals are pleasant. To begin at the outset, I hate starting the engine. My gasoline mower is balky, and if the temperature is under sixty degrees, it will not start at all, unless left in the sun or even brought into the kitchen to warm the gasoline. Furthermore, I am left-handed and left-footed, and power mowers are made for the right-handed majority of this world, who have the correct limbs in the correct places for pulling the cord to start an engine.

I am, however, now a convert. I love to mow my lawn, so much so that for the past month I have mowed it not just weekly but every other day. But I have not changed—my mower has.

It happened like this. One night in mid-June, I was sitting on the deck, thinking about the sounds of summer—the bird songs each morning at dawn, the distant screech of owls from locations impossible to determine, the katydids that would fill the afternoon and evening air in mid-July, the crickets a little later in the summer, who on some cool mornings would hide in the folds of the morning paper. All these sounds seem eternal somehow, or at least when I hear them in my mid-fifties they call up immediate memories of summers when I was six or seven or eight.

The sound of the gasoline mower, however, is a parvenu, dating back only to the early 1950s. And it replaced a much more pleasant, even harmonious sound, from the days when homeowners mowed their lawns with reel mowers, pushing them by hand. Neighborhoods

then were filled on Saturday mornings with the reassuring whir of
steel against steel. The grass was shaved blade by blade, blades of
grass precisely cut by blades of steel, rather than decapitated by a
metal propeller with a sharp edge.

I wanted to hear that sound once again, so I picked up a catalog
from Smith and Hawken in California, found a reel mower that
looked just fine, dialed an 800 number, and ordered one.

Delivery took a week—during which time my mind and soul
swelled with thoughts of righteousness and ecological awareness.
Cutting the fescue and the white clover and the crabgrass would no
longer help deplete fossil fuel. When I mowed the lawn, I would
no longer spew carbon monoxide and other toxic gases into the
atmosphere. The new mower would furthermore provide some good
exercise.

But when the box arrived and I unpacked the new machine,
solid and responsible virtue was replaced by sheer aesthetic delight.
The mower was as shiny and red in its enameled metal as the scooters
and wagons I had as a child, and as the two-seater sports car I never
managed to get as a young man. I pushed it across a short stretch
of grass, and its rubber tires and precisely machined wheels on ball
bearings made using it no chore at all—and precious little exercise.

It cuts grass cleanly, with no tattered leaf edges like the power
mower left. And the sound is wonderful to hear, a soft whir no louder
than a whisper.

I am no Luddite. I wouldn't return to the days of windup
Victrolas and give up my CD player for anything. I can't imagine
getting rid of my computer and going back to typewriters and carbon
paper. I couldn't do without my fax machine.

But I've given the power mower to one of my sons.

What Avon and Procter and Gamble Won't Tell You

I KNOW the incongruous when I see it, and I saw it at a roadside fruit and vegetable stand near my house some years ago, one Friday before Memorial Day. On a shelf right above the Vidalia onions and the local asparagus, there were a couple of dozen bottles of bath oil—Avon Skin-So-Soft, to be specific. A hand-lettered sign with eight exclamation points proclaimed them to be "available now, great insect repellant." When I mentioned to the checkout clerk the obvious mistake, he said it wasn't a mistake at all. "Try it," he advised. "Just mix it half and half with water, rub it on your arms and legs and hair, and stop swatting bugs."

It made no sense at all, so I bought a four-ounce bottle. My garden has its indigenous fauna, as well as its flora both native and exotic, and much of the fauna is out to get me all summer long. Gnats, mosquitoes, the little triangular biting flies called strawberry flies because they abound in strawberry season, and the dreaded greenhead flies of midsummer, whose thirst for human blood rivals

Count Dracula's—all of these in combination sometimes tempt me
to give up gardening and take up stamp collecting.

In that late May, the gnats were in full possession of my garden,
and the strawberry flies had just arrived. No matter how improbable
the idea might sound, anything that might bring relief from them
was worth a try. Modifying somewhat the old biblical injunction, I
anointed mine self lightly with Skin-So-Soft and went outside to do
some pruning. There was a thick cloud of gnats near the shrubbery,
but they left me alone. So did the strawberry flies. Meanwhile, my
wife, in another part of the garden, was pulling up the first crop of
crabgrass—and swatting gnats. I anointed her with Avon's oil, and
the gnats immediately left her alone.

The stuff worked. What's more, it seemed to work better than
any of the insect repellants we had on hand. It also smelled better.

But the evidence for the anti-gnat properties of Skin-So-Soft
was strictly anecdotal, and I don't trust anecdotal evidence, since it
leads to stories about flying saucers and eight-year-old boys who
perform emergency surgery with can openers in those tabloid newspapers the congenitally credulous buy at grocery store checkout
counters.

So I decided to consult an authority, my pharmacist, asking if
he had heard about a bath oil that kept insects away. "Oh yes," he
said, "Avon Skin-So-Soft. We don't sell it here, but my wife gets it
from her Avon representative. We use it all summer whenever we
go outside."

On Tuesday after Memorial Day, I called Avon Products in
Manhattan and asked for the publicity department. The very pleasant woman who answered turned out to be hesitant about this
particular use of the company's product. Yes, of course, she had
heard some rumors that some customers were convinced it kept
annoying insects at bay. There would seem to be considerable word
of mouth to that effect, in some parts of the country. But Avon
advertised it only as a skin moisturizer, period.

I said I was puzzled. If people were in fact buying Skin-So-Soft to keep from being bitten whenever they went out to garden or to fish, and if the product was effective, then why didn't Avon proclaim its merits publicly? She said there were a couple of reasons. One was that it would probably have to seek governmental approval. The other was that Avon was purely a cosmetics company. Its business lay exclusively in making people look better, smell better, and feel luxurious in the bathtub or shower. Gnats and mosquitoes somehow didn't fit the image the company wanted in the public mind.

Next, I called the Food and Drug Administration in Washington. My first highly placed source there said that officially she knew nothing about Skin-So-Soft. But she had just joined a wildflower study group and on the advice of her fellow members had bought a bottle before going on her first field trip. She suggested that I talk with someone else, so I placed another phone call. My second source knew nothing, either officially or unofficially. He also laughed several times during our conversation, being quite amused by the idea that a company like Avon would be reluctant to speak out about the unintended usefulness of one of its products. Before we hung up, he asked me to repeat the name of the bath oil: he had a fishing trip coming up in Maine and he'd try anything that might keep the blackflies away.

I thought by this time that I was probably one of a handful of people in the whole country in possession of this arcane information about Skin-So-Soft. I also thought it was my duty to pass it on, so I mentioned it to the first seven people I ran into during the day's errands. Starting with the postman and ending with a clerk at a garden center, they all professed surprise that I didn't know about the stuff. My belated discovery was, it turned out, nothing but the evidence of my ignorance.

There's a bit more to say, however. I'm on the telephone an hour a day at least, mostly long-distance. And for the next couple of weeks, every conversation included a question to the party on the other end of the line: do you know anything about a bath oil that repels biting insects?

Some, perhaps 50 percent, piped right up and said, "Sure, it's called Skin-So-Soft." One person added that he bathed his dog with it and it seemed to drive fleas away. The rest had never heard of it, so I gave them the good news, the secret of my success in being able to work in the garden, at last free of insect annoyance.

There is more to this story, although the discovery came years later, at a roadside nursery near Beaufort, South Carolina, on a day in early May. Hella and I had been smitten by the Confederate jasmines we had just seen blooming everywhere in Charleston— wonderful vines with lustrous evergreen foliage and multitudinous little creamy blossoms that scented the warm spring air with their luxuriant sweetness. (I have no doubt that some of my fellow native southerners plant Confederate jasmine in every blank spot they can find on a wall or a wrought-iron fence or gate purely because of its name. *Jasmine* is a magic word, to begin with, and *Confederate* calls up images of the gray uniforms worn by the losing side in the Civil War—or the War of Northern Aggression, as some of the handful of Dixie diehards still alive in that part of the country call it. But Confederate jasmine's common name is doubly misleading. It's not a jasmine—*Jasminum*—at all, but a trachelospermum, *Trachelospermum jasminoides*. And, despite what *Wyman's Gardening Encyclopedia* and some other references say about the Confederate part of its name, the name has nothing to do with Jefferson Davis or Robert E. Lee. It comes from the old Confederation of Malay States, where this plant from south China was widely planted, growing as lustily as it does in the Low Country of South Carolina.)

These imposter jasmines in Charleston had jogged our memories. We had grown a fine trachelospermum specimen as a houseplant, which had thrived for years until it up and died on us, for no reason we could figure out. So we stopped at that roadside nursery, hoping it would have a replacement growing in a pot for us to bring home. The old woman who owned the place allowed as how, yes sir, she did have a few jasmines out back, behind the shed. We started out, through some knee-high grass, and I started worrying. I worried about a copperhead. But mostly I worried about chiggers.

Of chiggers, I need say nothing to people who have lived in the South. They know all about chiggers. Northerners may need an explanation, however. We have chiggers in New Jersey, but in nowhere near the numbers we have mosquitoes. Chiggers are found in the Pine Barrens, often on blueberries or sweetferns, which aren't ferns at all, but *Comptonia peregrina,* a low shrub with pleasantly aromatic leaves. Occasionally when somebody walks through the woods in this part of the world, a chigger will fall from a tree and set about its task of burrowing under the skin of its mammalian victim. There it lives for a time, raising a bump and a powerful itch. In the South, chiggers claim a much larger share of the world. They live in grass, as well as trees, and during any given summer there are probably a billion chiggers for every man, woman, and child. Chiggers are serious business. Mosquitoes, by comparison, are pikers. They bite humans (at least the females of some species do), they gorge on blood, and then they fly away. A mosquito bite looks like a chigger bump, but it's just a tiny wound, and the itch goes away fairly soon. Chiggers, however, take up residence inside the body, and they stay around a goodly period of time, gorging on blood at their leisure. The itch stays until they depart, and it's more unpleasant than the itch a mosquito bite brings on.

I grew up during World War II, but my most vivid childhood memories are of another war—the one against the chigger enemy. There were only two weapons, sulphur and clear nail polish. Sulphur, which chiggers hate as much as they love human blood, was used in two ways. It was spread as a dust on grass and shrubbery to drive the enemy away. It was also consumed internally. My mother was a firm believer in dispensing to her children daily doses of sulphur tablets starting in spring, on the theory that sulphur built up in the blood to the point that a child changed from tasty chigger feast to something a chigger would sooner starve than eat. We still got chiggers, but maybe there were fewer of them than there would have been without those tablets—which had some side effects best left undescribed here. The nail polish was applied to a chigger bump as soon as one appeared, despite the sulphur. It smarted a bit at first, but then it cut off the air supply to the chigger, bringing it to an entirely just end by suffocation.

It all came back to me as we walked through the tall grass, so I asked the woman, "You got chiggers here yet?"

"Lawdy-do, we do got chiggers here," she replied. But then she said that chiggers didn't worry her none, because she had the bounce.

I wondered if people down South had discovered some new way of walking, some springy little step that made chiggers keep their distance, but she went on to explain. The bounce was Bounce—the trade name for Procter and Gamble's little tissues used in dryers to soften fabrics and reduce static cling. She just rubbed a sheet of it on her arms and legs before going outside in the morning and never got a single chigger all summer long. She handed us a sheet of Bounce from her pocket, and we followed her example. We got our *Trachelospermum jasminoides,* but no chigger bites.

Of course when I got back to New Jersey and started asking questions, I discovered that I was as tardy a learner about Bounce as I had been about Skin-So-Soft. I also discovered that Bounce discouraged mosquitoes, gnats, no-see-ums, and biting flies, in addition to chiggers. One of my neighbors said he used it ever since he went to Disney World and saw some employees rubbing themselves with the tissues.

I made a test, during early June, a time when without protection it can take about five seconds in the garden to be located and bitten by half a dozen insects. I used the scientific method. I rubbed a sheet of Bounce on my legs. I anointed my left arm with Skin-So-Soft. I left my right arm untreated. I walked outside, quickly accumulating a congregation of tiny creatures ready to gorge themselves, all on the right arm.

Bounce worked. What's more, it worked just as well as Skin-So-Soft, which is unpleasantly oily and smells like cheap drugstore perfume. I said good-bye to Avon and hello to Procter and Gamble.

I MUST MAKE a disclaimer here, for fear of steering anyone wrong. Neither Skin-So-Soft nor Bounce can be chemically inert, or they would have no effect on insects. They obviously contain perfumes, to which susceptible people may develop allergies. I may become allergic, one of these days, but until then, I will gratefully use Bounce to keep mine enemies at bay.

But there is a larger point here. The history of the human race is in part the history of the serendipitous discovery of remedies for ancient woes in unexpected places. No one knows who discovered that this plant was edible, this other one inedible or even toxic. No one knows who discovered that by rubbing two sticks together a fire could be started, and that fire could be used to cook food. The antibiotic properties of certain molds existed long before we learned about them and put them to use.

Cause and effect is a mysterious notion. In our daily lives, we rely constantly on the idea that some things cause others to happen, but I suspect that David Hume was right: the idea of causality is a mental habit that has wobbly foundations, no matter how useful it may be.

I don't know who noticed that Skin-So-Soft worked to repel insects, or who came to the brilliant conclusion that a sheet of paper intended to soften clothes did the same thing. But to these people, whoever they are or may have been, I tip my hat and say a grateful word as I kneel among the weeds of June.

The Pleasures
of the Bog

MY FAVORITE PLACE in our garden used to be of scant interest, duller than a pair of kindergarten scissors. It was a side yard to the west of the house, where the clothesline lived. There was a long and narrow rectangular bed defined by half-sunken concrete bricks the previous owner of the house put down before we moved in, which we planted during our first years of gardening here mostly in easy annuals, like zinnias and marigolds. Facing it, across a narrow lawn of scruffy turf, there was a deep hedge of mildew-infested lilacs. Every year, the lilacs advanced a foot or two toward the house, foretelling a day to come when there would be only a small pathway between hedge and house.

Clearly something had to be done about that diminishing part of the garden, but I have a well-practiced habit of noting that something is wrong and then doing nothing whatsoever about it. Hella is different. She will put up with something that doesn't please her for a time, but only for a time. A day always comes when she jumps in and takes action.

I knew on that Saturday afternoon some Junes ago that she was taking action when I was reading the newspaper in the living room and heard some heavy sawing going on in the side yard in the midst of the lilac hedge. I went out to investigate, discovering that Hella was attacking it with a pruning saw. It looked like a major project to start on a hot summer day, so I sensibly went back inside to continue with the newspaper. The pretense that what Hella was doing was something I could just ignore lasted about ten minutes, so I went to the shed, grabbed a spare pruning saw, and offered my assistance.

By late that afternoon, the lilac hedge had retreated five feet back toward the fence on the property line, and Hella had turned her attention to the very center of the hedge. Like Nature, she abhors straight lines and things in rows, so she decided to cut a deep and curving bay into the hedge.

"What are we going to do here?" I asked.

"Something will come to us," she said, "once we've opened up this space."

Something did come to us, the very next day. The bay would become a bog—a man-made bog where we could grow the moisture-loving plants that find our sandy soil inimical to their well-being. We had in the shed a large pool liner of butyl rubber. We had acquired it with the intent of digging a decent-sized pond for koi and for water lilies and other aquatic plants, but then we scaled down our ambitions, settling instead for a very small kidney-shaped fiberglass pool that we installed by the deck. The pool's edges were concealed with hostas and ferns, and the koi turned out to be a few small goldfish, the water lilies a potted papyrus and some water lettuce floating about. The butyl rubber had sat, like an unfulfilled New Year's resolution, in the shed ever since. But the thought struck us that if a sheet of rubber could line a pool and contain its water, it could as easily contain the muck of a bog, provided that we slashed it slightly to allow for a minimum of drainage.

Sandy soil has its liabilities, but when a chore involving digging arrives, it's a benediction. That Sunday, two people with a shovel apiece took only a few hours to dig an impressive pit, three feet deep, vaguely kidney shaped, roughly nine feet long and four feet across. The rubber liner went in. I shoveled in some dirt to anchor it, while Hella trimmed it around the edge, leaving just enough to ring the bog-to-be, six inches beyond the lip of the hole. At the bottom of the hole, I laid one of those leaky hoses made from recycled automobile tires, to provide deep moisture, making certain that one end of the hose was outside the bog. We hooked it up to a regular garden hose, turned on the water, and started shoveling the dirt back in.

To mix the sandy soil into a properly boggy consistency, we took off our shoes and tromped around barefoot, feeling the ooze between our toes. It was immensely satisfying, a wonderful return to the mud pies of childhood.

Next we covered the edges of the new bog with broken fieldstones, and the gathering of plants began. From the perennial border I retrieved a number of sick and unhappy moisture-loving plants that were gasping for life. Cardinal flowers, chelones, rodgersias, and other plants got a new home. So did a Japanese iris and a yellowing ginger lily from a pot on the deck. A friend who has a natural bog brought us some dwarf cattails and ferns. To soften the edges of the bog we added more ferns and some clumps of liriope.

It was an almost instant success. The cardinal flowers and other plants perked up right away. The foliage of the ginger lily turned green and produced many stalks of huge white blossoms that looked like moths and perfumed the night air with a delicious sweetness. Tracks in the mud showed that our resident raccoon approved, even if his gratitude was insufficient to cure him of his habit of knocking over our garbage cans for nocturnal feasts.

One thing in a garden always leads to another, and so it was with the bog. I exterminated the lawn and replaced it with shredded bark, as soft to the feet as forest duff. Then it occurred to me that we could plant things that relished dry soil and good drainage in front of the bog. I planted some low sedums, many different ornamental thymes, and hens-and-chickens. We removed the annuals from the bed, planting instead artemisias 'Powis Castle' and 'Huntington', which don't spread by underground runners, and a collection of summer- and autumn-blooming alliums. We let the planting, which went on to include santolinas and lavenders and winter heaths, spill over the concrete into the shredded bark. Next to the two small steps that lead down into the side yard from the deck, we planted little shrubs—dwarf crape myrtles and the dwarf ferny-leafed nandina 'San Gabriel'. A trip to South Carolina somewhat later provided us with a park bench modeled after those on Charleston's Battery and a rope hammock from Pawleys Island.

Over the years, we have renewed the bark and continued to add more plants, mostly little ones that need to be seen close at hand to be appreciated. The bog has become a jungle of ferns, irises, and chelones, and it undergoes fascinating changes of light during the day as the sun moves across the sky. A dull side yard has become a place to live, a true garden room.

A Demon of
a Machine

SIX YEARS AGO I indulged myself with one of the many mechanical, electric, and electronic toys I justify as necessary tools. My grown sons began at about that time to hail as symptomatic my increasing fascination with these devices, beginning but by no means ending with a microwave oven. "Dad's playthings," the younger commented, "show that he's well into his middle years."

This one, however, was an electric chipper-shredder. My son was wrong. At just under three hundred dollars it was a wise investment. It would pulverize leaves into tiny pieces that would turn into dark, rich compost in a month or two. Twigs and small branches would be turned into chips for mulch for perennial beds and shrubs, keeping down weeds and conserving moisture.

Thanks to this demon of a machine, the garden would be tidier than ever before. There would be very little expenditure of either electricity or time. I estimated that half an hour's worth of chipping and grinding per week during the growing season—and probably twice that during fall cleanup—would do the trick. The machine would pay for itself within a few months, as I could stop buying commercial mulches like pine bark at the local garden center.

I believed all these things on the strength of advertisements in gardening magazines showing someone feeding branches into the hopper of such machines and then spreading the mulch around a garden, with a beaming face suggesting that it was no work at all.

My estimates were all wrong. My garden, a small one on a lot only 100 by 150 feet, could produce enough grindable and chippable material in July to keep me busy for six or seven hours. And it isn't easy work. To be chipped, branches first have to be sawed or cut with loppers, then hauled to the machine. Feeding it a steady supply of woody material, furthermore, uses a set of muscles I had never used before, because I didn't know I had them. For two days after a session of grinding and chipping, I ached sufficiently that the very idea of going into the garden was painful.

The machine, moreover, had a strange habit of clogging when I fed it too much soft vegetation at a time. The heavy metal housing that protected its operator's life and limbs had to be removed with a wrench and then lifted off to clear the chute of soggy material. It might be ten or fifteen minutes before the shredding could resume.

I decided on a return to the status quo ante. All leaves, grass clippings, and kitchen waste except for bones and fats would go directly as is to the compost heap. Small limbs and branches would go out to the curb, tied in bundles thirty inches long, for the town garbage trucks to cart away. The chipper-shredder found a place in a far back corner of the shed, almost out of sight and completely out of mind.

Then, long after the disappointing machine was put away, Hella found a small item in our local newspaper, where the closing of most of New Jersey's municipal landfills has been a big story for over a year. Our town, she informed me, was about to stop picking up vegetative waste, no matter how neatly it might be tied in bundles and left at the curb.

A Demon of a Machine

She said we ought to give the shredder another try. I said hmm. Within an hour, I heard from my upstairs study the loud whir the machine makes as it revs up and then the screaming noise of small branches going through the chipper. She had cut down one of two fair-sized yews neither of us liked, as they were plunging a front room into darkness half the day to the detriment of houseplants in the window. I came downstairs and went into the garden.

It will clog up right away, I told her. She told me that she had read the instructions that came with the machine, something I had never done. The trick, she said, is to put soft material through only in small batches, alternating with woodier and drier stuff.

She—and the instruction book—were right. Nothing clogged.

Feeling that it was probably ungentlemanly and bad domestic policy to boot just to sit and watch all the chipping and the shredding, I fetched the loppers to attack the other yew. Within four or five hours we had a sizable pile of erstwhile yews to use as mulch.

"We'll both ache tomorrow," I said.

"Aching is good for people," she said, "when it comes from exercise—and you could stand a little."

On sunny weekend days, we prune and lop, and then we grind and chip. The mulch is building up in an impressive way. Hackberry branches, dead lilac twigs, pine boughs that blocked a path—these and other nuisances are put to better uses as transformed by a machine that has hardly clogged at all. I don't even ache—much.

My wife I think loves this machine a lot more than I do. We both have done the work, even if I have managed to be away part of the time, so that we are hardly equal partners in the labor. She smiles as she feeds a branch or a handful of twigs into the hopper. I don't really smile.

But I do feel some satisfaction. Our vegetative waste is now being recycled, right on the premises. We have eliminated at least a part of our household's demands on scarce space in the landfill.

It is good to feel like part of the solution, not of the problem.

Scowling Cats,
a Bright Flash
of Wings at
the Window

WHEN THE LAST maple leaf has fallen, when there's virtually nothing flowering in the garden except the stalwart winter heaths, and when the first snows have come, sensible gardeners will come inside for their fallow season. But still, through our windows, we can take joy in both movement and color out of doors, if we have been provident and put up bird feeders on their suction cups on the panes of glass.

I am no expert on birds. I can tell a blue jay from a cardinal, as can any child of four, and I know enough about starlings and their pushy and nasty ways to curse whoever it was who imported them to our shores in the nineteenth century because he thought America ought to have every bird mentioned by Shakespeare. But for several years I mistook purple finches for redpolls and had trouble distinguishing between chickadees and nuthatches. I still get puzzled, studying the pictures in Roger Tory Peterson and observing some little bird perched on a contorted hazel near our back door that might be a pine siskin—or might not.

Until just recently, we had many a problem with the half-dozen clear plastic feeders at our kitchen and dining-room windows. Squirrels often knocked them loose in their frenzy to stuff themselves on sunflower seeds or peanut hearts. Sometimes the birds themselves would dislodge them in their quick escape, when Thurber or Samantha, our inside cats, leaped to the window for a closer look.

All of this has changed, since we found the Rolls-Royce of window feeders. It is called the Meta Bird Feeding System. Tim Lunquist invented it in his basement shop in 1987 as a Christmas gift for his six-year-old son. It took no time at all for it to reach mail-order catalogs and the tonier sorts of hardware stores and garden centers.

This is a window feeder that differs substantially from any others I have seen. It is quite large, being twenty-six inches high, five inches deep, and fourteen inches wide. Its peaked roof, with a removable chimney for filling the storage tubes at the sides that dispense food to its three feeding trays, makes it look like a roadside shrine, perhaps one to Saint Francis, considering the huge numbers of birds it attracts. The one-way mirror at its back means that I can see them without their seeing me or fluttering away at the slightest movement inside the house. It affixes to the window with six suction cups, and it can be placed high enough that squirrels can't get into it, but have to stay on the ground waiting for some messy starling to throw seeds out in its greedy way.

Our cats are most unhappy. They leap to the sill in their accustomed manner, but the birds just ignore them and continue to feed a few inches away. Samantha avoids the dining room as a place of frustration and sudden, unexpected loss of power over tinier creatures. During the hours of daylight, Thurber wears the closest thing to a scowl I've yet seen on a cat, as finches, cardinals, and possibly pine siskins congregate to enjoy their feast in perfect tranquillity.

Bibliography

Barton, Barbara J. *Gardening by Mail: A Source Book.* Third edition. Boston: Houghton Mifflin, 1990.

Betts, Edwin Morris. *Thomas Jefferson's Garden Book.* Philadelphia: The American Philosophical Society, 1944.

Breck, Joseph. *New Book of Flowers.* New York: Orange, Judd, 1900.

Earle, Alice Morse. *Old Time Gardens.* New York: Macmillan, 1901. Reprint. Detroit: Singing Tree Press, 1968.

Gerard, John. *The Herball, or Generall Historie of Plants.* Second edition. London: 1633. Facsimile. New York: Dover, 1975.

Hedrick, U. P. *A History of Horticulture in America to 1860.* Second edition, with an addendum by Elisabeth Woodburn of books published from 1861–1920. Portland, Or.: Timber Press, 1990.

Kingsley, Charles. *Madam How and Lady Why: Lessons in Earth Lore for Children* (1869). London: Dent Everyman's Library, n.d.

Lacey, Stephen. *The Startling Jungle.* Boston: Godine, 1990.

Lawrence, Elizabeth. *Gardening for Love: The Market Bulletins.* Durham, N.C.: Duke University Press, 1987.

———. *Gardens in Winter.* New York: Harper, 1957.

———. *The Little Bulbs: A Tale of Two Gardens.* New York: Criterion Books, 1957. Reprint. Durham, N.C.: Duke University Press, 1986.

———. *Lob's Wood.* Cincinnati, Ohio: Cincinnati Nature Center, 1971.

———. *A Rock Garden in the South.* Edited by Nancy Goodwin, with Allen Lacy. Durham, N.C.: Duke University Press, 1990.

———. *A Southern Garden: A Handbook for the Middle South.* Chapel Hill: The University of North Carolina Press, 1942.

———. *Through the Garden Gate.* Edited by Bill Neal. Chapel Hill: The University of North Carolina Press, 1990.

McMahon, Bernard. *The American Gardener's Calendar.* Eleventh edition. Philadelphia: Lippincott, 1857.

Parkinson, John. *Paradisi in Sole* (1629). Facsimile edition. London: Methuen, 1904.

Ruskin, John. *Modern Painters.* Edited by David Barrie. New York: Alfred A. Knopf, 1988.

Scott, Frank C. *The Art of Beautifying Suburban Home Grounds.* New York: D. Appleton & Co., 1870.

Thaxter, Celia. *An Island Garden.* Boston: Houghton Mifflin, 1894. Facsimile edition. Boston: Houghton Mifflin, 1988.

Tull, Delena. *A Practical Guide to Edible and Useful Plants.* Austin, Tx.: Texas Monthly Press, 1987.

Warner, Charles Dudley. *My Summer in a Garden.* Boston: Field, Osgood & Co., 1870.

Wilder, Louise Beebe. *Adventures with Hardy Bulbs.* New York: Macmillan, 1936, 1990.

———. *Color in My Garden.* New York: Doubleday, 1927. Reprint. New York: Atlantic Monthly Press, 1990.

———. *The Fragrant Path.* New York: Macmillan, 1932, 1990.

Sources and Resources

Except for people who live in areas that are unusually rich in fine local nurseries specializing in uncommon plants, American gardeners who wish to move beyond the horticultural least common denominators of their neighborhoods are almost forced to resort to mail-order nurseries. Fortunately, the United States has been enjoying for a decade at least a remarkable increase in the number of such concerns. A reasonably complete list of these is contained in Barbara J. Barton's *Gardening by Mail: A Source Book* (third edition, Boston: Houghton Mifflin, 1990), although new nurseries keep coming into being at a rate that suggests a fourth edition of this useful reference may soon be in order.

I would not know how to garden without using mail-order nurseries. There are a few pitfalls, of course, but with experience they may be avoided. One rule is to listen to one's fellow gardeners in their comments about certain nurseries that have achieved lasting notoriety for taking in gullible gardeners by offering great claims, but small deliverance. If a catalog comes unsolicited, by bulk mail, and promises amazing results for a few pennies, it should be regarded with suspicion. A high count of adjectives that hype everything offered is another dangerous sign. The absence of scientific names for any plant is another. I tend strongly to the view that there are no bargain plants. It has also been my general experience that the nurseries from which I have been most satisfied charge anywhere between one and five dollars for their catalogs. The people who run them are serious plantsmen, and they expect that their customers will also be serious people who recognize the unfairness of asking noncustomers to be subsidized in their desire for a catalog by people who are real patrons.

Some nurseries accept orders by telephone; some even have 800 numbers. Some accept credit cards. But some very fine nurseries indeed extend no credit and require advance payment in full accompanying a written order.

What follows is my personal list of mail-order nurseries—and seed companies—with which I have had nothing but good experiences, or that gardening friends I respect and trust have repeatedly praised.

B and D Lilies, 330 P Street, Port Townsend, Washington 98368. Catalog $4.00. The lily-bulb industry in the Pacific Northwest has hit on hard times, and even scandal of the kind that attracts the attention of *The Wall Street Journal,* in the last few years. There's no scandal associated with this family-run business, and I hope no hard times either. The catalog would tempt a flower-hating, ascetic saint off a rock to revel in the pleasures of the eye—and often the nose. If I ran into an ex-saint, showing the telltale signs of guilty pleasure in the pollen stains on his (or her) cheek, I'd remind him that the lily was associated with the Virgin Mary. If he (or she) had gone pagan, I'd switch to Juno or even Aphrodite. But my point is lilies, not theology. B and D has them, old and brand-new, and they ship healthy, solid, first-rate bulbs in the fall, which establish themselves by the following summer, and then in years to come go on from glory unto glory.

Bluestone Perennials, 7211 Middle Ridge Road, Madison, Ohio 44057. Catalog free. Here's the first of several exceptions to the rule about paying for catalogs. Bluestone offers a wide range of perennials, sold as small plants for very reasonable prices. Gardeners thirsting for perennials and lots of them, but suffering from the pangs of a constricted wallet, may find relief here. It may take a year or two for these plants to come to maturity, but a full-grown phlox is a full-grown phlox, no matter when and where it reached that size.

Caladium World, P.O. Box 629, Sebring, Florida 33870. Catalog free. Caladiums are dandy plants to perk up the dead of summer with multi-colored leaves in shades of green, white, pink, and red. Except for gardeners who live in frost-free areas, these tuberous tropical plants are best treated as annuals and planted after the soil warms past seventy degrees. Caladium World offers a good selection at reasonable prices.

Canyon Creek Nursery, 3527 Dry Creek Road, Oroville, California 95965. Catalog $2.00. This is one of my favorite catalogs, and favorite nurseries. When I read the catalog, I feel that I am listening to a gardening friend share his enthusiasms with me. There are lots of unusual perennials, with a strong specialty here in violas, dianthuses, and euphorbias. The list of hardy fuchsias is unusually rich.

The Cook's Garden, P.O. Box 65, Londonderry, Vermont 05148. Catalog $1.00. This catalog offers a tantalizing number of vegetables of European and Oriental origin that you won't find in any grocery store.

Crownsville Nursery, 1241 Generals Highway, Crownsville, Maryland 21032. Catalog $2.00. This nursery's offerings are never the same from one year to the next, and there's always much to tempt me. Order as soon as the catalog arrives, as some perennials offered are in short supply.

The Daffodil Mart, Route 3, Box 794, Gloucester, Virginia 23061. Catalog $1.00. For some sixty years, the Heath family in tidewater

Virginia has been virtually synonymous with daffodils in America. Brent and Becky Heath, the third generation in the business, offer an enormous number of daffodil cultivars of British, European, and American breeding. The catalog celebrates the daffodil in particular, but other bulbs of spring are well represented, as well as those that bloom in the summer and fall.

Henry Field Seed and Nursery Company, 407 Sycamore Street, Shenandoah, Iowa 51602. A long-established, rather old-fashioned nursery.

Forestfarm, 990 Tetherhod, Williams, Oregon 97544. Catalog $2.00. Here one finds woody plants, often quite rare, sold very reasonably in small sizes. For patient people—and an impatient gardener is an unhappy one who might be advised to take up some pastime with more immediate rewards, whatever that might be—the wait is worth it. They will probably end up with a healthier plant than they could have bought in a five-gallon container three years earlier.

Gossler Farms Nursery, 1200 Weaver Road, Springfield, Oregon 97478. Catalog $1.00. Studying this catalog's rich array of witch hazels, magnolias, and other flowering shrubs or small trees always makes me wish I reckoned my garden in square miles, not square feet.

Heaths and Heathers, P.O. Box 850, Elma, Washington 98541. Send SASE for catalog. This nursery sells what its name leads you to suspect, and nothing else. But the assortment of both kinds of plants is extremely rich. With enough heaths and heathers properly chosen, a garden can be in bloom 365 days of the year in many parts of the country.

Holbrook Farm and Nursery, Route 2, Box 223, Fletcher, North Carolina 28732. Catalog $2.00. Holbrook's catalog is sage, low-key, and rich in good humor, as is its owner, Allen Bush. Allen loves to talk plants and is the only person in the nursery trade I know who has set aside an hour late each weekday afternoon to answer the phone. Holbrook sells a rich selection of perennials for both sun and shade and has introduced to American gardens such plants as heuchera 'Palace Purple' and *Patrinia scabiosifolia*.

Kelly's Plant World, 10266 E. Princeton, Sanger, California 93657. Send SASE for catalog. Cannas, cannas, and more cannas. Anyone who thinks cannas are fusty Victorian plants, garish in color and useful only in circular beds dotted senselessly around on a lawn, will find surprises here.

Klehm Nursery, Route 5, Box 197, South Barrington, Illinois 60010. Catalog $4.00. The specialty here is peonies, long associated with the name of the Klehm family, but there are also many cultivars of bearded iris, daylilies, and hostas. In recent years the nursery has imported from Germany superior forms of many other perennials.

Lamb Nurseries, 101 East Sharp Avenue, Spokane, Washington 99202. Catalog free. For years I have found the true meaning of temptation in the tall and skinny catalog this nursery puts out. Good sedums, sempervivums, dianthuses, violets, phloxes, and more.

Logee's Greenhouses, 55 North Street, Danielson, Connecticut 06239. Catalog $3.00. Tropical or tender houseplants are the mainstay. Fancy begonias, mandevillas, passifloras, jasmines, and many other houseplants to winter over inside and then bring out to live on the deck are found here.

Montrose Nursery, Box 957, Hillsborough, North Carolina 27278. Catalog $2.00. Montrose is one of the most beautiful gardens I know, but it is not open to the public. Nancy Goodwin, who founded it in the mid-1970s to sell seed-raised species of hardy cyclamen to help protect these lovely plants in their native habitats, has since busied herself in propagating other rare perennials for the benefit of other gardeners. Without plants from Montrose, my garden would be less interesting,

I fear. The emphasis here is on perennials that can thrive in the long and sultry summers of the North Carolina Piedmont, but many of them do equally well in the long and sultry summers of New Jersey.

Niche Gardens, 1111 Dawson Road, Chapel Hill, North Carolina 27514. Catalog $3.00. Niche, for those who wonder, isn't the name of the owners. They happen to be Kim and Bruce Hawks. They were looking for a niche for their nursery, its own little corner of the gardening world, and they found it. They sell other things in addition, but their specialty is native North American perennials, grown from seed, not collected in the wild.

Park Seed Company, Greenwood, South Carolina 29647. Catalog free. It wouldn't be midwinter without the Park catalog arriving to bring on December and January dreams of gardens bright with summer annuals and bursting with luscious, rich red, juicy tomatoes bursting on the vine.

Pinetree Garden Seeds, Route 100, New Gloucester, Maine 04260. Catalog free. Pinetree sells at reasonable prices small packets of vegetable and flower seeds, on the hunch that someone who wants eight zucchini plants would just as soon not have ten times that number of seeds at five times the price. Some heirloom vegetables have been kept going for over a decade by this company, and it carries a substantial number of good books on gardening.

Sandy Mush Herb Nursery, Route 2, Leicester, North Carolina 28748. Catalog $4.00. Herbs, scented geraniums, ornamental and culinary sages are all sold by this nursery on the other side of nowhere in the mountains of North Carolina.

Shady Oaks Nursery, 700 19th Avenue N.E., Waseca, Minnesota 56093. Catalog $1.00. No surprise here. The specialty is plants that thrive in shade, from light shade to true gloom.

Shepherd's Garden Seeds, 6116 Highway 9, Felton, California 95018. Catalog $1.00. The catalog is lively, devoted to herbs, especially basils, to edible flowers, and to vegetables Farmer Brown doesn't raise and Safeway doesn't sell. The founder, Renée Shepherd, obviously sets a fine table as well as tending a terrific vegetable patch. The catalog gives many recipes for imaginative things to do with herbs and vegetables once harvested. Try the potatoes roasted with olive oil, garlic, and rosemary, or the lemon basil pesto dressing.

Siskiyou Rare Plant Nursery, 2825 Cummings Road, Medford, Oregon 97501. Catalog $2.00. Siskiyou is a fine source for alpine plants and for small native American shrubs.

Sunlight Gardens, Route 1, Box 600-A, Andersonville, Tennessee 37705. Catalog $2.00. A good assortment of seed-grown native American perennials is found here. Some, on the USDA endangered list, like *Echinacea purpurea tennesseensis,* indigenous only to Davidson County, where the explosive growth of Nashville has made it almost vanishingly rare, are raised and sold under federal and state permits.

Andre Viette Farm and Nursery, Route 1, Box 16, Fishersville, Virginia 22939. Catalog $2.00. This all-purpose perennial nursery specializes in daylilies, hostas, irises, peonies, Oriental poppies, ferns, and grasses, but it's hard to think of any major perennial not found here. It sells on the spot, as well as by mail order, and the nursery has beautiful display gardens and a splendid view of the Shenandoah Valley and the Blue Ridge Mountains.

Note: I must add that praising and listing the mail-order nurseries that have served my garden and Hella's does not mean that a locally acquired plant is beneath consideration, or that a local nursery has nothing to offer. Some nurseries that require their customers to come to them have extremely useful, beautiful, and rare plants to offer. Hillside Nursery, to name one that I know, is a fine example. It doesn't ship, I guess because it has all that it can deal with in the sophisticated horticultural territory of Norfolk, Connecticut. A few miles from our own door, a promising perennial nursery, Wildflowers, has sprung up. The owners do much of their own propagation, and they are avid searchers for worthy plants, like red valerian, or *Centranthus ruber*, which appears in few mail-order catalogs and which it alone sells in my neck of the woods. The message here is buy locally, if you can, by mail-order if you must, but remember that UPS turns distant nurseries that ship into virtual next-door neighbors.

Index